Several more
lives to live

CONTRIBUTIONS IN AMERICAN STUDIES
SERIES EDITOR: Robert H. Walker

Michael Meyer

Several more
lives to live

THOREAU'S POLITICAL
REPUTATION IN
AMERICA

818.
309
MEY

Contributions in American Studies, Number 29

GREENWOOD PRESS
Westport, Connecticut • London, England

Library of Congress Cataloging in Publication Data

Meyer, Michael.
  Several more lives to live.

  (Contributions in American studies ; no. 29)
  Includes bibliographical references and index.
  1. Thoreau, Henry David, 1817-1862—Criticism and interpretation—
History. 2. Thoreau, Henry David, 1817-1862—Political and social views.
I. Title.
PS3054.M43 1977   818'.3'09   76-56622
ISBN 0-8371-9477-6

Library of Congress Catalog Card Number: 76-56622
ISBN: 0-8371-9477-6

First published in 1977

Greenwood Press, Inc.
51 Riverside Avenue, Westport, Connecticut 06880

Printed in the United States of America

To the memory of
Theodore C. Miller

I left the woods for as good a reason as I went there. Perhaps it seemed to me that I had several more lives to live, and could not spare any more time for that one.
Thoreau, "Conclusion" to *Walden*

The highest law gives a thing to him who can use it.
Thoreau, *Journal* (VIII, 19)

An honest misunderstanding is often the ground of future intercourse.
Thoreau, *Journal* (I, 229)

Contents

Acknowledgments

I have enjoyed good teachers as well as good readers, and I am grateful for them. The late Theodore C. Miller introduced me to the serious study of American literature, and as a result of his example and character I discovered for myself what he valued so much and understood so well. To Milton R. Stern and John D. Seelye, for their continued generosity, support, encouragement, and confidence, I owe a debt that goes well beyond my gratitude for their scholarship, their remarkable teaching, and their suggestions which made an early version of this study a better version. I am also grateful to others for reading various stages of the manuscript: Irving P. Cummings, for reading carefully and letting me know when I was not writing the way he was reading; Donald B. Gibson, for detailed and helpful discussions on politics and literary criticism; and A. William Hoglund, for his shrewd sense of the past, matched only by his understanding of the present and his willingness to share it. In addition, Walter Harding graciously agreed to read the manuscript just before it went to press and made helpful suggestions. An even more significant help to me, however, was my use of his work on Thoreau, particularly the continuing bibliographies in the *Thoreau Society Bulletin*. Without them, this study would have been much less complete and would have taken considerably longer to put together. One other reader must also be acknowledged: my colleague just across the hall, Perry M. Robinson, whose interest in my work I have greatly appreciated. Of the many libraries that I used in the course of this study, several have been consistently helpful: the Harvard College Library, the Yale University Library, the Concord Free Public Library, and especially the reference librarians at the Wilbur Cross Library, University of Connecticut, and the J. Murrey Atkins Library, University of North Carolina at Charlotte, for obtaining scores of items available to me only by way of interlibrary loan services.

And finally, I am indebted to Patricia Ryan Meyer, my wife, for more than could ever be acknowledged here. She knows that too, and that is yet another reason why I am grateful to her.

Several more
lives to live

Introduction

To attend chiefly to the desk or schoolhouse
while we neglect the scenery in which it is
placed is absurd. If we do not look out we shall
find our fine schoolhouse standing in a cow-
yard at last.

Thoreau, Journal (XII, 387)

In the 1890s Henry David Thoreau's English biographer, Henry
Salt, could write somewhat optimistically that if Thoreau "is a
good deal misapplied at present, time will set that right."[1] Not yet.
Thoreau has come to be regarded in the United States as a national
resource, as public property. An advocate of national parks, he has
almost become one himself because he seems to be in everybody's
camp. Although there are numerous surveys of American criticism
that have described, analyzed, and accounted for Thoreau's reputation, none has examined in detail the American response to
Thoreau's social and political thought.   It may be that Thoreau
will always be "a good deal misapplied," but there is some solace in
the realization that if time has not set right his reputation, its passage has, at least, provided a different angle of vision from which to

understand his reputation. It is the passage of time, and particularly America's recent political past, that has offered a clearer perspective on Thoreau's reputation as a social and political thinker.

During the 1960s the land that Fitzgerald once described as "a fresh green breast of the new world" vanished for many Americans when we rediscovered the underside of America the Beautiful, and it was a view of the country from the bottom up that went beyond the economic despair of the 1930s. *War, racism, poverty,* and *oppression* were words that became clichés during the past decade; they also became synonymous with the word *America,* rightly or not. We grew tired not only of the clichés but also of what they described. Epithets were chronically used because the problems seemed to be chronic. In the sixties the country gave birth to a conception of itself that previously had been creditable only among those that George F. Babbitt had labeled the "long-haired gentry who call themselves 'liberals' and 'radicals' and 'non-partisan' and 'intelligentsia' and God only knows how many other trick names!" Nightly, the vision of America as the historical realization of a paradise regained, the vision of America as God's country, receded before millions of Americans who watched the seven o'clock news: the soaring eagle had its wings clipped by history. We discovered, finally perhaps, that America was not the New Jerusalem, that it did not have a Manifest Destiny, that it could not make the world safe for democracy, and that it could not expect, like Babbitt, its true patriots to "get out and root for Uncle Samuel U.S.A.!"[3] One hundred years after Whitman's *Democratic Vistas* Americans were painfully aware that it was "about time for more solid achievement, and less windy promise." The crucial difference, however, between the mood of the sixties and Whitman's—or other periods of internal disillusionment—is that many Americans were voicing this complaint. The mass demonstration replaced the solitary singer. The "divine average" finally came around, but unlike Whitman, they did not find "that a kelson of the creation is love"; instead, they found politics.

Every age is a political one, but ours is consciously so. Today we tend to make sense of ourselves and the world from a political perspective. Whereas the Puritans saw the hand of Providence or the claw of Satan informing every natural event, our own age has opted for politics as the most powerful means of explaining phenomena. In its zeal and wonder America's discovery of politics has been similar to the scientific discovery of air; it seems to be everywhere.[4] Nearly every kind of human activity is currently being reassessed from a political perspective. No doubt the Puritans would have been hard pressed to make sense of Kate Millet's study, published in 1970, entitled *Sexual Politics.*

Although it is certainly true that the seventies have witnessed a decline in political activism, particularly among university students, the number of politically oriented studies published in the past few years demonstrates that there is no indication of a decline in political consciousness, particularly among university teachers. At least for the time being, politics has assumed some of the explanatory power that religion and science once held. Without question this assessment of contemporary political consciousness is an oversimplification, but it is not, I think, a misrepresentation.

Americans have come to see themselves in a political context that includes institutions and activities which previously seemed immune to politics. Churches, universities, and even academic research, both scientific and humanistic, have been under fire for either taking political stands or remaining silent (silence has also been taken to represent a political stand). Political demands have been made upon professional organizations such as the American Medical Association, the American Historical Association, and the Modern Language Association (MLA). Generally, these organizations have been strongly criticized for not addressing themselves to contemporary social problems.[5] At the 1968 annual meeting the MLA was split, on the one hand, by those who insisted that the studying and the teaching of literature are and ought to be objective and, on the other hand, by those who argued that such objectivity is neither possible nor desirable, because it is an implicit endorsement of the social and political status quo. The dissidents argued that a studious effort to remain apolitical was, indeed, a political position. The years since 1968 have proceeded like the final chapters of a Dickens novel: some members of the profession have increasingly insisted that its activities are interrelated with all kinds of characters and plots that previously had been relegated to lowlife.[6] As Henry Nash Smith cautiously and judiciously pointed out in his 1969 presidential address to the MLA: "The dissidents among our members are challenging assumptions that have gone too long without being reexamined. Provocation is good for us if it obliges us to explain — to ourselves as much as to others — why we consider our scholarship and our teaching to be worthwhile." [7] The political consciousness pervasive in America has had the effect of directly or indirectly urging many professionals to take stock of what they are doing professionally and what it means politically. For literary critics and scholars this means forcing scholarly and critical prejudices into the open so that they can be dealt with candidly and honestly.

Literary criticism (I use this term to include scholarship as well) usually is and should be objective in the sense that its methodology must be honest and accurate: one does not, for example, purposely quote out of context, stack evidence, or suppress data which damages one's own argument. Criticism is not always objective, however, if what is meant by objectivity is an ability on the part of the critic to transcend time, space, matter, circumstances, and history; no criticism is completely ahistorical or totally free from the assumptions and fashions of its own age. How else can one account for the literary reputations of such major American writers as Emily Dickinson, Herman Melville, Henry James, and William Faulkner? [8] Any criticism reflects the critic in his time and cultural setting. To assume that one's vision is pure is a pure vision. Even Emerson, who, as "transparent eyeball," disclaimed "all mean egotism" and claimed "I am nothing; I see all," still came back from nature with burrs on his trousers and footprints under his shoes. This less than Olympian point of view does not necessarily constitute failure on the part of the critic; it is rather a necessary condition that is part of life. To acknowledge this is only common sense; to deny it is foolish. Just as literature must be understood, at least in part, in the context of history, so must literary criticism be viewed as a participant in the process of history if we are to be honest with ourselves. [9]

My study of the response to Thoreau's social and political thought is, in one sense, a response to the needs (and fashion) of my own times. The persistent claims dealing with the politics implicit in ostensibly apolitical professional organizations and activities cannot be ignored, nor should they be. I am not concerned, here, with the question of whether or not literature studies should or should not have a political ideology. However, I am concerned with the fact that politics has informed some of the critical response to Thoreau. At this moment, an examination of the influence of politics on the writing of criticism is both useful and necessary. It is useful because such a study will add to an understanding of Thoreau's reputation, and it is necessary not because such criticism continues to be written but because it is sometimes unconsciously written. I take my cue from Thoreau: "When a dog runs at you, whistle for him." Indirectly, time and the events of the past decade have helped to place much of the criticism on Thoreau in a clearer perspective. By using a political frame of reference, we can re-examine the facts of his reputation in order to yield some insights into both Thoreau's reputation and the relationship between politics and criticism.

For the purposes of this study the term *politics* is used in its broadest sense; it refers to the total complex of man's interactions in society. When one asks what characterizes the politics of an age, one is concerned not only with its governmental structures and political parties but also with ideas and attitudes concerning the nature of man and his relationship to the universe and his fellowman; at the same time that these broader questions are considered, it is also important to determine whether or not change is thought to be desirable, and, if it is, what the mode of change is to be. No attempt is made here to define *politics* rigidly because it is unlikely that any particular, exclusive definition would be better than any other. Although my use of *politics* does not recommend itself for its precision and sophistication, it is, I think, comprehensible. Does one, after all, really know any more about a horse because Dickens' Gradgrind insists upon defining it as a "Quadruped Graminivorous"?

Since the seventeenth century, American historiographers have frequently attempted to find in history a usable past that might help them in providing a new dynamic approach to the country's problems. [10] Critics have sometimes done the same in literature but usually not as consciously. By focusing on the criticism of *Walden* and Thoreau's social and political essays, but not to the exclusion of Thoreau's other works, this study describes the American critics' attempts to find a "usable" Thoreau. The explicit and implicit political assumptions of the critics and their respective times have, in many instances, generated the uses to which Thoreau has been put. The purpose of the analysis is not to prove that the real Thoreau is the Father of Our National and State Parks or the true American Folk Hero of the New Left; instead, the study attempts to define the possibilities and significances of Thoreau's social thought for each generation of critics past and present.

In dealing with these critics it is necessary to be aware of some of the political assumptions they make, but no attempt is made to expose their personal politics; such a task would be unfair and pointless, if not impossible. Emily Dickinson's concise observation that "No bird resumes its egg" serves as a useful reminder of the need for tact. The concern of this study is with generatons of critics — their political innocence, not their guilt — and the historical context in which the criticism was written. In unscrambling the relationships between the criticism of Thoreau and the politics contemporary to it, it is often possible to perceive more connections between the two than have previously been noted. As the political needs and level of political consciousness in the country have changed and developed, so has the criticism.

Thoreau is particularly useful as the focal point of this kind of study because of the range of his interests; he wrote about everything from woodchucks to John Brown. Moreover, like Emerson and Whitman he refused to be intimidated by "foolish" consistencies. Avoiding contradictions was for little minds; Thoreau contained multitudes and celebrated them in his writing. In *Walden* he mourned that "in this part of the world it is considered a ground for complaint if a man's writings admit of more than one interpretation."[11] It is precisely because of the range of his interests and his tendency to "admit of more than one interpretation" that Thoreau has been the subject of many critics who have attempted to use him as "a rallier of causes."[12] If Thoreau could complain in 1852 that "I am never invited by the community to do anything quite worth the while to do," it was only because he could not possibly have been aware of his posthumous reputation.[13] Walter Harding sums up this point nicely; it is a point frequently made and as well worn as the path from the center of Concord to Thoreau's hut, but it is a path infrequently taken by those who write about Thoreau:

> unfortunately altogether too many students of Thoreau have
> not been willing to accept the fact that Thoreau did not for-
> mulate and unify his thinking. Approaching his writings with
> a preconceived notion that there was a unity to his ideas, they
> have attempted to impose a consistency where no consistency
> existed. They have accepted those ideas of his that fitted their
> own particular orthodoxy and silently rejected the rest. Thus
> they have been able to "prove" that Thoreau was a stoic or an
> epicurean, a pacifist or a militarist, a pessimist or an optimist,
> an individualist or a communist. There is hardly an ism of our
> times that has not attempted to adopt Thoreau . . . .[14]

In addition to lending himself to such use, Thoreau encouraged
it: "Use me . . . if by any means ye may find me serviceable;
whether for a medicated drink or bath, as balm and lavender; or
for fragrance, as verbena and geranium; or for sight, as cactus; or
for thoughts, as pansy."[15] Thoreau wanted to be used in the same
way that he used Walden Pond, as "God's Drop," and he has been
in many a prescription for Americans ever since. For this reason an
examination of the image of Thoreau that has developed in
America must take into account not only the critics and their respective historical contexts but also the popular response to Thoreau's social and political thought. The popular response serves, in
some respects, as a useful and accessible index to the historical factors which inform the academic criticism. Although the focus of the
book is on the criticism, the fabric of Thoreau's reputation is an in-
terweaving of all three.

This study picks up the thread of Thoreau's reputation in the
1920s and proceeds to the early 1970s. The decade of the 1920s is a
sensible starting point for several reasons. Academic interest in
Thoreau's social and political thought did not begin to develop
significantly until the late twenties. Prior to that time Thoreau was
viewed primarily as a nature writer — or worse. In a relatively
early comparison of "English and American Criticism of Thoreau,"
James Playsted Wood pointed out that long before 1920 English
critics

recognized in Thoreau a thinker — a man whose ideas and practices of liberty and independence, whose moral judgments, were important. All the time that American writers were haggling over the eccentricities of his personality, maligning or defending him for speaking with an accent that resembled Emerson's or for accepting pies from his mother's larder while living as a hermit at Walden, the English had seized on the essentials of his thought and life. [16]

In addition to there being little American interest in the social and political aspects of Thoreau, there was also little native interest in American literature before the twenties; it was considered to be too easy, too modern, and too provincial. [17] Until the late twenties and the first issue of *American Literature*, the idea of American literature as a formal academic subject and discipline was as absurd as Mark Twain in Oxford robes. Most respectable, serious scholars would have no truck with it. There were earlier exceptions of course — notably Fred Lewis Pattee — but the predominant attitude toward American literature was a cautious one. In the late twenties, for example, the proposed thesis topic of a Harvard Ph.D. candidate was turned down because "too much" had already been written on that particular American writer. The candidate was F.O. Matthiessen; the writer was Walt Whitman. [18] Consequently, a separate study of the American academic response to Thoreau's social and political thought before the 1920s would be so brief as to be negligible. From the twenties on, however, academic interest in Thoreau has developed from a small cottage industry to a booming big business. Thoreau's stock has had its ups and downs since, but it has never crashed.

In charting the course of the ups and downs of Thoreau's reputation I have attempted to present the historical context which influenced the criticism as economically as possible. In place of copious details and descriptions, the reader will find impressionistic devices used to evoke the spirit, atmosphere, and milieu of the periods that I deemed relevant to the formation of the critical and popular responses to Thoreau. The commentaries about Thoreau, however, are examined in detail and quoted whenever the tone or rhetoric of a passage loses its significance and impact by being paraphrased.

It is inevitable that my own view of Thoreau's politics and social thought emerges in the course of this study, but it is only secondary to the description and explanation of the history of his political reputation. The purpose of this study is to chart a history of Thoreau criticism rather than to produce a reading of Thoreau. Although I have frequently taken issue with the critics directly and attempted to refute their use or reading of Thoreau, when I have done so it was for the purpose of demonstrating that a more complete reading and consideration of Thoreau might have precluded or qualified their particular use of him. Readers who hope to find a definitive Thoreau in these pages, a Thoreau who is simple to place and understand, a Thoreau whose currents of thought run deeper than the sum total of the critics, will be disappointed.

I have made no attempt to advance systematically a particular view of Thoreau's politics because it became clear, as I wrote, that the complex nature of the subject would require a book of its own, a book that would shrewdly accept Walter Harding's point that Thoreau "did not formulate and unify his thinking." Such a book would have to explore not only the contradictions and competing ideas in Thoreau's own writing and life, but it would also have to relate him to his own historical moment — rather than running a twentieth-century security check on him — in order to place him in a context that would help to determine how typical or extreme his positions were on particular issues and reform in general. After reading the critics it seems that perhaps one way of resolving some of the nearly endless conflicting judgments and assessments concerning Thoreau's politics might be to relate Thoreau more to his own contemporaries than to ours. More studies are needed which connect Thoreau's political thought to that of such Transcendental figures as Orestes Brownson, Theodore Parker, Margaret Fuller, and George Ripley, rather than to twentieth-century thinkers influenced by Thoreau. Such studies are, however, clearly beyond the scope of this book.

Pursuing Thoreau's politics can be as frustrating and maddening as chasing a loon — or a white whale; he was a grand apolitical, political-like man who resists tidy summations. As of this writing, it is remarkable that no book-length treatment — from any point of view — has yet been published which examines and assesses Tho-

reau's politics. It is a book that is long overdue for Thoreau studies.
I like to think that this one will hasten it along.[19]

NOTES

1. Henry Salt, *The Life of Henry David Thoreau*, rev. ed. (1896; rpt. Hamden, Conn.: Archon Books, 1968), p. 197.

2. Although the following chronological list of books, articles, and theses concerning Thoreau's reputation is not exhaustive, it does suggest the bulk and the range of such studies: Henry Seidel Canby, *American Estimates* (New York: Harcourt, Brace, 1929), pp. 97-109; Austin Warren, "Lowell on Thoreau," *Studies in Philology*, 27 (July 1930), 442-462; James Playsted Wood, "English and American Criticism of Thoreau," *New England Quarterly*, 6 (December 1933), 733-746; Henry Seidel Canby, *Thoreau* (Boston: Houghton Mifflin, 1939), pp. 441-455; Margaret F. Hauber, "Thoreau, the Humanitarian," unpublished master's thesis (Rutgers University, 1939), pp. 75-90; Charles Child Walcutt, "Thoreau in the Twentieth Century," *South Atlantic Quarterly*, 39 (April 1940), 168-184; Walter Harding, "A Century of Thoreau," *Audubon Magazine*, 47 (March-April 1945), 80-84; Randall Stewart, "The Growth of Thoreau's Reputation," *College English*, 7 (January 1946), 208-214; John Quincy Reed, "Thoreau's Literary Reputation in the Twentieth Century," unpublished master's thesis (University of Pittsburgh, 1948); Walter Scott Houston, "An Analysis of Some of the Criticism of Henry David Thoreau," unpublished master's thesis (University of Alabama, 1948); Leonard Gray, "The Growth of Thoreau's Reputation," *Thoreau Society Bulletin*, 42 (Winter 1953), 3-4; Walter Harding, *Thoreau: A Century of Criticism* (Dallas, Tex.: Southern Methodist University Press, 1954); Bruce E. Burdett, "The Cult of Thoreau: Its Background, Development, and Status," unpublished master's thesis (Brown University, 1955); Walter Harding, *A Thoreau Handbook* (New York: New York University Press, 1959), pp. 175-213, et passim; Theodore Haddin, "The Changing Image of Henry Thoreau: The Emergence of the Literary Artist," unpublished doctoral dissertation (University of Michigan, 1968); Hubert H. Hoeltje, "Misconceptions in Current Thoreau Criticism," *Philological Quarterly*, 47 (October 1968), 563-570; Wendell Glick, *The Recognition of Henry David Thoreau* (Ann Arbor: University of Michigan Press, 1969); Joseph Schiffman, "*Walden* and *Civil Disobedience*: Critical Analyses," *New Approaches to Thoreau: A Symposium*, ed. William Bysshe Stein

(Hartford, Conn.: Transcendental Books, 1969), pp. 56-60; Lewis Leary, "Thoreau," *Eight American Authors*, ed. James Woodress, rev. ed. (New York: Norton, 1971), pp. 129-171; and Theodore Haddin, "Thoreau's Reputation Once More," *Thoreau Journal Quarterly*, 4 (January 15, 1972), 10-15.

3. This millennial view of America has been described and analyzed by many historians and critics (borrowing a phrase from Dwight MacDonald, there is a possibility for a "Book-of-the-Millennium Club" here). It hardly needs documentation, but if it is desired it will be found in David E. Smith, "Millenarian Scholarship in America," *American Quarterly*, 17 (Fall 1965), 535-549.

4. Consider a sampling of titles from a recent edition of *Books in Print* (New York: R.R. Bowker Co., 1975, IV). This list is only a small fraction of the entire listing and consists of only those titles that have *politics* as the first alphabetized word: *The Politics of Affluence, The Politics of American Science, The Politics of Architecture, The Politics of Authenticity, The Politics of Consumer Protection, The Politics of Culture, The Politics of Education, The Politics of God, The Politics of Literature, The Politics of the Family, The Politics of the Ocean, The Politics of Therapy,* and *The Politics of Truth.*

5. Theodore Roszak's *The Dissenting Academy* (New York: Pantheon, 1967) offers a general (and partisan) overview of the problem by presenting essays written by professionals from various academic disciplines which deal with the social responsibilities of their respective professions. The specific charges leveled against the MLA at the 1968 annual meeting are reported in the *New York Times*, December 28, 1968, p. 18; December 29, 1968, p. 36; December 30, 1968, p. 20; and December 31, 1968, p. 16. For a summary of the results of those charges see Doris Grumbach, "What Matters to the MLA," *New Republic*, January 6 and 23, 1973, pp. 21-23.

6. For representative discussions dealing with the relationship between literature and politics see Frederick Crews, "Do Literary Studies Have an Ideology?" *PMLA*, 85 (May 1970), 423-428; and Rima Drell Reck, "The Politics of Literature," in the same issue of *PMLA*, 429-432. An issue of *College English*, 31 (March 1970), entitled "A Phalanx from the Left" is devoted exclusively to politics and literature; for "Comment and Rebuttal" see 32 (November 1970), 204-236.

7. "Something Is Happening But You Don't Know What It Is, Do You, Mr. Jones?" *PMLA*, 85 (May 1970), 422.

8. For an explanation of the literary revival of these writers which takes into account the assumptions, values, and tastes of their respective critics see Michael Zimmerman, "Literary Revivalism in America: Some Notes

Toward a Hypothesis," *American Quarterly*, 19 (Spring 1967), 71-85.

9. Egon Schwarz argues convincingly that a refusal to recognize and consciously deal with this historical dimension of literary criticism can result in criticism "shot through with implicit, unconscious, and unreflected value judgments that amount to mere prejudice." "Hermann Hesse, the American Youth Movement, and Problems of Literary Evaluation," *PMLA*, 85 (October 1970), 985.

10. Warren I. Susman provides a succinct overview of this idea in "History and the American Intellectual: Uses of a Usable Past," *American Quarterly*, 16 (Summer 1964), 243-263. He points out that "history is often used as the basis for a political philosophy which while explaining the past offers also a way to change the future" (p. 244).

11. *Walden*, ed. J. Lyndon Shanley (Princeton: Princeton University Press, 1971), p. 325. Hereafter references to *Walden* will be cited within parentheses in the text. Whenever available the new Princeton edition of Thoreau's writings has been used. In connection with my use of the Princeton edition, it should be noted at the outset that Wendell Glick's edition of *Reform Papers* (1973) has as the title for "Civil Disobedience" a "more defensible [editorial] choice" for the essay; Glick uses the 1849 title of the copy-text, "Resistance to Civil Government." Throughout this study, however, I use the more well-known title, "Civil Disobedience," when referring to the essay. Since there is no evidence to make a conclusive case for either title (see Glick, pp. 320-321), I have chosen "Civil Disobedience" because nearly all the commentaries I discuss refer to the essay by that title.

12. Lewis Leary, "Thoreau," *Eight American Authors*, ed. James Woodress, rev. ed. (New York: Norton, 1971), p. 133.

13. *The Journal of Henry D. Thoreau* (1906; rpt. 14 vols. in 2, New York: Dover, 1962) IV, 252. Subsequent references to the *Journal* will be cited within parentheses in the text. This Dover reprint is an unabridged republication of volumes VII to XX of the 1906 "Walden edition" of twenty volumes. The *Journal* is also numbered from I to XIV, which is the numbering used here.

14. Walter Harding, *A Thoreau Handbook* (New York: New York University Press, 1959), p. 132.

15. *The Writings of Henry David Thoreau* (Boston and New York: Houghton Mifflin, 1906), I, 304-305. Subsequent references to the first six volumes of this "Walden edition" will be cited within parentheses in the text.

16. *New England Quarterly*, 6 (December 1933), 742. Stewart, Harding, and Leary, among others, support this assessment; a useful overview and

discussion of Thoreau's reputation before 1920 will be found in Burdett, pp. 1-51 (see note 2).

17. See Willard Thorp, "Exodus: Four Decades of American Literature Scholarship," *Modern Language Quarterly*, 26 (March 1965), 40-61.

18. George Abbott White, "Ideology and Literature: *American Renaissance* and F.O. Matthiessen," *TriQuarterly*, 23/24 (Winter/Spring 1972), 431.

19. After I completed this study, Robert Dickens published *Thoreau, the Complete Individualist: His Relevance—and Lack of It—for Our Time* (New York: Exposition Press, 1974), which he describes as, among other things, "a thorough descriptive and critical study of Thoreau's social and political philosophy" (p. 5). This is a surprising claim given that Dickens does not discuss Thoreau's social and political thought until page 61 of his book, a book that contains fewer than one hundred pages of text.

chapter 1

THOREAU IN THE TWENTIES: "WHAT ARE YOU GOING TO DO WITH SUCH A FELLOW?"

The business of America is business.

Calvin Coolidge, 1925

In my experience nothing is so opposed to
poetry—not crime—as business. It is a negation
of life.

Thoreau, *Journal* (IV, 162)

The social and political climate of the 1920s was not conducive to the growth of Thoreau's reputation. Whereas Thoreau's business was beans and beyond, America's business was business, and there was little commerce between them. But there had been three decades before.

America had made its pact earlier with Thoreau in the 1890s when he was seen as a prefiguration of the growing reaction against urban life. This "unique individual, half college-graduate and half Algonquin," as Oliver Wendell Holmes called him, was just what the doctor ordered for Teddy Roosevelt's generaton of Rough Riders. For an overstuffed civilization that wanted to avoid flabbiness, Thoreau was a voice from the past that spoke for the

American Cult of the Primitive. His stay at Walden Pond and his writings on nature made him a venerable veteran of the strenuous life for a peripatetic, athletic kind of age, an age curiously out of tune with Thoreau's flute, an age characterized by "Ta-ra-ra-boom-dee-ay," yet an age that found him useful. [2] Thoreau's reputation as a nature writer bloomed at a time when Americans turned to nature as a tonic to relieve their inability to digest completely the raw facts of urban life. The frontier was closed, and the wilderness was no longer perceived as a threat; instead it was "the preservation of the World" (*Writings*, V, 224). This view of Thoreau was clearly at the expense of much of his other writings, but it was no mere illusion, because interest in Thoreau as a nature writer was based primarily upon excerpts from his *Journal*, edited by H.G.O. Blake, who entitled them *Early Spring in Massachusetts* (1881), *Summer* (1884), *Winter* (1887), and *Autumn* (1892). From a social and political perspective this is bowdlerized Thoreau, but for Americans looking for a pleasant literary path from the city back to the regenerative woods of Concord, it was all of Thoreau they needed.

Thoreau was made party to a pact that he had never signed, a circumstance typical of his career. Unfortunately his reputation as a nature writer was one from which he could never sign off, simply because he was dead. Of course Thoreau wrote about and valued nature, but it is as meaningful to say *only* that as it would be to describe Melville as a fish warden. There were exceptions to this view of Thoreau as a bachelor of nature, but criticism that focused on his social and political thought was generally either so ignored or pruned by the nature buffs that it was scarcely visible. One of several notable exceptions before the 1920s was John Macy's chapter on Thoreau in *The Spirit of American Literature* (1913). Macy duly noted that the "growing cult of the open air" and "the increasing host of amateur prodigals returning to nature" had "given fresh vogue" to Thoreau's nature writings, but he believed that this was a distortion of Thoreau. Macy, who insisted that criticism should be "witty, eloquent, instinctive, humorous . . . beautiful, provocative, and irritating," obviously enjoyed unloading established literary canons. In addition to championing Thoreau's social thought, he also praised Twain and Whitman over Bryant. His observations on the function of criticism appear in an essay entitled "The Critical Game," a title that informs his attitude toward criticism on Thoreau.

Macy views Thoreau as "the one anarchist of great literary power in a nation of slavish conformity to legalism, where obedience to statute and maintenance of 'order' are assiduously inculcated as patriotic virtures by the social powers which profit from other peoples' docility." Macy felt that the overwhelming interest in Thoreau's nature writing at the expense of his social writing was generated by a fear of being considered "disloyally 'un-American.' " He makes his point by targeting Harvard University, ostensibly one of the leading centers of free inquiry in America:

The essays on "Forest Trees" and "Wild Apples" were to be found in a school reader twenty-five years ago. But the ringing revolt of the essay on "Civil Disobedience" is still silenced under the thick respectability of our times. The ideas in it could not today be printed in the magazine which was for years owned by the publishers of Thoreau's complete works. Boston Back Bay would shiver! It would not do, really, to utter aloud Thoreau's ideas in a society whose leading university, Thoreau's alma mater, has recently ruled, "that the hall of the university shall not be open for persistent or systematic propaganda on contentious questions of contemporaneous social, economic, political, or religious interests." [3]

Thus while Thoreau's nature writing gained in popularity, the "flaming eloquence of his social philosophy" was ignored. Though Macy was not the first to point out that Thoreau's social philosophy was unwelcome in a politically conservative atmosphere, he did so with the most vehemence.[4]

With the publication of the 1906 Walden edition, which included fourteen volumes of the *Journal*, a more complete Thoreau was made available to readers. Blake's nature excerpts were seen by some critics as precisely that — only excerpts. Although students of American literature gradually became more aware of Thoreau as a social critic, Macy's complaint that Thoreau was perceived primarily as a nature writer was valid until the late twenties. In

1919 N.C. Wyeth noted that "In all forewords and prefaces that appear in the various editions of his books, this *Naturalist* idea dominates almost to the complete exclusion of [any other aspect of Thoreau.]"[5]

The history of Thoreau's reputation in the twenties consists primarily of a dialogue among commentators who choose to see Thoreau as a nature writer and those who choose to see him as a social and political thinker. Thoreau's political reputation was slow to develop, and even as it did develop, commentators who focused upon his social and political thought generally expressed reservations about their new found ally. Owing to the predominantly conservative political atmosphere of the twenties, there was an ambivalent attitude toward Thoreau's politics until fairly late in the decade when Vernon L. Parrington's *Main Currents in American Thought* firmly established Thoreau's reputation as a social thinker.

Very early in the decade Odell Shepard sought to remedy the predominant emphasis on Thoreau as a naturalist.[6] Shepard argued that before Thoreau could be placed "as one of the three or four most original men of letters in America," it would be necessary to dispel two misconceptions concerning him (p. 339). The first misconception was that Thoreau was a mere shadow of Emerson, and the second was that he was only a naturalist. Contrary to previous generations of American critics, Shepard insisted that it was precisely when Thoreau "forgets the woodchuck, concerning which others now know more than he did, and begins to speak of men, that it behooves us to listen" (p. 342). In defoliating Thoreau, Shepard emphasized him as a "practical philosopher" who could teach us "how to live" and whose head was not in the clouds but in the streets of Concord. Shepard points to "Civil Disobedience," "Slavery in Massachusetts," and the John Brown episode as indications of Thoreau's participation in history despite his aversion to politics. Though Shepard mentions this social and political aspect of Thoreau, and in so doing presents a more balanced view of him, he is not given to the enthusiasm of Macy. Shepard has serious reservations concerning the efficacy of Thoreau's social philosophy, because "one fears that he seldom knew the sober and durable pleasure that comes of pulling one's full weight in the world's united ef-

fort. Moreover, he was a reformer without a programme, a wor-
shiper of the deed who never began to act" (p. 339). Shepard is
troubled by Thoreau's unwillingness to accept a social identity, because he believes that it is through a collective effort that the world
is reformed. Shepard seems to have an ambivalent attitude toward
Thoreau; he wants to see Thoreau as more than a bird watcher, but
he has difficulty reconciling Thoreau's political posture with that of
the twenties because Thoreau refuses to be a good citizen.

The predominant politics of the twenties, the conservatism and
the general fear of left-wing unorthodoxy, is too well known to require a summary here.[7] The "Red Scare," the Sacco and Vanzetti
case, the Ku Klux Klan, and the Scopes trial are only a few of the
more famous manifestations of the political conservatism of the decade. In addition to the searching out of un-American activities,
there was an almost militant effort to be as American as possible.
This took many forms — sometimes they were ugly white-hooded
forms — but one of the more amusing is the example set by the wife
of the President of the United States, as reported in *Time* (without a
trace of irony). Mrs. Harding, attending a Shriner's parade in
Washington, D.C., stood up more than one hundred times to salute
the Stars and Stripes as they streamed past, and the women nearby
uniformly followed her patriotic gesture. "Said Mrs. Harding:
'Why shouldn't the women of America pay the same respect to the
flag as the men do? No citizen of this country is a better American
than I am. I purpose hereafter, as long as I live, to salute the
American flag!' "[8] While Mrs. Harding ceaselessly hoisted herself
and saluted the flag, the average citizen had to be content to express
his patriotism by demonstrating that he worked for American
values.

Public service — whether affiliated with the Boosters Club, the
B.P.O.E., the Good Citizens' League, the Kiwanis, or the Republican party — was all the rage. The twenties might be most
remembered for its flappers, bathtub gin, bootleggers, tommy
guns, jazz, and zany collegiates, but these were not the only
characteristics of the age; indeed they were reactions to the predominant characteristics. There was also the Volstead Act. If Fitzgerald was the unofficial spokesman of the roaring twenties, then
Harding and Coolidge were the official spokesmen of the decade's

respectability and orthodoxy. In 1922 President Harding confidently and officially assured his fellow countrymen that "If I could plant a Rotary Club in every city and hamlet in this country I would then rest assured that our ideals of freedom would be safe and civilization would progress."[9] Harding is an easy target, but it is enough to point out that he was serious.

The "Standardized American Citizen" was not expected — quoting another President — to "rock the boat." Instead, Americans were supposed to man the oars of the ship of state, with the Republican party platform as its rudder and the business community as its executive officers. This was no outward bound voyage but one "Back to Normalcy." It is not difficult to imagine that Thoreau's response to this demand would have been similar to that of a Bartleby aboard an early version of the *Good Ship Lollipop*: "I would prefer not to." *Normalcy* was a word that Thoreau, of course, had never even heard. One indeed fears that Thoreau, as Shepard points out, "seldom knew the sober and durable pleasure that comes of pulling one's full weight in the world's united effort." For his reputation could not possibly thrive in a decade that demanded "united effort."

William Lyon Phelps, a famous professor of literature at Yale, who valued Thoreau because he insisted upon being independent of the world's opinion, sharply confirms Shepard's sense that Thoreau rubbed against the American grain of the twenties: "Thoreau is upsetting, disturbing, like a mosquito in the night. Many have decided that he is either negligible or a nuisance. He is still accused of conceit and selfishness. The moral watchword of the twentieth century, 'Service,' did not appeal to him."[10] As much as Phelps celebrates Thoreau's buzziness over busyness, he, like Shepard, feels compelled to take a swat at his gadfly: "I should like it better if he had not insisted so much on his own happiness; sometimes I think he protests too much" (p. 88). Thoreau seems to be as disturbing to Phelps as he is to those who accuse him of conceit and selfishness. Phelps's objection to Thoreau is, essentially, no different from that of those who worship service. In short, one cannot point an accusing finger at the country and still have both hands on an oar.

·Although Shepard gives his verson of public service an international twist by invoking the "world's united effort" (a liberal sensibility left over from Wilsonian politics), the discomfort he feels with Thoreau is similar to that felt by the superpatriots, the 100 percent Americans. Thoreau's apparent refusal to be a good citizen, to pull his own weight, made his political posture suspect to both liberals and conservatives. To liberals the refusal seemed conservative and isolationist; to conservatives it placed Thoreau outside the safe, predictable majority. Phelps was correct in noting that

When a man finds that he can be quite happy in solitude, and proclaims the fact, he is sure to be condemned. Society feels uncomfortable when informed of its superfluousness, or of its stupidity. The average man suspects that such men as Thoreau are dangerous, because so self-sufficient. He is not flattering to our self-esteem. (p. 80)

In 1842 Emerson made this same point in his essay "The Transcendentalist," and he added that "Society will retaliate." The conservatives of the twenties had more objections to Thoreau than the fact that he was a loner, and they too would retaliate. Or at least that was the fear of their contemporary liberals.

In the pages of *The Freeman*, a magazine begun in the early twenties which shared the liberal values of *The Nation* and *The New Republic*, but which saw itself as more radical than either of them,[11] Thoreau was seen as a champion of liberal values in a conservative age: "Thoreau came nearer to being the incarnation of the independence which has been our national watchword, than any American we can think of; and we do not forget Paine, Jefferson, Franklin, Lincoln, and others of our varied galaxy."[12] The brief one-page article from which this excerpt is taken suggests that if newly arrived Europeans are to be subjected to Americanization, then perhaps Americans ought to be also, "and if the choice of textbooks were confided to us, we should like first of all — and perhaps last — to put Thoreau's works in the students' hands." *The Freeman* writer would also choose the students who might learn from the "eighteen-carat Americanism of Thoreau." The class would consist of, among others, notables such as John D. Rockefeller, Jr.,

Adolph S. Ochs, Bishop Manning, J.P. Morgan, and Judge Gary, all busily reading Thoreau on education, morality, technology, and dollar chasing. But such a school could not last long, because

It requires no highly developed fancy to picture the rough dispersal of the class by the agents of American Daugherty, headed by American Burns, supported by posses representing the American Ku Klux Klan, the American Legion and the American National Civil Federation. They would certainly regard the textbooks as seditious. Thoreau! — sounds like some damned foreigner!

There is no hard evidence that I am aware of to support this assertion; it is, rather, an extrapolation of known conservative political views and activities applied to Thoreau. There are no extreme right-wing denunciations of Thoreau in print during the twenties, because he probably was not read by conservatives and because he had no large popular following (as he eventually would have in the 1960s) which might have made a denunciation necessary. Indeed, Thoreau was not very well known in the early 1920s among any group, regardless of its political persuasions. An anonymous reviewer in *Scribner's Magazine* confirms this in an offhand but convincing manner: "Thoreau, no doubt, is still read now and then; I know some who even keep his books on a shelf of intimates and occasionally quote him."[13] No limbo would have been more hellish for a writer who wanted to be used. Nevertheless, *The Freeman* writer's fancy makes sense, and, more to the point, demonstrates that even though Thoreau was disinclined to join liberal causes, they were inclined to join him.

The Freeman championed Thoreau because he was seen as an earlier American freeman who shared its views on a number of issues ranging from labor and capital to college education and technology. The magazine had even invoked Thoreau's name in a full-page subscription advertisement for itself. Both *The Freeman* and Thoreau would "help American culture" if only they were read.[14] *The Freeman's* delight in discovering Thoreau as a trailblazer for its own values is demonstrated in an article which, ignoring the popular fallacy of viewing Thoreau as a nature writer, finds "Thoreau

the Radical": ". . . to our amazement in this year of grace and enlightenment, 1920, we discover this odd fellow, living in all places
in Concord, Massachusetts, in the heart of chill New England [*The
Freeman* was a New York magazine], the graduate of Harvard college — to be a radical — a stupendous radical!"[15] Here was a Thoreau whom most Americans had not been aware of before. The
author concludes the article with a rhetorical question for his
reader: "What are you going to do with such a fellow?" The decade's overwhelming response to this question was that it would
have nothing to do with such a fellow. Neither Thoreau the radical
nor *The Freeman* was much read in the early twenties. But Thoreau
the nature writer and *National Geographic Magazine* were.[16]

In 1920 the readers of *National Geographic* were presented with
a fifteen-page winter ramble through Thoreau's New England.[17]
H.W. Gleason's photographs, coupled with descriptive passages
from Thoreau's writings, chronicled a typical New England winter
in and around Concord. Gleason, who provided the photographs
for the 1906 edition of the *Journal*, begins his photographic essay
with something of a defense for including a relatively provincial
Thoreau in a magazine that normally featured adventures in exotic
places such as Samoa, China, Paris, or Zanzibar: "The *National
Geographic Magazine* being pre-eminently a magazine of travel, it
is not inappropriate to call the attention to its readers to the jour-
neyings of one of the most original, observant, and wholly enter-
taining travelers whom the continent has produced" (p. 165). Thoreau is praised as a superb nature writer whose descriptions are so
vivid that one can go to Concord and environs to snap pictures of
almost the very things he describes. Thoreau, writes Gleason, "has
given us an unsurpassed picture of New England outdoor life . . ."
(p. 168). Gleason's photographs are intended to complement, not
surpass, Thoreau's descriptions. Yet one tends to remember the
pleasant photographs of winter brooks and stone walls more than
the prose. It seems that the impact of such an article on the reader is
to assure that if Thoreau is remembered at all, he is recalled as a
verbal illustrator of nature, and if a picture is worth a thousand
words, Gleason has, in effect, written a 15,000-word piece on Thoreau as a nature writer. Thoreau country, like Robert Frost country, has always been a resource for its writers, but it has also been a

liability for its writers' reputations. It has led one Thoreau enthusiast, James O'Donnell Bennett, to assert that "for a complete understanding of Thoreau, three days in Concord and in Walden woods
are worth many books." [18] "Study Thoreau" becomes "Study
Nature." There is some truth to this assertion (any writer's intentions are better understood by a sympathetic reader), but it leads at
best to only a partial, not a complete, understanding of Thoreau. It
leads to this:

He [Thoreau] is the bonniest, gravest, honestest spirit in our
literature, and his great book [*Walden*] has the sunshine, the
crisp snow, the bird notes, the morning light and the morning
fragrance of Walden pond bound in with every one of its
nearly 400 steadying, exhilarating comforting pages. It lives
and sings. (p. 326)

Bennett's exuberance here is genuine, but like Thoreau's wood-
chopper his mind seems to be asleep. Writing for a popular audience, he ignores Thoreau's social criticism of American materialism
and its consequences. This is expurgated Thoreau.
    However, as Norman Foerster has suggested in his "Thoreau as
Artist" (1921), the "magical truth" of Thoreau's nature writing "has
won him many a devoted reader who finds himself indifferent to,
or exasperated by, Thoreau's personal piquancy and his paradoxical satire of human society." [19] The poet-naturalist is always safe
and never upsetting. The naturalist John Burroughs serves as an
example of what Foerster only suggests. Burroughs calls Thoreau to
task for his scientific inaccuracies, but generally he finds Thoreau's
value to be in his descriptions of nature. At the same time that Burroughs praises Thoreau for his nature writing, he also criticizes
what Foerster labels his "personal piquancy and his paradoxical
satire." Burroughs argues that "We could have wished him to have
shown himself in his writings as somewhat sweeter and more
tolerant toward the rest of the world, broader in out look, and
more just and charitable in disposition . . . ." [20]
    It is worth noting that Foerster, a well-known New Humanist in
the tradition of Paul Elmer More and Irving Babbitt, discusses the
art of Thoreau's prose in "Thoreau as Artist" only in connection

with his nature writing and not his social criticism. Two years later in his lengthy chapter on Thoreau in *Nature in American Literature* he all but ignores Thoreau's social thought, presumably because "his relation to his fellow man . . . must be held against him . . . he was inveterately self-centered." [21]

Although Foerster's emphasis on Thoreau's spiritual use of nature rescues Thoreau from those who would see him only as a naturalist (p. 120), Foerster also takes Thoreau's "romanticism" away from him and replaces it with those "perennially vital" traditions of the Western world, "the classical and the Christian" (p. 142). This allows Foerster to present Thoreau as "more nearly an exponent of humanism" (p. 140); it allows him, in other words, to present him as an ally. Foerster must avoid Thoreau's social thought because it is more romantic than classical in its insistence upon man's perfectability and man's infinite possibilities. Thoreau's social thought is not classical, insofar as either of the terms *romantic* and *classical* have any political meaning, and they do.

T.E. Hulme's essay "Romanticism and Classicism" categorizes the basic political values that cluster around each term. The classical is associated with discipline, restraint, orthodoxy, tradition, and social organization; the romantic is allied with freedom, self-expression, spontaneity, and the primacy of the individual over established institutions. [22] The categories that Hulme describes are the basis for the distinctions that are usually made between conservative and liberal politics. New Humanist values, classical values which align themselves with conservative politics, [23] seem to generate Foerster's emphasis upon Thoreau as a "true son of the Puritans" (p. 131) who (despite "his sense of the inalienable divinity of men" [p. 137]) was a lover of individual restraint and discipline "Uniting the spirit of the Puritans with the purpose of the Greeks . . . . " Foerster is correct in describing this aspect of Thoreau — clearly, he was not one of the roughs — but Foerster neglects the romantic Thoreau who insisted that one should "Grow wild according to thy nature" (*Walden*, p. 207) and follow one's "genius, which is a very crooked one, every moment" (*Walden*, p. 56). Foerster sees more of the Puritan than the antinomian in Thoreau, more of the " 'all round' man of the Greeks" (p. 135) than the man who made a career of his "crooked" genius. Because Thoreau's

romanticism — his faith in an organic response to life — does not
correspond to Foerster's conception of Thoreau as a humanist, he
must weed Thoreau of such unwieldy growth and prune him to
conform to a conservative termperament.

The only mention of Thoreau's politics is given a distinctly conservative turn; observing that Thoreau, like Socrates, was obeying
"an unwritten law superior to that of the state," Foerster writes that
Thoreau's repudiation of a government that supported slavery was
based upon his belief that " 'They are the lovers of law and order
who observe the law when the government breaks it' " (p. 131).
The quotation chosen by Foerster is a revealing one, and it is the
only one. There is no sloppy "emotional Humanitarianism" dis-
played here (a phrase used to describe Whitman and "European
romanticists" [p. 138]); instead, the outlaw, the man who will not
pledge allegiance to a government that supports slavery, is presented as a (higher) law-and-order man. Reading Foerster, one
would never know that there is in Thoreau a strong anarchistic impulse which is not so restrained and measured. This is not to say
that Thoreau is an anarchist, but it is to point out that he can be absorbed into a New Humanist tradition only by filtering out some of
his romantic qualities. Were it not for Foerster's likening Thoreau
to Socrates, one might think that Thoreau's interest in classical
literature was focused upon Creon instead of Antigone.

Foerster was writing for an academic audience of scholarly
gentlemen (with the exception of critics like Macy, whom Foerster
criticized in his *American Criticism* [1928] because Macy's Whit-
manesque, undisciplined approach to the problems of the day was
not what the disordered postwar decade needed[24]). For such an
audience, an audience that valued restraint and discipline, Foerster's description of Thoreau must have been attractive:

In his natural history studies . . . he aimed at exact observation and record, and succeeded in a larger measure than one
would expect of a man who was more philosopher and poet
than scientist. His wide reading, also, was not a matter of di-
version but rather of enlightenment and still more of discipline; especially was this true of his study of the Latin and
Greek authors in the original (the dead languages did not die

over again for him when he left college) and his reading of the
"scriptures of the nations."

But the chief discipline of all, including, indeed all others,
was obedience to his genius — not the "genius" of the German
romanticists but the Socratic inner witness, the "heavenly
monitor" of Milton. (p. 130)

A man with these qualities could have completed a Ph.D. almost
anywhere during the twenties. The reassurance that Thoreau was a
serious student of both life and letters redeemed him from the
charges of profligacy of the sort that his disapproving Aunt Jane
clucked over years before when she complained: "I wish he could
find something better to do than walking off every now and
then." [25] Thoreau had to wait a good deal longer than Emerson for
his invitation back to Harvard.

In contrast to the academic sensibility of the early twenties,
which made Thoreau out to be a disciplined student who, as a result, had found "something better to do," there was on a more
popular level a celebration of Thoreau's "walking off every now
and then." To Charles J. Finger, Thoreau was *The Man Who
Escaped from the Herd* (1922). The *herd* was a particularly popular
term in the twenties used to suggest the conformist societal pressures that were brought to bear upon artists or sensitive individuals
of any vocation. Raymond Weaver uses the term in his biography
of Herman Melville to explain Melville's unpopularity in the nineteenth century: ". . . the herd must always be intolerant of all who
violate its sacred and painfully reared institutions." [26] Finger's
pamphlet emphasizing Thoreau's individualism was one of hundreds of small pamphlets in the then famous Little Blue Book series
under the general editorship and ownership of E. Haldeman-Julius.
What Henry Ford was to the automobile and the masses, Haldeman-Julius was to "Culture" and the masses. Like the little red
books of Mao Tse-tung, the purpose of the Little Blue Books was
nothing less than cultural revolution; indeed, the first Little Blue
Book was, oddly enough, red. In order to appreciate the significance of Thoreau's being included in this popular series, it is first
necessary to be aware of the importance of the Little Blue Books.

In one of the numerous advertisements that appeared in newspapers and magazines of the twenties, Haldeman-Julius, capitalizing upon Sinclair Lewis' successes, asks in huge type:

Are You a Babbitt?

Do Intelligent and Sophisticated People Laugh at You When You Leave? Do They Repeat Your Crudities and Smile Knowingly? Are You Barred from the Company of the Cultured Because Intellectually You Are a Main Streeter? [27]

One needn't be if one can spare a nickel or a dime for a Little Blue Book that can be read while waiting for a train or sitting in a dentist's office. In an address to his potential readers, Haldeman-Julius writes that he is offering these "Books Which Will Send You on the Road to Culture" for the reader's sake, not his. He is not in it for the money, but rather because "I have dedicated my life to the work of bringing culture to the people." And he proudly adds: "In the words of the Baltimore Sun: 'That Individual, E. Haldeman-Julius, is doing more to educate the country than any ten universities put together.' " Perhaps this is an exaggeration, but he did sell over 300 million of his Little Blue Books. [28]

The topics of these books varied tremendously. Because Haldeman-Julius wanted to introduce his readers to the best of the world's achievements in all areas of life, there are the usual pamphlets one might expect on the arts, science, politics, and great writers, but because Haldeman-Julius also considered himself an iconoclast — he was a socialist — there are many pamphlets by unorthodox writers who perhaps would not otherwise have had access to so large a popular market. Clarence Darrow, Upton Sinclair, Havelock Ellis, and Bertrand Russell were among the contributors. One of the more iconoclastic titles of the series, written in part by the editor himself, was *The Serious Lesson in President Harding's Case of Gonorrhea.* [29] Like any good iconoclast Haldeman-Julius had a knack for the catchy title.

In the context of this liberal publishing enterprise it is not surprising then to find a pamphlet on Thoreau, a writer who was also an enemy of the Babbittry of his own time. In his pamphlet Finger explains how Thoreau introduced him to the possibilities of a non-materialistic life. His introductory sentence is almost apocalyptic: "On the 12th of July, 1817, a thinker was turned loose on this planet."[30] There is a promise of something revolutionary here. His Thoreau is a good deal more loose than Foerster's.

Finger's account is a personal testimony of the value of Thoreau's life style. He learns how to do without "a different tie for each day of the week" (p. 4), and with his family he leaves "complex" Cleveland for the Ozarks to live the simple life for a year. Finger quotes liberally from Thoreau not only on the simple life but also on government, education, and literature. He describes Thoreau as an "unterrified Jeffersonian democrat" (p. 18) who was not afraid to speak up for his principles, "an intellectual rebel from the first. He was ever against sham religion, sham propriety, sham knowledge" (p. 61). Finger makes every attempt to portray Thoreau as a radical apart from the herd (though not a "fanatic" or "wild-eyed reformer" [p. 28]). Thoreau's "outspoken boldness astonished and alarmed his friends" (p. 63), but not Finger. His Thoreau is associated with a set of values very different from that of Foerster's Thoreau. The Puritan and Greek very nearly give way to Sacco and Vanzetti. However, it is also necessary to point out that Finger, like most of his contemporaries of the twenties, was not willing to emphasize Thoreau as too much the simple separate person. He sums up Thoreau's signing off for two years at Walden Pond with this: "He was, in short, a private citizen attending strictly to his own business" (p. 31). As much as Finger praises Thoreau for being the man who escaped from the herd, his diction suggests that the decade will not allow it. Finger does not seem to be able to decide whether Thoreau ought to be praised for keeping his nose clean or for nearly getting it bloodied. His ambivalence affects the reader so that one is left somewhat confused over whether Thoreau was simply a private citizen who had no interest in rocking the ship of state or a near anarchist who withdrew from the herd and whose business was in the streets. Neither view accounts for Thoreau's complexity — or Finger's own ambivalence — but it is safe to conclude that Finger's readers tended to remember Thoreau more as the private citizen than the anarchistic protester. Thoreau's involvement in politics eluded the American public of the twenties. The man who escaped from the herd turned out to be a bit of a hermit but not a radical. Even H.L. Mencken, who bumptiously attacked the *Herdenmoral* of the twenties, wrote to Theodore Dreiser as late as 1939 confessing that he knew "relatively little about Thoreau" and "the range of his ideas," having "always thought of him as a sort of nature lover." [31]

Given the fact that the Sacco-Vanzetti case lasted seven years, it is not unreasonable to suppose that if Thoreau was remembered as anarchistic, his name would have been invoked in behalf of the anarchists in magazines and newspapers. There may have been some scattered references to Thoreau and the trial, but there were many more instances of Thoreau's being described in popular periodicals as a naturalist. And when not presented as a naturalist, he was the self-reliant, Franklinesque, thrifty Yankee whom the *New York Times* found particularly attractive.[32] The Little Blue Books were popular, but Finger's seems to have had little or no obvious effect in changing Thoreau's reputation. The radical Thoreau was to be found only sporadically in low-circulation magazines such as *The Freeman* or *The New Student*.

Like *The Freeman*, *The New Student* was a short-lived radical periodical, running from 1922 until 1929. *The New Student* was published by student intellectuals for students who were more interested in voicing their objections to American conservatism than in cheering at college football games. A typical classified advertisement page serves as a useful index to the magazine's predominant sympathies and interests. The advertisements listed are "Organizations That Will Help the Inquiring Student." Among them are Committee on Militarism in Education, the American Civil Liberties Union, the League for Industrial Democracy, the Prevention of War Literature, the Proportional Representation League, the Women's International League for Peace and Freedom, and the Worker's Education Bureau of America. In addition, there are ads for the *Nation*, the *New Leader*, the *New Masses*, and the *Labor Age*.[33] These are the influences upon the new student at the old State U. that turned George F. Babbitt red, white, and blue.

Eliseo Vivas' article in *The New Student*, "Thoreau: The Paradox of Youth," is introduced by a short anonymous piece that sums up both Thoreau's reputation and the place of American literature studies in the United States of the late 1920s.

> In the current issue of *The American Mercury*, a contributor complains that the literature of our country is not receiving sufficient recognition in the colleges. American literature, he says, is rated as "about equal in importance to Scandinavian literature," and "one tenth as important as English literature." *The New Student* has long recognized this seeming defect in our college teaching and has set about to stimulate a demand for more such courses by showing how some of the older writers are relevant to our lives. The article by Mr. Vivas in this issue is on Henry Thoreau, one of the most important writers of the "golden day" who is now achieving the recognition long denied him. (p. 2)

The phrase *golden day* refers to Lewis Mumford's influential study, *The Golden Day: A Study in American Experience and Culture* (1926), which locates the golden day in America before the Civil War when American culture, according to Mumford, was more balanced between the material and the spiritual. Mumford presents Thoreau as an alternative to American materialism, which he considers to be one of the major problems that the country faces. Although Mumford's book was influential, his chapter on Thoreau was not especially significant, since it did not go beyond earlier commentaries on Thoreau. However, it did help to introduce Thoreau to those readers who shared Mumford's view of American materialism.

The New Student echoes the predominant sense of a number of writers on Thoreau that 1927-1928 witnessed a noticeable growing interest in Thoreau. The publishing of Brooks Atkinson's *Cosmic Yankee* and Odell Shepard's *The Heart of Thoreau's Journals*, both in 1927, prompted a *New York Times* reviewer to note that

> the work of revaluing Thoreau, of giving him that significance in American life and letters which belongs to him by every right of genius, has only begun. Thus far the rallying to

his standard has been infrequent and sporadic, but it grows steadily in strength and numbers. This is a Thoreau year.

The recognition given to Thoreau in *The New Student* was due to his "radicalism and his anarchism" (p. 6). Vivas cites Thoreau's repudiation of the Mexican War in "Civil Disobedience" as one of the first native attacks upon American imperialism, and it is "more relevant" in the 1920s than it was in Thoreau's time: "What would he have to say today, after Wilson's macabre hypocrisy of the war to end war, and the development of Pan-American politics, and the ruthless suppression of liberty which has followed? (p. 6). Without going into any significant details about Thoreau's politics, Vivas asserts that "The notable thing about his political criticism is that it anticipated in all significant details, in all its essentials, the criticism of contemporary radicals and liberals, and in many respects went far beyond." Though Vivas finds Thoreau attractive as a strong antidote for the "lily-livered respectable liberals of today" (p. 6), he too shares the decade's reservations about Thoreau's withdrawal from the world. He finds Thoreau paradoxical.

The paradox of Thoreau, according to Vivas, is that the youthful idealism and high aspirations which account for his relevancy are also responsible for his ineffectiveness, "narrowness of vision and loss of wisdom" (p. 8). His extreme idealism isolated him from mankind. In the final analysis Thoreau is ineffective because he was incapable of empathizing with his fellowman:

His intolerance indicates an obtuse nerve in his vision, an inability to understand fully. A man who sees the world with a little detachment and a small modicum of human sympathy, and who seeing, does not forget that he, too, is human, and therefore an heir to the weakness that rankles him in others, never runs the risk of fanaticism. (p. 7)

This qualified view of Thoreau places Vivas within the ranks of contemporaries like Shepard, Phelps, and Finger, who also have ambivalent attitudes toward Thoreau. Vivas' reservations, however, seem more carefully considered. He knows exactly what it is that bothers him about Thoreau: Thoreau's extreme ideals are

inoperative in the real, everyday world, and because he will not
compromise his ideals at all, they have no effect upon the world;
they are politically useless. Vivas sees Thoreau sacrificing his
political effectiveness to his own insistence upon individual moral
purity.

To compromise is vile when compromise is the result of lazi-
ness and cowardice, as it is in the majority of cases. But not to
compromise is often as cowardly and foolish. It is foolish because it ends in futility. The business of the world will be
done. It will be done badly because it will be done for men by
men. But it will be done. (p. 8)

Melville's Captain Starry Vere might have said the same about
Thoreau. A person must act within the world as it is, if the world is
ever to approach what it ought to be. From Vivas' point of view,
Americans can consider themselves fortunate that Thoreau was
only the captain of a huckleberry party instead of engineering for
all America. Vivas sees the idealistic impulse that informs Thoreau's political thought as praiseworthy, but, paradoxically — and
Vivas is aware of the paradox — that same idealistic strain can be a
liability, because "men like him run the risk of aiming too high —
as others aim too low, due to the meanness of their natures —, of
wishing to encase the universe in their own noble, exalted, but narrow forms" (p. 15).
  As much as Vivas aligns Thoreau with the sensibilities of liberals
and radicals of the twenties, he resists signing Thoreau on: "The
reader of Thoreau . . . must regret that the wisdom he garnered for
himself cannot also be made use of by others" (p. 15). Vivas concludes that the idealism which informs Thoreau's political thought
is useful and necessary, but the idealistic mode — "fanatical exaltation" (p. 7) — is useless and counterproductive. Vivas, more than
Thoreau, was interested in changing the world and did not worry
as much about the world changing him.
  Regardless of whether one completely agrees with Vivas' approach to Thoreau's politics, it is perhaps the most thoughtful and
balanced brief account of the subject during the entire decade. It
deserves more attention. Unfortunately, in 1927 there was a study

which attracted considerably more attention; it was a popular book entitled *Henry Thoreau: The Cosmic Yankee* written by J. Brooks Atkinson, the author of *The Freeman* article who had asked his readers earlier in the decade what they would do with such a "stupendous radical." Seven years after *The Freeman* article — the same span of time that begins and ends the Sacco-Vanzetti trial — Atkinson answered his own question.

"Yes," he wrote, Thoreau was still "a radical." [35] His fundamental truths and the principles by which he lived his life "roar like rebellion in a complex civilization" (p. 7) and "assault our eardrums like the glycerin bombs of anarchy" (p. 43). Throughout his book Atkinson writes that he admires Thoreau, but if he does it is not the politicized Thoreau. Earlier Atkinson had strongly suggested in his *Freeman* article that Thoreau warranted a chorus of hurrahs for being a "stupendous radical," but Atkinson, writing for a popular audience — surely more to the right than the readers of *The Freeman* — changes his tune when he considers Thoreau's politics in the *Cosmic Yankee*. His reservations, like Vivas' begin with Thoreau's unwillingness to be a member of society; but whereas Vivas employs understanding and tact in his analysis, Atkinson uses a cudgel. He describes Thoreau's seclusiveness as

the sentiment of a self-contained, unsocial being, a troglodyte of sorts; and taken in conjunction with the chilly condemnation of social government in "Civil Disobedience," and the ex-cathedra, snake-in-the-grass vituperation of "Life Without Principle" I think it portrays accurately enough the intellectual Thoreau. (p. 47)

Atkinson's denunciation of Thoreau's politics is the most dramatic attack of the decade. What do you do with a "stupendous radical"? You hit him over the head with abusive epithets:

For the hostility and the jeering of "Civil Disobedience," "Life Without Principle," and "Slavery in Massachusetts" betoken nothing more admirable than want of sympathy, and arid understanding. Was not Thoreau a little pious in these papers? Was he not setting himself up? Was he not pusillanimous, vindictive, and feline in his attack? (pp. 49-50)

Thoreau's politics, for Atkinson, were "unworthy of the poet who sang of Nature in *Walden*" (p. 50). He cites passages in which Thoreau comments on money-getting, government, and the California gold rush, and he views them as the mark of a "limited" man. After quoting Thoreau, he writes:

In such passages we miss the give-and-take, the camaraderie of men all headed hopefully in the same direction, that informs the writings of men who know more of their neighbors. "Come, come, Henry!" I feel like saying, "if Nature countenances these little failings and forgives all with her sweet beneficence, how much more then ought you, the disciple of Nature, to yield and try to understand as well." (p. 50)

The tone here is considerably different from Vivas' thoughtful objection to Thoreau; one is led back toward the Rotary luncheon and the Good Citizens' League with Atkinson. There are few passages in Thoreau criticism that are as disconcerting and as slippery with what Thoreau called "slimy benignity" (*Journal*, V, 264) as this one. When Atkinson is not abusive, he is seductive. He tries very hard to convince us that he admires Thoreau as a dissenter (pp. 100-101), but when Thoreau dissents in a political way, Atkinson is annoyed and impatient because "Nearly all of Thoreau's political thoughts reveal the less worthy side of his character" (p. 51). [36]

In place of the paradox of Thoreau presented by Vivas, with the *Cosmic Yankee* one is confronted with the contradictions of Atkinson. The book is full of contradictions, because Atkinson strongly attacks Thoreau's politics while at the same time minimizing his own attacks so that he can praise the self-reliant, nature-loving Thoreau. The contradictions in the book are primarily the result of Atkinson trying to say two things at once that are mutually exclusive. The first is that Thoreau is useful because he speaks to the regimented, conforming,materialistic conditions of Americans in the 1920s, and the second is that when Thoreau addresses himself to such matters from a political perspective he is being pusillanimous, vindictive, and just plain grumpy and nasty. In almost Emersonian fashion, Atkinson attempts to keep a trembling balance between the snake-in-the-grass Thoreau and the surveyor-in-the-grass. Like Emerson, Atkinson finds his compensatory resolution in building an altar to beautiful necessity when, two years later, he writes a *New York Times* book review of an edition of "Civil Disobedience."[37] Despite Atkinson's earlier condemnation of the essay, fate seems to have generated some public interest in it.

In the review Atkinson gingerly avoids commenting upon the contents of "Civil Disobedience" and, instead, praises the type, the format, and the general appearance of the edition, because *"if* [my emphasis] such an essay is worth doing, it is worth doing well." Atkinson's "if" is a big one, and he raises his noble doubt not just once but twice. His concluding sentence reads: "If it is good that such a declaration has been written, it is good to have it reprinted in a trenchant design." Beautiful necessity indeed; at least Emerson did not completely ignore the snap of his tiger or the crackle of the bones within the coil of his snake. Atkinson, when he does not attack Thoreau's politics, offers his "lucubrations" to the altar of beautiful editions, and that altar is not to be found in the street but upon one's coffee table. Here is a reviewer who asks his readers to judge a book by its cover. Atkinson knows when to stop; he does not cut the pages.

A contemporary of Atkinson's did cut the pages, and the effects on Thoreau's political reputation were radical. At the same time that Atkinson was alternately condemning or avoiding Thoreau's political thought, Vernon Louis Parrington was presenting Thoreau's social and political thought as part of a liberal usable past in *Main Currents in American Thought* (1927). Whereas Atkinson serves as an enclosing summation of the twenties' negative view of Thoreau's politics, Parrington looks forward to what the thirties would have to say about Thoreau. In a sense, *Main Currents* is, as one literary historian suggests, the "tentative introduction to a decade of leftist literary interpretation."[38]

Parrington did not need a depression to see that America was facing an economic dilemma, a dilemma that was not new to the twenties but which characterized American history from its beginnings. He did not share Atkinson's optimistic assumption that there was in America a *"camaraderie* of men all headed hopefully in the same direction." Parrington might have wanted to believe this, but he could not, because for him the "idea of a beneficent progress," which he located in the eighteenth century, "came to be interpreted" by the twenties "as material expansion with constantly augmenting profits; and the idea of democracy came to be interpreted as the right to use the government of the whole for the benefit of the few." Hence, Parrington believed that the Jeffersonian democratic principles of the early republic were in danger.[39] He felt compelled to speak out against this, and he did: "Officially I am a teacher of English literature, but in reality my business in life is to wage war on the crude and selfish materialism that is biting so deeply into our national life and character . . . ."[40] He wrote books that were designed both to inform and reform his fellow countrymen, and in order to generate reform he first had to establish a need for it in America. Instead of the smooth, pacific development envisioned by those who tended to gloss over social, political, and economic conflicts in American life, Parrington saw conflict — founded in economic conditions — as the warp and woof of American history. American thought and writing according to Parrington, were to be seen in the context of this conflict: "Ideas are not godlings that spring perfect-winged from the head of Jove"; that is, they cannot be understood independently of the country's social, political, and economic developments. Instead, "they are weapons hammered out on the anvil of human needs."[41] The history of American intellectual thought revolved around the question of who was in possession of the hammer.

The two principal opposing forces in this conflict were, in their broadest categories, liberal and conservative. With the former, Parrington associated democracy, reason, freedom, progress, imagination, and vision; these were the main currents of American thought. That which was not liberal went against the current and was a "floundering bark," or a "barnacled craft." These barriers to progressive reform were elitist, irrational, limiting, and dogmatic.[42]

Parrington organized his three volumes of *Main Currents* around these two categories. Up through the nineteenth century, he ranked on the liberal side such writers as Roger Williams, Franklin, Jefferson, Cooper, Thoreau, Twain, and Whitman. The conservatives were men like John Cotton, Edwards, Hamilton, Poe, Lowell, Longfellow, and James. These writers were judged primarily according to their political dispositions rather than their literary abilities; Parrington's emphasis was on reform, not form.

Richard Ruland, using Parrington's own phrases, neatly sums up the ameliorative purpose of *Main Currents*, a work written at a time when industrialism, centralized government, and the machine were perceived by Parrington as threats to liberalism:

The ideas Parrington saw as germinal to the American tradition he explicitly affirmed as "liberal rather than conservative, Jeffersonian rather than Federalistic" —" democracy as a humane social order, serving the common well-being." He was looking for men who still had something — the right thing — to say to his own generation, and, as he put it himself, "very likely in my search I have found what I went forth to find." For Parrington, "the promise of the future has lain always in the keeping of liberal minds that were never discouraged from their dreams." [43]

One of the writers who met these requirements for Parrington was Thoreau.

Parrington transforms what several of his contemporaries considered to be Thoreau's selfish tenacity into a virtue. Thoreau's unwillingness to compromise was not a sign of perversity but of principle. A man never discouraged in pursuing his own dreams was to be admired; if he was not, then it was not Thoreau's problem but his critics': "To the inmates of Bedlam a sane man will appear queer." [44]

Thoreau is one of Parrington's heroes because he too was aware of the importance of economics in shaping life and thought. *Walden* is "the handbook of an economy that endeavors to refute Adam Smith and transform the round of daily life into something nobler than a mean gospel of plus and minus" (p. 400). Parrington stresses the social criticism in *Walden* and has little to say about Thoreau's use of nature in it except that (like Jefferson) he was a man of soil who loathed the corruption of cities which were "wedded to the economy of industrialism and exploitation" (p. 402). By implicitly associating Thoreau with Jeffersonian agrarian values, Parrington elevates Thoreau to an exalted position in his scheme of things. Moreover, Thoreau is a "child of Jean Jacques" (p. 402). Parrington believed, like many of his contemporaries, that Rousseau had had a strong influence on Jefferson, the Declaration of Independence, and democratic thought in the eighteenth century.[45] By presenting Thoreau as a descendant of both Jefferson and Rousseau, Parrington was able to praise Thoreau without reservation. If, according to Parrington, Thoreau "was at heart a Greek" (p. 402), he was not the kind that Foerster described in his *Nature in American Literature*; Thoreau's link to Hellenist sensibilities was by way of Jefferson and the eighteenth century, and that link was clearly of a romantic cast. Unlike Foerster's Thoreau, Parrington's "Greek turned transcendental economist" (p. 401) had a strong romantic streak in him.

Obviously, Parrington does not try to tailor Thoreau's thought to make him more acceptable to the conservative sensibilities of the 1920s. Nor does he worry about Thoreau not pulling his weight in the world's united effort. In contrast to Odell Shepard, he neither apologizes nor expresses any reservations about Thoreau's aloofness. However, in a footnote he quotes a *Journal* entry which serves as Parrington's own muted refutation of the prevailing notion in the twenties that Thoreau would do nothing in the service of humanity. The quotation reads in part:

I must confess I have felt mean enough when asked how I was to act on society, what errand I had to mankind. Undoubtedly I did not feel mean without a reason, and yet my loitering is not without defense. I would fain communicate the wealth of my life to men, would really give them what is most precious in my gift. . . . I know no riches I would keep back. I have no private good unless it be my peculiar ability to serve the public . . . . (p. 411)

Parrington finds in Thoreau the makings of a good citizen even if he was a citizen of somewhere else.[46] He does not flinch in describing Thoreau's political thought in "Civil Disobedience" as being that of a "philosophical anarchist" (p. 409), because he does not find it un-American.

What Parrington had to say about Thoreau's political thought was not entirely new. His treatment of Thoreau in *Main Currents* is essentially a more scholarly version of Finger's 1922 pamphlet on *The Man Who Escaped from the Herd*. Finger, it will be remem-

bered, praised Thoreau's economy and called him an "unterrified
Jeffersonian democrat" who was not afraid to make public his "anarchistic" political ideas. Parrington, however, goes a step further
to point out how Thoreau fits into an American liberal tradition, a
tradition which had earlier been associated with Thoreau in the
pages of *The Freeman*. Parrington places Thoreau in the liberal
tradition by tracing the political ideas in "Civil Disobedience" back
to William Godwin's *Political Justice* (p. 409), which helped inform
Jefferson's "idea of political justice and the conception of a
minimized political state" (p. 11). By making this connection Parrington is able to make Thoreau sound almost as though he had
been one of the Founding Fathers:

In Thoreau the eighteenth-century philosophy of individualism, the potent liberalisms let loose on the world by Jean
Jacques, came to fullest expression in New England. He was
the completest embodiment of the *laissez-faire* reaction
against a regimented social order, the severest critic of the
lower economies that frustrate the dreams of human freedom.
(p. 413)

For Parrington, Thoreau turns out to be a stupendous liberal.
    Parrington's liberal Thoreau was the prototype of the radical
that Thoreau was to become in the 1930s, a phenomenon entirely in
keeping with Parrington's intentions. His use of the term *liberal* in
Main Currents looks forward to the thirties; he once explained in a
letter written in 1928, "I could see no harm and some good in using
the term, and warping it pretty well to the left. As a matter of fact,
in my first draft of *Main Currents* I used the word radical throughout, and only on revising did I substitute the other." [47]
    Parrington's brief chapter on Thoreau is the first significant
American attempt to find Thoreau's politics — his "potent liberalisms" — useful. The chapter is only fifteen pages long and makes
no attempt to analyze Thoreau's politics, but it is significant because *Main Currents* was so widely read and influential in the thirties. [48] Charles Beard, the famous Progressive historian, reviewed
Main Currents in 1927 and anticipated what the intellectuals of the
thirties would find attractive in it. Parrington, wrote Beard,

is about to start an upheaval in American literary criticism. He has yanked Miss Beautiful Letters out of the sphere of the higher verbal hokum and fairly set her in the way that leads to contact with pulsating reality — that source and inspiration of all magnificent literature. No doubt, the magpies, busy with the accidence of Horace, the classical allusions of Thoreau, and the use of the adverb by Emerson, will make a big outcry, but plain citizens who believe that the American eagle could soar with unblinking eyes against the full-orbed noonday sun if he had half a chance will clasp their hands with joy and make the hills ring with gladness. [49]

From Beard's point of view *Main Currents* offers to Americans their own potential greatness. America's greatest writers — those who fit into Parrington's idea of the liberal tradition — perform the same function as did Thoreau in writing *Walden*. The motto with which Thoreau begins *Walden* sums up Parrington's purpose in writing *Main Currents* as much as Thoreau's own: "I do not propose to write an ode to dejection, but to brag as lustily as chanticleer in the morning, standing on his roost, if only to wake my neighbors up." It is no wonder then that Parrington, believing his own generation to be asleep in the 1920s, found in Thoreau a liberal sensibility that served as an antidote to the timid materialism of modern American life. Thoreau's "transcendental declaration of independence" (p. 400) was for Parrington a major pumping station along the pipeline leading from eighteenth-century liberal Jeffersonian democratic thought. Parrington was well aware of the volatile quality of Thoreau's economic and political thought which sweeps away the "comfortable compromises" (p. 409) that most people live by, but he was under no illusion that American life was being fueled by Thoreauvian principles. Thoreau, by not living into the twentieth century, was "fortunate in not foreseeing how remote is that future of free men on which his hopes were fixed" (p. 413).

For Parrington, freedom, not nature, was the prerequisite for an understanding of Thoreau. The recognition that he was truly "One of the great names in American literature" (p. 413) could come only by seeing Thoreau as more than a "bachelor of nature" or a "poet-naturalist" whose political ideas were a mere excrescence of his thought.

Parrington concludes the chapter with a sentence that serves as a fulcrum for Thoreau's shifting reputation in the late twenties; few would dispute Thoreau's greatness: "Yet only after sixty years is he slowly coming into his own" (p. 413). Since Thoreau's reputation as a nature writer had been firmly established by 1927, what Parrington is referring to here is Thoreau's coming into his own as a social and political thinker. The issue concerning Thoreau's reputation that emerged in the late twenties was not whether Thoreau was great but why he was considered to be so.[50] The influence of *Main Currents* and its unqualified praise of Thoreau's social and political thought definitively launched Thoreau into American political waters. The liberal and left-wing critics of the thirties, who had read Parrington, reread Thoreau and found a friend. The 1930s was a time when Americans would greet Thoreau at the beginning of a great career; as the twenties crashed, Parrington's "transcendental economist" experienced a windfall produced by the convulsive quakes on Wall Street. As stocks and bonds decreased in value, Thoreau's words and ideas increased in meaning. In terms of Thoreau's reputation, the crash of 1929 was a fortunate fall.

Parrington had constructed the castle of Thoreau's reputation as a social thinker in the thin air of the materialistic, conservative twenties, but his work was not lost, because the thirties were to put the foundations under it.

NOTES

1. Roderick Nash in "The American Cult of the Primitive," *American Quarterly*, 18 (Fall 1966), 517-537, discusses the back-to-nature movement of the period and the manifestations of it which range from the Boy Scouts and outing clubs to *The Call of the Wild* and *Tarzan of the Apes*. This discussion is connected in some detail to Thoreau's reputation by Theodore Haddin in his unpublished dissertation (University of Michigan, 1968), "The Changing Image of Henry Thoreau: The Emergence of the Literary Artist," pp. 9-37. Nash specifically deals with Thoreau in his *Wilderness and the American Mind* (New Haven, Conn.: Yale University Press, 1967),

pp. 84-95, which also reprints "The American Cult of the Primitive." For a general overview see Peter J. Schmitt, *Back to Nature: The Arcadian Myth in Urban America* (New York: Oxford University Press, 1969).

2. The "muscular spirit" of the 1890s is described intelligently (and delightfully) by John Higham, "The Reorientation of American Culture in the 1890s," in *The Origins of Modern Consciousness*, ed. John Weiss (Detroit, Mich.: Wayne State University Press, 1965), pp. 25-49.

3. *The Spirit of American Literature* (1913; rpt. New York: Johnson Reprint Corporation, 1969), pp. 171-188. All quoted material is from pp. 171-174. "The Critical Game" appears in Macy's *The Critical Game* (New York: Boni and Liveright, 1922), pp. 11-27.

4. Some other early views similar to Macy's are cited and discussed in Bruce E. Burdett, "The Cult of Thoreau," unpublished master's thesis (Brown University, 1955), pp. 39-49.

5. Though Wyeth's essay, "Thoreau, His Critics, and the Public," was written in 1919, it was not published until it appeared in *The Thoreau Society Bulletin*, 37 (October 1951); hereafter cited as *TSB*.

6. "The Paradox of Thoreau," *Scribner's Magazine*, 68 (September 1920), 335-342. In order to minimize interruptions in the text, hereafter page references to the works I discuss will be cited in parentheses within the text after the first complete entry in the notes. This method will be used throughout each chapter.

7. Particularly useful, because it is written from a literary point of view, is Frederick J. Hoffman, *The Twenties: American Writings in the Postwar Decade*, rev. ed. (New York: The Free Press, 1966). For a study of the conservative political atmosphere of the early twenties see Robert K. Murray, *Red Scare: A Study in National Hysteria, 1919-20* (Minneapolis: University of Minnesota Press, 1955).

8. "The Stars and Stripes," *Time*, June 18, 1923, p. 1.

9. Quoted in James D. Hart, *The Popular Book: A History of America's Literary Taste* (New York: Oxford University Press, 1950), p. 236.

10. "Thoreau in 1854," *Howells, James, Bryant and Other Essays* (1924; rpt. Port Washington, N.Y.: Kennikat Press, 1965), p. 80.

11. "Miscellany," *The Freeman*, 1 (March 1920), 15. *The Freeman's* political position—its philosophical anarchism, its nonviolent attitudes, its rejection of direct political action, and its emphasis upon man's natural right to *use* land—is described by Franklin Luther Mott, *A History of American Magazines* (Cambridge, Mass.: Harvard University Press, 1968), V, 88-99. The magazine's attitude toward politics is similar to Thoreau's, as he was perceived in the twenties. Susan J. Turner's *A History of The Freeman, Literary Landmark of the Early Twenties* (New York:

Columbia University Press, 1963) focuses on the literary criticism of the magazine but does not mention Thoreau. One learns from Turner's book that Macy, one of the earliest critics to politicize Thoreau, was the "general reviewer of literature; from winter, 1921, to spring, 1922" (p. 106).

12. "Americanizing the Titmen," *The Freeman*, 6 (December 1922), 343.

13. "Thoreau on the 'Kindly Relations,' " *Scribner's Magazine*, 67 (March 1920), 379.

14. *The Freeman*, 6 (March 1923), 624.

15. J. Brooks Atkinson, *The Freeman*, 1 (July 1920), 469.

16. *The Freeman* "never passed seven thousand circulation" (Mott, p. 98); *National Geographic*, however, had "more than a million in the twenties," according to Theodore Peterson, *Magazines in the Twentieth Century* (Urbana: University of Illinois Press, 1964), p. 393. Albert Jay Nock, one of the editors of *The Freeman*, once beamed about "How the millennium would be hastened if 100,000 new readers were added to our list in 1921!" (quoted in Mott, p. 99). If Nock was correct, the world is in trouble; *The Freeman* folded on March 5, 1924, four years and two weeks after it had begun.

17. H.W. Gleason, "Winter Rambles in Thoreau's Country," *National Geographic Magazine*, 37 (February 1920), 165-180.

18. *Much Loved Books: Best Sellers of the Ages* (New York: Boni and Liveright, 1927), p. 458.

19. "Thoreau as Artist," *Sewanee Review*, 29 (January 1921), 12.

20. *The Last Harvest* (1922; rpt. New York: Russell & Russell, 1968), p. 126.

21. *Nature in American Literature: Studies in the Modern View of Nature* (1923; rpt. New York: Russell & Russell, 1958), p. 136.

22. T.E. Hulme, "Romanticism and Classicism," in *Speculations: Essays on Humanism and the Philosophy of Art*, ed. Herbert Read (London: Routledge & Kegan Paul, 1924), pp. 113-140.

23. A succinct statement connecting New Humanist sensibilities with conservative politics will be found in Merle Curti, *The Growth of American Thought*, 3rd ed. (New York: Harper & Row, 1964), pp. 624-626. The movement's relationship to American literary criticism is discussed in Walter Sutton, *Modern American Criticism* (Englewood Cliffs, N.J.: Prentice-Hall, 1963), pp. 26-50, 219-224; and Richard Ruland, *The Rediscovery of American Literature: Premises of Critical Taste, 1900-1940* (Cambridge, Mass.: Harvard University Press, 1967), pp. 11-56.

24. Foerster discusses Macy in the final chapter of *American Criticism: A Study in Literary Theory from Poe to the Present* (Boston: Houghton Mifflin, 1928).

25. Quoted in Henry Seidel Canby, *Thoreau* (Boston: Houghton Mifflin, 1939), p. 22.

26. *Herman Melville: Mariner and Mystic* (New York: George H. Doran and Co., 1921), p. 18.

27. *Life*, September 27, 1923, no page.

28. Albert Mordell, the compiler of *The World of Haldeman-Julius* (New York: Twayne, 1960), includes a "Foreword" by Harry Golden which provides a brief but informative sketch of the publisher's career and a history of the Little Blue Books (pp. 5-7). For more detailed accounts see Andrew N. Cothran's unpublished 1966 doctoral dissertation for the University of Maryland, "The Little Blue Book Man and the Big American Parade: A Biography of Emanual Haldeman-Julius"; and Dale M. Herder, "Haldeman-Julius, The Little Blue Books, and the Theory of Popular Culture," *Journal of Popular Culture*, 4 (Spring 1971), 881-889.

29. E. Haldeman-Julius, *The Serious Lesson in President Harding's Case of Gonorrhea* (Girard, Kans.: Haldenman-Julius Co., 1931). The lesson, incidentally, was that there was a need for sex education in the United States.

30. Charles J. Finger, *Henry David Thoreau: The Man Who Escaped from the Herd* (Girard, Kans.: Haldeman-Julius Co., 1922), p. 3.

31. Guy J. Forgue, ed. *Letters of H.L. Mencken* (New York: Alfred A. Knopf, 1961), p. 431.

32. For Thoreau as a naturalist, see: "The Gardener's Calendar for October," *House and Garden*, October 1924, p. 98; F. White, "Thoreau's Observations on Fogs, Clouds and Rain," *Nature Study*, 17 (October 1921), 296-298; Gladys A. Harper, "The Moon and Thoreau," *Nature Study*, 18 (November 1922), 317-319; "Fern Notes from Thoreau's Notebooks," *Nature Study*, 19 (May 1923), 178-193; and J.S. Wade, "Henry Thoreau and His Journal," *Nature Magazine*, 10 (July 1927), 53-54. The Franklinesque Thoreau will be found in: "A Concord Man of Leisure," *New York Times*, September 12, 1920, sec. 2, p. 2; E.W. Coombs, "New Views of Thoreau," *New York Times*, November 14, 1920, sec. 8, p. 12; "Thoreau's Pond," *New York Times*, January 30, 1921, sec. 2, p. 2. Naturalist and thrifty Yankee, Thoreau was also a hero to tuberculars in J.A. Myers, *Fighters of Fate: A Story of Men and Women Who Have Achieved Greatly Despite the Handicaps of the White Plague* (Baltimore: Williams and Wilkins, 1927), pp. 118-139. For a general discussion of the conservative tone of most mass magazines of the twenties, see Sherilyn Cox Bennion, "Reform Agitation in the American Periodical Press, 1920-29," *Journalism Quarterly*, 48 (Winter 1971), 652-659, 713.

33. *The New Student*, March 7, 1928, p. 15. All references are to this

issue of the magazine. "Thoreau: The Paradox of Youth" is on pages 5-8, 15.

34. "Thoreau Comes into His Own," *New York Times*, November 20, 1927, sec. 4, p. 1. For additional views on Thoreau's popularity see J.S. Wade, "Henry Thoreau and His Journal," *Nature Magazine*, 10 (July 1927), 54; and F.I. Carpenter, who connects the growing interest in Thoreau to the parallel interest in American literature in general: *New England Quarterly*, 1 (April 1928), 252-254.

35. J. Brooks Atkinson, '*HHenry Thoreau: The Cosmic Yankee* (New York: Alfred A. Knopf, 1927), p. 6.

36. It is remarkable that no reviewer of *Cosmic Yankee* challenged Atkinson's assessment. There is only the mild demur by a *New York Times* writer that "One wishes Mr. Atkinson had not dismissed the political thought of Thoreau quite so summarily, even though it was something of an excrescence on the surface of his intellectual and spiritual life . . . ." (November 20, 1927, sec. 4, p. 18). Since this comment is not developed, one must assume that because the reviewer saw Thoreau's political thought as merely an "excrescence," it was not worth refuting Atkinson. There could be no reason to argue with a commentator on Thoreau's politics when those same politics were considered unimportant anyway. Oddly enough, even a highly sympathetic treatment of Thoreau's civil disobedience manages to avoid discussing the significance of Thoreau's politics: See John Cournos, "Hater of Shams; In Jail with Thoreau and His Thoughts," *Century*, 116 (June 1928), 140-146. Cournos tells a pleasant story about Thoreau's arrest and what he did in jail but little more.

37. *New York Times*, January 13, 1929, sec. 4, p. 12.

38. Ruland, *The Rediscovery of American Literature*, p. 186. Ruland discusses Parrington on pp. 186-191. Several other helpful overviews of *Main Currents* will be found in Sutton, *Modern American Criticism*, pp. 89-92; Robert A. Skotheim, *American Intellectual Histories and Historians* (Princeton, N.J.: Princeton University Press, 1966), pp. 124-148; Richard Hofstadter, *The Progressive Historians: Turner, Beard, Parrington* (New York: Alfred A. Knopf, 1968), pp. 349-434; and Wesley Morris, *Toward A New Historicism* (Princeton, N.J.: Princeton University Press, 1972), pp. 35-51. My discussion of Parrington's "progressive" thought is based upon these studies.

39. *Main Currents in American Thought: The Beginnings of Critical Realism in America, 1860-1920* (New York: Harcourt, Brace, 1930), III, xxv. This edition of *Main Currents* contains all three volumes in one; each volume has its own pagination. Despite modern "psychology, with its discovery of morons, and its study of mob tendencies" which made a belief in

"human perfectability" and democracy seem "only a will-o'-the-wisp," Parrington affirmed that "Jeffersonian democracy still offers hope" (pp. xxviii-xxix). The kind of abiding faith that Parrington had in democracy sometimes met with militant resistance. A 1928 War Department Army *Training Manual* explains democracy to the troops as "a government of the masses. Authority derived through mass meeting or any other forms of 'direct' expression. Results in mobocracy. Attitude toward property is communistic — negating property rights. Attitude toward law is that the will of the majority shall regulate, whether it be based upon deliberation or governed by passion, prejudice, and impulse, without restraint or regard to consequence. Results in demagogism, license, agitation, discontent, anarchy." Quoted in Curti, *The Growth of American Thought*, p. 677. Given this view of democracy, it is not difficult to understand why Parrington felt it necessary to provide a historical rationale for liberal thought.

40. Quoted in Hofstadter, *The Progressive Historians*, p. 349.

41. Vernon Parrington, Jr., ed. "Vernon Parrington's View: Economics and Criticism," *Pacific Northwest Quarterly*, 44 (July 1953), 99.

42. Skotheim, *American Intellectual Histories and Historians*, pp. 126, 140-141.

43. Ruland, *The Rediscovery of American Literature*, p. 187.

44. Vernon L. Parrington, *Main Currents in American Thought: The Romantic Revolution in America 1800-1860* (New York: Harcourt, Brace, 1930), II, 400.

45. Hofstadter discusses Parrington's enthusiasm for Jefferson and Rousseau: *The Progressive Historians*, pp. 423-425.

46. Significantly, Lucy Lockwood Hazard, in *The Frontier in American Literature* (1927), uses the same quotation from Thoreau to answer critics who argue that Thoreau was selfish. Unlike Parrington, however, Hazard finds *Walden* "fascinating as the adventure of a solitary pioneer," but "fallacious as the guidebook for a general migration. An idyll of the golden age of transcendentalism, it is an ineffectual protest against the gilded age of industrialism" (New York: Barnes & Noble, 1941), p. 170. Parrington, on the other hand, is not concerned with Thoreau's individual failure or success, but rather with what he has to contribute to the liberal tradition; hence he can praise Thoreau's civil disobedience even though someone else paid his poll tax (a fact that Hazard seizes upon), thereby putting an end to his confrontation with the state.

47. Quoted in Hofstadter, *The Progressive Historians*, p. 430.

48. Skotheim documents the popularity of *Main Currents* and notes, particularly, its influence among left-wing intellectuals of the thirties: *American Intellectual Histories and Historians*, p. 148.

49. "Fresh Air in American Letters," *Nation*, May 18, 1927, p. 562. This passage is quoted in Hofstadter, *The Progressive Historians*, p. 392. Beard's denunciation of "Miss Beautiful Letters" as "verbal Hokum" was an attitude shared by Parrington, who called it in the second volume of *Main Currents* the "narrow field of *belles lettres*" (p. xiii). Neither Beard nor Parrington was satisfied with literary studies which valued form over content and ignored social and philosophical concerns in a writer's work. Certainly the few academic specialized articles devoted to Thoreau in the twenties would not have met their requirements; see, for example: T.M. Raysor, "The Love Story of Thoreau," *Studies in Philology*, 23 (October 1926), 457-463; J.A. Russell, "Thoreau: The Interpreter of the Real Indian," *Queens Quarterly*, 35 (August 1927), 37-48; Clarence Gohdes, "Henry Thoreau, Bachelor of Arts," *Classical Journal*, 23 (February 1928), 323-336; Albert Keiser, "Thoreau's Manuscripts on the Indians," *Journal of English and Germanic Philology*, 27 (1928), 183-199; and Raymond Adams, "Thoreau and Immortality," *Studies in Philology*, 26 (January 1929), 58-66. With few exceptions — Parrington being the most notable — academics of the twenties avoided Thoreau's social and political thought.

50. One writer did, however, challenge Thoreau's greatness; the broadest denunciation of Thoreau in the twenties is by Llewelyn Powys, "Thoreau: A Disparagement," *Bookman*, 69 (April 1929), 163-165. Powys finds Thoreau "much overrated." He considers Thoreau a fraud, a "dilettante of the bluebird and bobolink," whose writing was mere "Sunday School" talk. He concludes that Thoreau "was neither a profound thinker nor a great writer, and that is the truth." Powys' brief article does not develop any of his charges; the article is significant primarily because no one bothered to respond to it. Thoreau's reputation had been too firmly established to be threatened by such a total condemnation.

chapter 2

THOREAU AND THE "ART OF LIVING" IN THE 1930s

Let me assert my firm belief that the only thing
we have to fear is fear itself.

Franklin D. Roosevelt, 1933

Nothing is so much to be feared as fear.

Thoreau, *Journal* (II, 468)

In the 1930s Thoreau's reputation enjoyed a new deal. *Walden*, addressed to poor students and the mass of discontented men, found a larger audience during the depression than it had in the twenties. After the economic collapse of 1929 the moneychangers had fled from what President Roosevelt called "their high seats in the temple of our civilization," and the business of America was no longer only business. The President's first inaugural address in 1933 called for a restoration of social values to replace "mere monetary profit" in American life. His audience, many of whom were either unemployed or losing their farms, was told that "Happiness lies not in the mere possession of money." No one, of course, was willing or able to argue the point, since most Americans felt in one way or another the effects of the depression. Nearly everyone could sing the words to the decade's anthem, "Brother Can You Spare a Dime?" Roosevelt told his countrymen what they already knew:

Values have shrunken to fantastic levels; taxes have risen; our ability to pay has fallen; government of all kinds is faced by serious curtailment of income; the means of exchange are frozen in the currents of trade; the withered leaves of industrial enterprise lie on every side; farmers find no markets for their produce; the savings of many years in thousands of families are gone.[1]

Under the weight of these circumstances, Americans had to make the best of a grim situation; they had to make a virtue out of necessity. It was their President who helped them to cope with unemployment and poverty. Although Roosevelt was committed to legislation that was designed to revive the economic level of the country, he also emphasized that the sum total of human life could not be reduced to a bank account statement. By telling his countrymen that true happiness was not found in "the mere possession of money," he was, indirectly, officially establishing a national consciousness that would be receptive to Thoreau. Who's afraid of the big bad wolf? As the majority of Americans believed: not Roosevelt. And as many Americans would learn: not Thoreau.

Walter Harding has summed up this aspect of Thoreau's growing popularity in the thirties:

It was in the depression years of the thirties that Thoreau really came into his own. A friend of mine once commented, "Thoreau is the only author I know of that I can read without a nickle in my pocket and not feel insulted." Certainly the simple life forced upon many people by financial necessity through those years turned many of them to reading Thoreau with a new insight, and for the first time Thoreau was treated *generally* [my emphasis] as a social philosopher rather than just a nature writer. [2]

Thoreau was on the minds of many Americans of the thirties, because he taught them how to do without material things. He simplified his America by eliminating money getting, ornate furniture, fashionable clothing, and all the other vestments associated with a life devoted to Mammon. Since Mammom was almost dead in the thirties, it was relatively easy not to serve him and so Americans looked to new gods.

It is difficult to measure precisely just how much the depression psychology of the thirties contributed to Thoreau's reputation on a popular level. Thoreau was part of high school and college curriculums, and even if he was not much read, he was at least known to the majority of literate Americans in the thirties. Familiarity with Thoreau was probably very much like catching a cold; he was in the air. Perhaps the best contemporary index in support of this assertion is to be found in *Reader's Digest*, a magazine that built its success upon its ability to capitalize on what was in the air.

In 1937 *Reader's Digest* condensed parts of Van Wyck Brooks's *The Flowering of New England*, a book that had appeared on bestseller lists the same year.[3] The pages which the editors chose to condense from Brooks's very popular book were on Thoreau. Brooks's treatment of Thoreau is a pleasant biographical sketch filled with interesting anecdotes from previous biographies. Brooks keeps up a steady chatter about Thoreau's relationship to Emerson, his friends, flora and fauna, travel, and the experience at Walden Pond. There is not a word of explanation about Thoreau's politics and very little about his social thought except that he developed an individualized, simplified economy for himself.[4] The *Reader's Digest* condensation presented some biographical information and the rationale for Thoreau's stay at Walden Pond; the article was entitled "Thoreau, Master of Simplicity."[5]

The Thoreau that was presented to the readers of this mass-circulation magazine (circulation was well over a million by 1937) conformed to both the needs of the thirties public and the conservative politics underlying the editorial policies of *Reader's Digest*. The editorial criteria for their selections were three: (1) the reader should feel that the material is applicable to him; (2) the material should be of "lasting interest" so that a reader might pick it up at a later date and still enjoy it; and (3) the material should be constructive rather than dispiriting, depressing, or defeatist.[6] Thoreau was to be digested by the American public of the thirties because he was

a master of the art of living, which for that decade necessarily involved simplicity and frugality. An examination of the table of
contents of the *Reader's Digest* for the thirties yields numerous articles dealing with the "art of living"; in fact, the very phrase is a
standing category in the index of the magazine for the thirties.

Three years after the Brooks condensation, and shortly after
Henry Seidel Canby's 1939 biography of Thoreau had been a popular success, *Reader's Digest* editors managed to trim *Walden* to
seven pages. The editors apparently took Thoreau at his word
when he wrote in "Where I Lived and What I Lived For" that "If
you are acquainted with the principle, what do you care for a
myriad instances and applications?" The preface to the condensation describes *Walden* as "The record of an experience in serene
living, a venture in simplicity and discipline as timely today as it
was nearly 100 years ago." The excerpts provide the reader with
Thoreau's reasons for going to Walden, how he lived simply, and,
perhaps most importantly, how he learned that poverty is not
poverty. The selections from *Walden* put in Thoreau's own words
what Brooks had earlier described. *Walden*, according to the
editors of a magazine who knew a good deal about American reading habits, "is a book of which everyone has heard, but which few
now read. Yet . . . its importance and durability seem to increase
with each year. . . ." Curiously the growth of Thoreau's popular
reputation in the thirties was not directly related to a wide readership.[7] The American reading public had a vague sense that Thoreau spoke to their condition in some way, but they left it up to the
journalists, anthologists, literary historians, and critics to articulate
how he was relevant to their lives.

Although not all commentators on Thoreau were convinced that
his social and political thought was relevant to Americans of the
thirties, there was some agreement on the questions to be raised in
dealing with the problem. If the answers were radically different,
the questions that were explored tended to be similar. The most important single issue concerning Thoreau's reputation in the thirties
was the question of what mode of reform he advocated: should reform be achieved by individual action or by collective means? This
question was extremely important to Americans of the 1930s — not
because Thoreau's reputation depended upon the answer — but be-

cause Roosevelt's administration did. Thoreau commentators tended to accept or reject Thoreau's politics on the basis of their own commitment to a particular mode of reform. Their votes are tallied in the remaining pages of this chapter.

After Parrington's 1927 chapter had placed Thoreau within the main current of American liberal thought, there appeared in 1930 a collection of Thoreau's writings which contributed to Parrington's portrait of him as a liberal thinker. The collection, selected and introduced by James MacKaye, was entitled *Thoreau: Philosopher of Freedom: Writings on Liberty by Henry David Thoreau*. The book's subtitle is redundant; perhaps it was necessary to emphasize Thoreau's liberal thought twice in order to make sure that the reader would be aware that he was about to read a Thoreau who was more than a bachelor of nature. MacKaye, like Parrington, wanted to introduce a more useful Thoreau than the naturalist or literary master. It is Thoreau's "contribution to the philosophy and art of living that is emphasized" in MacKaye's book. [8]

The selections which MacKaye offers present a Thoreau whose "teaching is of especial value in these days of constantly increasing complexity of life" (p. xv). There is in the collection a hint that Thoreau's writings can be used as a *handbook* (Parrington's term). The title page includes a quotation from Thoreau that serves as an introduction to the selections: "I wish to communicate those parts of my life which I would gladly live again."

Turning to the first selection in the book, the unemployed reader of the early 1930s finds this from one of Thoreau's college exercises on the "commercial spirit": "Let men, true to their natures, cultivate the moral affections, lead manly and independent lives; let them make riches the means and not the ends of existence, and we shall hear no more of the commercial spirit" (p. 4). Thoreau's call for a shift in priorities coincided with his reader's shift in circumstances, and any reader who had the jitters must have been comforted when he read that "The order of things should be somewhat reversed; the seventh should be man's day of toil, wherein to earn his living by the sweat of his brow; and the other six his Sabbath of the affections and the soul . . ." (p. 4). A reader of the 1930s might have felt some compensation in the fact that even if he was despairing about his economic status, at least Thoreau communicated those parts of his own life which suggested that he might not be too unfortunate after all. MacKaye reprints only one entire chapter from *Walden*, and that is "Economy." Clearly, "Economy" is the most didactic chapter of *Walden*; it serves as both a critique of a complex materialistic society and as a handbook for an individual economy. There are in addition to "Economy" about ten pages of extracts from *Walden* (pp. 203-215), but they reinforce the themes in "Economy." MacKaye begins the excerpts with a sentence that could serve as the rubric of his own intentions in putting the book together: "A Man is rich in proportion to the number of things which he can afford to let alone" (p. 203). Nearly all of the other selections in MacKaye's book are related to economics — with the exception of three essays: "Civil Disobedience," "Slavery in Massachusetts," and "A Plea for Captain John Brown."

MacKaye's enthusiasm for Thoreau's politically oriented essays is noticeably less than for his economics. He finds the usefulness of Thoreau's politics minimal, because in their extremism his politics represent a "departure from the middle ground of reason" (p. xii). Thoreau's economics are useful for MacKaye because they can be practiced by individuals no matter what their circumstances; Thoreau's politics, however, are not acceptable because the "sage of Walden" was also an "extreme individualist" who "never grasped the potentialities of cooperation" with his fellowman (p. x). In this, Mackaye followed commentators of the twenties. It is one thing for a person to regulate his own economy and thereby free himself from want, but it is quite another to repudiate government. MacKaye argues that "To be free from all law is not to be usefully free" (p. xi). Though he does not label Thoreau an anarchist, he does tend to view his politics as anarchistic.

When MacKaye uses the words *freedom* and *liberty* in his title, he is not referring to political freedom and political liberty but to economic freedom, the liberty to do without. In the early thirties the majority of Americans were more concerned with their chickenless pots than with chicanery in government, and MacKaye's book reflects that concern.[9] He has no problem with Parrington's "transcendental economist," but he has second thoughts about Thoreau as a "philosophical anarchist" because

such a position strikes him as unreasonable. Thoreau had too much
of "a tinge of otherwise-mindedness" in his complexion to please
MacKaye (p. xiii).

A contemporary of MacKaye's, Russell Blankenship, also emphasized Thoreau as a philosopher of freedom, but whereas
MacKaye dismisses his economist's politics, Blankenship lauds
Thoreau as "our great social rebel, our foremost protestor against
the tyranny of institutions," in his *American Literature as an Expression of the National Mind* (1931).[10] Blankenship, a student of
Parrington who follows his "daringly liberal point of view" (p. ix),
writes his history of American literature in order to relate it to its
"social environment" and demonstrate its best liberal qualities (pp.
x-xi). Like Parrington, he is not interested in "that esoteric goddess
known as esthetic beauty" (p. x). Out of ten pages devoted to Thoreau, Blankenship devotes one brief paragraph to Thoreau's style
(p. 311), while the rest is concerned primarily with his social criticism. He rallies Parrington's heroes around Thoreau:

In a very real sense Thoreau was the spiritual and intellectual
heir of the great liberals of the preceding age, Rousseau,
William Godwin, Paine, and Jefferson, writers whose belief in
the fundamental goodness of man led them to advocate a
state whose powers would be reduced to the minimum. (p.
307)

Blankenship makes explicit what Parrington had earlier implied.
Blankenship describes "Civil Disobedience" as an "explicit statement of philosophical anarchism" and as a "cap-stone on Thoreau's
work." He is not surprised that many of Thoreau's previous commentators "neglected entirely to mention the essay" because either
the commentators were not ready for Thoreau's radicalism or they
believed that their readers were not. In either case he finds the
omission inexcusable (p. 308). He therefore writes about Thoreau
in order to suggest the efficacy of his political thought.

Blankenship's pages on Thoreau are a tribute to Parrington, for
they totally agree with his assessments in *Main Currents*. Each
writer stresses Thoreau's social and political thought, and neither
feels compelled to qualify his praise. The reason for their complete

acceptance of Thoreau is that they were both staunch liberals who associated Thoreau's social thought with Jeffersonian liberalism. If in order to remedy the country's ills a dose of Jeffersonian liberalism was needed, and if Thoreau was an heir to that liberal tradition, then Thoreau, too, was good medicine. And given the general shift to the left in the thirties, Thoreau was not a bitter pill to swallow. Stanley T. Williams, writing in 1933, the year Roosevelt took office, noted that Thoreau's "attitude does not now appear radical, as in the days of our early mercantile culture. Proleptic, he expressed a mood of our civilization which today is vocal indeed." [11] Actually, Thoreau was still thought of as a radical by many, but — and this is where Williams is correct — his radicalism was no longer considered to be so shocking by most commentators of the thirties. His radicalism was studied even within the academy.

Although there is only one detailed study of Thoreau's radicalism in the thirties, a relatively brief study of Thoreau's anarchism by Eunice M. Schuster, it imputes radicalism to America itself. Her *Native American Anarchism* (1932) places Thoreau within a native tradition of left-wing individualism which extends from the antinomians of the seventeenth century to Emma Goldman of the twentieth century. [12] "Thoreau was an anarchist in the sense that he believed in the sovereignty of the individual and voluntary cooperation" (p. 51), but Schuster sees him as more than just a philosophical anarchist; she goes beyond Parrington's view: Thoreau "was not only an anarchist in thought, but also in action" (p. 46). Though Schuster's study is descriptive and makes no discernible attempt to use Thoreau — other than to demonstrate that anarchism in America was not the product of conspiracies abroad — she seems to be sympathetic toward him. Her treatment of Thoreau is the first American attempt to explore his anarchistic thought in any detail. It is not surprising that it comes in the thirties, since Americans in the twenties were generally more convinced that there was nothing native about anarchism.

Writers on the left tended to be exultant rather than censorious over Thoreau's social thought. Max Lerner, writing in 1934, has more than the nineteenth century in mind when he points out that implicit in Thoreau's

highly personal essays and nature soliloquies and journal entries is a devastating attack upon every dominant aspect of
American life in its first flush of industrial advance — the
factory system, the corporations, business enterprise, acquisi-
tiveness, the vandalism of natural resources, the vested commercial and intellectual interests, the cry for expansion, the
clanishness and theocratic smugness of New England society,
the hard-mindedness of the people, the unthinking civic allegiance they paid to an opportunist and imperialist government. [13]

Lerner does not avoid Thoreau's social thought as critics did in the
twenties; he goes in search of it by finding it implicit in everything
his "American philosopher" wrote. The emphasis Lerner places
upon Thoreau's social criticism is representative of the thirties' general treatment of Thoreau as a social philosopher rather than a
nature illustrator.

Thoreau commentators of the thirties, many of whom viewed
themselves as being left of center politically,[14] more often than not
pointed to Thoreau's political posture as one of the major proofs
that he was a giant among American writers. This was true, however, only of journalists and literary and social critics at large. Except for Schuster, academic criticism of Thoreau in the thirties
avoided Thoreau's social and political thought; there is no discus-
son of his social philosophy in academic literary journals during the
decade. The articles which did appear in such journals as *PMLA*
and *Studies in Philology* are, taken as a group, distinguished only
by their timidity.[15] None has found its way into subsequent collections of Thoreau criticism. Until the forties, the best criticism on
Thoreau (using any critical standard for excellence) is to be found
in journalistic pieces, or occasional chapters on Thoreau in books
— most of them written by critics outside the academy. This is not
to suggest that all nonacademic treatments of Thoreau were of excellent quality. They were not. Perhaps the fairest overall judgment
that can be made in distinguishing academic and nonacademic
treatments of Thoreau in the thirties is that the latter were, at least,
usually interesting, because the commentator frequently used
Thoreau to make a significant point. One either vigorously agrees

or disagrees with these various approaches to Thoreau, but one is rarely bored. Of course, the danger with this kind of criticism is that it many times says more about the critic and his own times than it does about the writer and his work. Occasionally, the commentator's commitment made apparent by such an approach is of interest primarily because it is bizarre rather than because it is challenging or compelling. One such approach appeared in the middle of the decade.

In "Thoreau, the Rebel Idealist" (1936) David Boyd, writing a brief biography of Thoreau for *Americana*, the American Historical Society magazine, presents him as "one of the most 'radical' men that American civilization has produced!"[16] Boyd's work is in keeping with the predominant liberal approach to Thoreau in the thirties, but the writer reveals himself more than he does Thoreau. He strings together quotations from previous studies which accent Thoreau's courage to act on his principles. Thoreau is the "village non-conformist" who was misunderstood in his own time but who — as Boyd is anxious to demonstrate — is understood by the author. Boyd tells the famous story of Thoreau accidently setting fire to approximately 200 acres of Concord woods and afterward writing that is as a "glorious spectacle." The woods were owned by farmers who had intended to sell the timber; it was part of their livelihood. Boyd has this to say about the farmers whose woods were burned:

The farmers were unable to distance themselves from their own personal interests and hence unable to appreciate the beauty of the fire. They all blamed Henry Thoreau for his carelessness. Wheeler's timber was gone. Now wasn't that too bad? (p. 109)

Boyd's effort to make Thoreau the hero of this episode is perhaps noble, but if one looks upon it with unanointed eyes, it is as bizarre as Queen Titania courting the ass-headed Bottom. Here is a most lamentable comedy because it is Boyd who is unable to distance himself, not the farmers of Concord. Boyd serves as an excellent example of a commentator on Thoreau who is so enamored of his subject (or of his idea about Thoreau) that he is blinded to common sense. Boyd's faith in his rebel idealist causes him to idealize Thoreau to such an absurd degree that one is ready to believe that reason and love keep little company together. Though reason did not accompany love in Boyd's treatment of his rebel, Thoreau did not lack fellow travelers in the thirties; but unlike Boyd they did not idealize him.

Parrington's chapter on Thoreau in *Main Currents* generated interest in Thoreau among Marxist critics. Parrington's pioneer work in relating American literature to its social, political, and economic environment appealed to Marxists because it was very similar to their approach to literature. Like the Marxists, Parrington attempted to explain the development of American literature in terms of social forces, particularly class conflicts.[17] One Marxist critic, Bernard Smith, looking back on Parrington's work in 1939, "emphasized Parrington's radicalism because it is probably the most significant aspect of *Main Currents*," and he went on to claim him as a fellow traveler: "I can state dogmatically that he had some acquaintance with Marxism had been influenced by it, and knew that his method was related to it. I have seen a letter by him in which he said as much.[18] But Smith was quick to point out that Parrington was not an "outright socialist or a true Marxist," because "he was too much the Western libertarian to stand exclusively for collectivism" (p. 42).

As another Marxist critic, Granville Hicks, had noted, though Parrington was "on occasion and to a certain extent, a Marxist" due to his awareness of economic forces and class conflicts, he deviated from the orthodox Marxist idea of the subordination of the individual to collectivistic proletarian goals, "because the basis of his [liberal] creed was a Jeffersonian trust in the individual."[19] This faith in the individual caused Parrington to turn to the literati rather than the proletariat as his primary source of hope for a better world. Hence, though he identified the problems in America as a Marxist would, his solution was based upon a sturdy individualism rather than upon a mass movement. For Marxists, Parrington was something of an embarrassment, because he was at once both part of the solution and part of the problem. Their view of Thoreau was similar.

The lengthiest Marxist treatment of Thoreau in the thirties appears in V.F. Calverton's *The Liberation of American Literature* (1932), and it is only ten pages long.[20] Calverton describes his book as the beginnings of the "spade work" necessary to develop a "Marxian approach" to American literature and culture that is conscious of the "class forces active in the creation" of them (p. xiii). The book, according to Calverton, is best thought of as "social history" rather than "literary criticism," because Calverton intentionally avoids aesthetic evaluations in order to proceed directly "to an analysis of the philosophy, or ideology . . . that underlay[s] the individual author's work" (p. xii). Naturally, the touchstone for Calverton's discussion of the authors he examines is Marxist ideology, and though Thoreau is to some extent praised, he does not entirely escape the blows of Calverton's hammer and sickle.

Calverton applauds Thoreau's antiestablishment stance. He quotes Thoreau on education, religion, the state, and the press and acclaims his views as "stinging words . . . quick with the dynamite of revolt — the revolt of the individual against the oppression of the society in which he lived" (p. 264). Calverton also rates Thoreau higher than his nineteenth-century contemporaries — particularly Emerson — because he was not afraid of manual labor, "the working hand" (pp. 263, 268); this placed him in a closer alliance, from Calverton's point of view, with the proletariat. In addition, Thoreau would not compromise his ideals:

In a sense, he was the best individual product of that petty bourgeois ideology of the frontier which captured the minds of so many of the literati of his day . . . he never became interested . . . in the acquisition of property, never built up a small fortune and never speculated in stocks as Emerson did, or built and sold houses as did Whitman in his early thirties. (p. 262)

But as much as Thoreau may have acted like a Marxist, he did not think like one, because the "anarcho-individualism" of Thoreau "inevitably led him to oppose movements or tendencies which demanded group action or emphasized social impulse" (p. 267). And as Granville Hicks noted: "Nothing in American literature is more admirable than Henry Thoreau's devotion to his principles, but the principles are, unfortunately, less significant than the devotion."[21]

According to Calverton the "doctrine" of Thoreau's individualism "was based upon a social error," since man is not by nature an isolate, but rather a "social animal" (p. 268). Thoreau's individualism is of no "practical value" because he was "not interested in individualists who organized themselves socially in order to defend their individual freedom" (p. 269). The Thoreau who wrote that "God does not sympathize with the popular movements" (quoted on p. 270) was of no use to a Marxist:

In his contention that "the gregariousness of men is their most contemptible and discouraging aspect," he showed how completely ignorant he was of the fact that it was that very gregariousness which made it possible for men to progress, and without which society could never have evolved and the human mind never have advanced. (p. 269)

Though Thoreau's individualism, like Emerson's and Whitman's, may have been a progressive force in the nineteenth century, it was for Calverton totally irrelevant for America in the 1930s; "it is nothing more than a hollow echo of a dead past" which

belonged to a different America and grew out of a different scene. Those who take it up to-day do so in hopeless protest against the America that is with us, believing that through its challenge they can save the country from its present economic destiny [and that destiny was, according to Calverton, to be the utter collapse of capitalism]. But their hope is as foolish and futile as that of the romantic Southerners who still believe in the possible restoration of old Dixie. (p. 298)

In linking Thoreau's individualism with "old Dixie," Calverton is clearly aligning it with what he takes to be the reactionary conservative forces in American life (see pp. 112-113). The political meaning of Thoreau's kind of individualism is associated with that of the Southern agrarians in *I'll Take My Stand* (1930), a book whose title captures some of the spirit of Thoreau's individualism. Mike Gold once called the writers of that book " 'humanist' blackshirts," and

Calverton did not disagree.[22] For Calverton, Thoreau, the stupendous radical of the twenties, had become by the third decade of the twentieth century an unsocial thinker who made fascism a possibility in America.

Calverton discredits Thoreau's individualism explicitly when he argues that it has no use in the twentieth century, but he also impugns it much more subtly by associating it implicitly with fascism (this despite the fact that he points out that "Civil Disobedience" inspired Gandhi [p. 270]). His parting shot at Thoreau's individualism is again more of an innuendo than an explicit charge, only this time it is not to imply that Thoreau was a prototypical fascist; rather, it is to suggest that his individualism was generated by mediphysics rather than metaphysics: "Any individual who could write that nature was 'more human than any single man or woman can be' . . . certainly revealed abnormal characteristics, possibly of a sexual nature, which unquestionably played a role in shaping the direction of his life as well as his thoughts" (p. 270). Calverton says that Thoreau's "psychological complexes" are, unfortunately, beyond the scope of his study, and so he buries the suggestion in a footnote where it goes unsupported; nevertheless the point is made. Calverton seems anxious to institutionalize Thoreau's anti-institutionalism. His use of psychology is not to explain Thoreau's motivations (that could be a perfectly legitimate approach); instead, his purpose is to discredit Thoreau's politics by hinting that they are the product of an abnormal mind. [23] This kind of tactic can be no more justified than red baiting.

Marxist critics of the thirties found Thoreau both interesting and exasperating. He was interesting because the Marxists believed he shared their critical views concerning society, and he was exasperating because most of them could not reconcile Thoreau's first-person "I" with Marxist ideology, a predicament that Thoreau seems to have anticipated with pleasure when he wrote that he "loved to see a man with a taproot, though it make him difficult to transplant" (*Journal*, IV, 16). As the Marxists pointed out, Thoreau could not be transplanted to their ideology because he was, from their point of view, anachronistic in his anticollective bias. For that reason the Marxists decided to leave Thoreau in the nineteenth century, where they felt he belonged. He was viewed as a thinker whose vision of American life identified its major social problems but whose solution to those problems was buried under nearly one hundred years of social change. Because Thoreau's social thought was useless, few Marxists paid any attention to him. [24]

Curiously, the Marxist objections to Thoreau were similar to those conservative commentaries of the twenties which voiced reservations about Thoreau's unwillingness to be a good citizen. Though the ideological differences between the Marxists and the commentators of the twenties were great, the demands that each group made upon Thoreau were not radically different. Whether it was the Good Citizens' League, Republicans or Democrats, conservatives or progressives, New Humanists or Marxists — all of them were frustrated and to a degree angered with Thoreau's refusal to sign on. However, there were some commentators in the thirties who championed rather than condemned Thoreau's suspicion and hostility toward collective action.

Attacks on Thoreau's individualism did not go unanswered in the thirties. Thoreau's reputation became a political as well as literary battleground. Critics of his individualism, "men-harriers" as Thoreau called them in *Walden*, were challenged by a group of conservative critics in the thirties who looked back nostalgically upon the individualism of Thoreau's "golden day" as a bit of "God's drop" for a decade characterized by what they felt was governmental encroachments upon the individual in the form of the welfare state.

The defenders of Thoreau's individualism in the thirties did not deny the existence of the economic problems facing the United States; they agreed with the collectivists that the country was in need of reform, but they parted ways over the means of reform. Their solution was not a collective one — neither the Marxist nor the Democratic New Deal variety — but an individualistic approach. The new deal that Thoreau enjoyed in the thirties was provided not so much by New Dealers as by some of their critics. These critics tended to be liberal in outlook, but their liberalism was suspicious of any form of government that interfered with an individual's freedom to direct his own life. In order to distinguish them from New Deal liberals, it is convenient to refer to them as libertarians rather than liberals. For the libertarians the best way to preserve a person's freedom was to limit governmental control over the individual; in short, the best government was that which governed least. These critics found a natural ally in Thoreau. [25]

Joseph Wood Krutch is representative of the libertarian reaction to the collectivistic Marxist solution to the country's problems. Perceiving the greatest threat to individualism to be among Marxists, he argues that the communists' insistence upon an artist's fidelity to their doctrines is no more than a rigid suppression of an artist's freedom, regardless of their utopian goals. Though an artist and his art are never entirely free from their environments, it is, according to Krutch, perverse to regard them as weapons or mere propaganda: ". . . a man *qua* Artist and *qua* Reformer are antithetical things, the reformer concerned largely with what he can do to the world, the artist primarily interested in what the world is doing to him." [26] Krutch insisted that neither the artist nor critic should be straitjacketed by an enforced allegiance to any orthodoxy.

Thoreau is, for Krutch, a paradigm of libertarian thought and action:

he quite openly distrusted those who would do good to others before they had discovered how to do good to themselves; and far from seeking some social discipline which would unite humanity into a manageable mass of essentially uniform creatures with predictable reactions, he desired, so he said, "as many different persons in the world as possible." [27]

The "social discipline" that Krutch has in mind is communism, which he sees as an enemy of "freedom, speculation, the useless arts, and the disinterested pursuit of knowledge" (p. 506). Krutch's approach to the complex problems of modern society is the exact opposite to that of the collectivists; his solution is Thoreau's "antisocial" (p. 506) stand. It is the individual who holds out whatever hope there is for amelioration, because man taken en masse is virtually doomed:

if it should by any chance happen that our world, instead of successfully organizing itself into one vast ant-hill, is destined to break up into a thousand fragments, it may still be those

individuals here and there persisting who will justify the sur-
vival of the fragments. Perhaps only the individual is saved or
is really savable. (507)

For Krutch the free individual was the only person capable of
salvation and worthy of it. This idea left the mass of men out in the
cold. In Krutch's scheme of things one had to be among the elect,
"here and there persisting," to be saved. There is a coldness here —
if not a self-righteousness — that is disturbing because it smacks of
a spiritual form of Darwinism; it is almost Calvinistic in its disdain
for the majority of human beings. It is strange to think of Thoreau,
who refused in *Walden* "to write an ode to dejection," being used
by a pessimist like Krutch, but it is a useful reminder that despite
Thoreau's Transcendental belief in the potential divinity of humanity, he frequently looked upon his fellows with contempt if they
were unable, or refused, to live up to their potentialities — and his
expectations. "Men," wrote Thoreau, "are the inveterate foes of all
improvement. Generally speaking, they think more of their hen-
houses than of any desirable heaven" (*Journal*, X, 351). There is not
much faith in the proletariat here. Like Krutch he believed that
united we fall, divided we stand.[28] It should be kept in mind, however, that Krutch refers to Thoreau not to disparage humanity but
to undercut the collectivistic "social discipline" of communism.
People cannot be saved, but an individual might be. This was a
function that Thoreau performed several times in the thirties.[29]
Krutch's use of Thoreau is an attempt to make nineteenth-century
individualism operative in the twentieth century; unlike Max
Lerner, he sees no basis for collectivism in his Thoreau.
    Henry Seidel Canby, the most prolific and influential writer on
Thoreau in the thirties, shares Krutch's negative reaction to Marxism in a review of Calverton's *The Liberation of American Literature*. Contrary to Marxist expectations, Canby asserts that collectivism in the United States may turn out to be a "possible Hell instead of a probable Heaven." What the country and its literature
needs is not Marxist analyses, "often based upon the winds of doctrine"; rather "we need more Parringtons" — a faith that individualism is not dead.[30] Canby's many writings on Thoreau attest to
his own libertarian faith in individualism.

In his writings about Thoreau, Canby strongly emphasizes Thoreau's nonconformity and his unwillingness to join in a united effort to bring about reforms of any sort. Yet he considers Thoreau's social thought to be more radical than any Marxist's "precisely because" he does "not threaten property or counsel spoiling the fat for the benefit of the lean, but go[es] to the root of the whole matter, where it is clear that a life conducted for worthy ends and according to principles of elementary justice is the ultimate that must be preserved *even if the state totters*" (my emphasis).[31] For anyone who might raise their institutional eyebrows at the dangerous implications of this brand of individualism, Canby offers one sentence: "You cannot quash such a theory by saying that it leads to anarchy" (p. 208). He points out that the country has not produced enough Thoreaus interested in self-reform to bring down the state and so Thoreau's ideas pose no actual threat to the state." And yet for Americans there is more dynamite in his writing than in all Marxism" (p. 209). Canby argues that the most radical kind of reform is individual reform; it is extremely difficult to achieve, however, because mechanized modern American life conspires against the individual.

Canby sees the freedom of the would-be individual of the thirties circumscribed foremost by the machine. There is also the crowded urban environment, and "artificial wants" created by the radio, moving pictures, newspapers, and magazines. Because of these trivialities, the individual is too easily distracted from the true business of a meaningful life and as a result frequently feels aimless and at loose ends in a materialistic, machine age (pp. 223-224). In the face of such insecurity, conformity to the orthodoxy of a party or the state is appealing but giving in would be to live a life without principle.

Canby offers Thoreau as a model for the individual who does not want to be ground up in the machine age either by the forces of industrialism or the forces of industrial reform:

There is really no other solution than his to the increasing ills of a state that we call sometimes progressive, but more often strenuous, nervous, febrile, aimless. The disease — which, like some selective malady, seizes upon our best, and fills sanitariums with nervous wrecks, homes with neurotics, cites with fine-drawn, irritable men, slaves of time whose hopes of leisure, and with leisure happiness, are always deferred — is susceptible to no other cure. Psychiatrists are patchers and repairers merely. They and the vocabulary of their science are inventions to describe the malady that Thoreau diagnosed. They cannot save the machine, and freely admit it. The only cure is moral, the only alleviation a robust discrimination in wants. (p. 206)

The solutions to an individual's problems, according to Canby, are all inside him; they are not on a couch or in a cell meeting or in a ballot box. The answers are to be discovered in a moral realm, not in a political arena. Thoreau's individual approach to living a good life is more relevant to Americans of the 1930s than any collectivistic ideology: "He states our problem, but we turn from his solution, not because it is impossible, but because it seems impossible to us" (p. 304). It is time that there were more Thoreaus before it is too late. "We must breed Thoreaus somewhere, or see this machine society stuffed and stifled by its own superheated desires" (p. 225). To be sure, that somewhere was not to be found within the ideology of either "socialism or communism, which are the parasites of industrialism" (p. 208), but within the simplified, unified, singular life of an individual.

In the thirties Thoreau's social thought was lubricated and well used by those who saw him as a social prophet inveighing against the threats to individualism posed by both industrial machinery and party machinery. As Canby pointed out, the machine was not at fault; it was the use to which the machine was being put that pointed to a decline in the role of the self-reliant individual in American culture (pp. 205-206). Similarly, though the goals of the collectivistic approaches to the country's economic and social problems may have been humane and idealistic, the means of attaining those ends — individual conformity — represented too great a sacrifice to libertarians.[32]

Political and industrial machines were pervasive concerns of the country and directly influenced the degree to which Americans were interested in Thoreau. *Time*, in reviewing Canby's *Thoreau*

(1939), a book that enjoyed the most popular success of any biography ever written about Thoreau, restated the major reason for the author's and his readers' interest in him: "What Thoreau really meant by his life" has become more apparent recently "under the triumph of indistrialism" and "the rise of dictatorships." In the 1930s this " 'friend of woodchucks and enemy of the state' emerges as the most read and most readable U.S. writer of his time." [33] The "triumph of industrialism" that *Time* refers to was frequently interpreted as a defeat for the individual. As one Thoreauvian put it to the 1930 graduating class of Wellesley College: ". . . the independence of the individual and the old philosophy of individualism to which Thoreau gave such eloquent expression at Walden Pond have been wiped out by the resistless march of the machine age." Although Americans cannot jump off their celestial railroad because their economy is coupled to it, Thoreau is not "completely out of date," because it is the spirit of his individualism that is important, not his specific solutions. This was a common theme of Thoreau commentators of the thirties. [34]

Inevitably, Thoreau's individualism, seen from the perspective of the complex mechanized, modernized, and homogenized thirties, resulted in a good deal of nostalgic looking back to a man and his era that seemed much better than the present. American individualism was in the past; the present represented a decline in American values. The individual seemed to mean very little in the corporate, collective thirties; the best he could do, perhaps, was to play Monopoly (patented in 1935). America's progress limited rather than liberated the individual.

The Thoreauvians who most directly expressed this sense of loss and limitation were those who went on pilgrimages to Walden Pond in an attempt to revitalize themselves in its simple natural setting. Instead of finding the conditions which awakened Thoreau's soul to the infinite possibilities of Self, these pilgrims found mounds of garbage, noisy automobiles, swarms of people, hot-dog stands, and any number of other manifestations of modern American civilization. There is no going back to the past, a fact that makes it doubly attractive, and for nostalgic pilgrims like the very popular E.B. White, a fact that gives the past a "certain credibility" which makes it seem more real than the present. [35] This nostalgic view, a mild, urbane form of escapism, has become a minor genre of writing about Thoreau which increased dramatically in the thirties and continues to be written. For these writers the pure Walden water is not so much mingled with the sacred water of the Ganges as it is with the Lethe.

There was a more ominous form of technology in the thirties than the Fords that sputtered their way to Walden Pond. There were the Italian tanks and the machine guns that smashed into Ethiopia, and the German dive bombers that descended upon Guernica. Machines were being used conspicuously by dictators for ruthless, inhuman purposes, and Thoreau was offered as an answer to both by Sinclair Lewis. Whereas V.F. Calverton hinted that Thoreau was a prototypical Fascist, Lewis insisted that he was fascism's nemesis whether it be in Huey Long's America, Mussolini's Italy, Hitler's Germany, or the emperor's Japan. Because Thoreau was one of our "captains of freedom," Lewis had no worries about setting him up as "the supreme Duce" even though "the very notion of dictatorship would be inconceivable" to Thoreau.[36]

Lewis is more interested in Thoreau for what he offers the present rather than for what he represents of a simplified pastoral past. He is not lulled into nostalgia, because even if Walden Pond were a pristine reality uncorrupted by empty beer bottles, blaring portable radios, and any of the other trappings of civilization, the man that went to it would not be. Lewis was too much of a realist to believe that solutions to complex modern problems could be found by making a private clearing in the wilderness. He makes this clear in an episode in *Babbitt*. Though *Babbitt* antedates Lewis' piece on Thoreau by fifteen years, it is useful in understanding why he prefers a political version of Thoreau to a pastoral one.

Lewis has Babbitt, who is leading a life of quiet desperation in complex, urban Zenith, long for a simple life in the woods where Babbitt saw himself "finding peace . . . in a life primitive and heroic."[37] The setting is not the woods of Walden Pond, however; rather it is the Maine Woods near "Katadumcook" (p. 148), a name that suggests Ktaadn and Chesuncook of Thoreau's *Maine Woods*. Babbitt looks forward to going off into the wilderness with the "half Yankee, half Indian" guide Joe Paradise: "If only he could but take up a backwoods claim with a man like Joe, work hard with his hands, be free and noisy in a flannel shirt, and never come back to this dull decency!" (p. 295). It will be remembered that Thoreau's Indian guide was actually named Joe Polis, a name strangely inappropriate for his Natty Bumppo-like gifts. Babbitt's Indian guide is also misnamed, but whereas Thoreau's "Polis" seems only inappropriate, Lewis' fictional "Paradise" is cruelly ironic. If Indian names are meant to characterize a man, he should have been named Polis.

Babbitt wants desperately to believe that his Joe is not "like a city man" (p. 297). He fights disillusionment when Joe sulks about their hiking into the wilderness instead of taking an easier way via boat powered by a chugging "Evinrude." Babbitt, wishing that he knew the woods the way Joe does, asks him the name of a little red flower they pass on the trail: he has to forget Joe's resentful answer quickly: "Well, some folks call it one thing and some calls it another — I always just call it Pink Flower." But he cannot forget Joe's response to Babbitt's asking him what he would do if he had a lot of money: "Would you stick to guiding, or would you take a claim 'way back in the woods and be independent of people?" For the first time during the trip Joe's face brightens and he enthusiastically replies: "I've often thought of that! If I had the money, I'd go down to Tinker's Falls and open a swell shoe store" (pp. 298-300). The next day Babbitt goes home.

Lewis found Thoreau-Polis considerably more useful that Thoreau-Paradise. Although Lewis, like other anticollectivists, emphasized that Thoreau conducted a "One-man revolution" in Nature, his "supreme Duce" was not an escapist seeking refuge in a impossible pastoral dream, but rather a thinker whose social thought was a guide for relationships among people — the polis. Unfortunately, Lewis does not explain how Thoreau's one-man revolution is translated into a broader social context. He places Thoreau in a political context, but he makes no attempt to describe how his Dictatorship of the Individual would operate on a political level. One is left with a sense of uncertainty about whether Thoreau would be fascism's greatest enemy or simply another — American — version of it.

Theodore Dreiser was another novelist in the thirties who was attracted to Thoreau, but unlike Lewis he was not interested in

Thoreau's social thought. For a collection of excerpts from Thoreau's writings that Dreiser edited in 1939, he wrote: "It seems to me that almost all his comments on men, society, the vindictive and critical side of his nature, his moral views, are not really essential to his greatness at all. . . ."[38] It is likely that Dreiser's interest in communism was responsible for this view. He was not one to read Thoreau dispassionately; in the introduction he manages to find in Thoreau's cosmology an affirmation of his own mechanistic philosophy: "Immutable [mechanical] law binds us all" (p. 10). This does not go very far in explaining Thoreau's Transcendentalism. Whereas Lewis is vague about Thoreau, Dreiser misreads him.

Lewis' vagueness concerning how Thoreau was to be applied to the problems of the thirties is representative of all the published commentary before the 1940s. Thoreau's social thought and politics were often invoked for a cause, but they were rarely discussed in any detail and never analyzed. With the exception of the Marxists, there was a tendency to be satisfied with awarding them an impressionistic approval rather than subjecting them to a vigorous analysis. One aspect of Thoreau's social thought — his simplified economics — was better understood and more generally discussed, because its application for the average American of the 1930s was obvious: cut down on expenses and be satisfied with less. Although this use of Thoreau ignored the Transcendentalism that informed Thoreau's economics, it was a clearly defined use of him, even if from a lower point of view than that of the "Master of Simplicity" himself. However, the libertarians who used Thoreau's individualism politically as an answer to communism and the corporate state did not explain clearly how his individualism was useful to *society*.

Canby is representative. He argues that Thoreau's anarchistic attitude toward society is "dynamite," but he also insists that it is no danger to society because there are so few Thoreaus, so few people of principle, that there is no actual threat to the state. Canby then goes on to warn Americans that "we must breed Thoreaus somewhere" before the individual is swallowed by "this machine society." This Thoreauvian fails to explain how a society populated by Thoreaus — Canby's remedy for its ills — would function. What about all that "dynamite"? If there were enough self-reformers to overturn a state, then what? This is not an unfair question to raise because it is built into Canby's argument. He offers Thoreau's social thought and politics for the specific ills of society, but he does not concern himself with specifics. Canby, like many of his contemporaries, simply avoided many of the problems that Thoreau's politics presented to a latter-day disciple. There was not one American analysis of even article length on "Civil Disobedience" or "A Plea for Captain John Brown," or any other Thoreau essay, prior to the 1940s. In the thirties there was a strong tendency to use Thoreau first and ask questions later.

NOTES

1. Franklin D. Roosevelt, *The Public Papers and Addresses* (New York: Random House, 1937), II, 11.

2. Walter Harding, *A Thoreau Handbook* (New York: New York University Press, 1959), p. 184. See also Randall Stewart's "The Growth of Thoreau's Reputation," *College English*, 7 (January 1946), 208-214.

3. Alice Payne Hackett, *60 Years of Best Sellers, 1895-1955* (New York: R.R. Bowker, 1956), p. 163.

4. Van Wyck Brooks, *The Flowering of New England, 1815-1865* (New York: E.P. Dutton & Co., 1936), pp. 286-302, 359-373, 423-428, 432-442.

5. *Reader's Digest*, 30 (May 1937), 25-29.

6. Theodore Peterson, *Magazines in the Twentieth Century* (Urbana: University of Illinois Press, 1964), p. 228. Information concerning the circulation of *Reader's Digest* will be found on p. 232.

7. "Walden: Or Life in the Woods," *Reader's Digest*, 37 (September 1940), 129-136. All quoted material is from p. 129. Thoreau's popularity and influence continue to be wider than his readership. Walter Harding, in a series of letters to famous authors asking how Thoreau might have influenced them, once queried Allen Ginsberg about his "special affinity" for Thoreau. Ginsberg replied that Thoreau "set [the] first classic US [*sic*] example of war resistance, back to nature, [and] tax refusal." Ginsberg added that he found himself "more and more indebted to Thoreau . . . without, oddly, having very much read in his texts" (*TSB*, 112 [Summer 1970], 7).

8. James MacKaye, *Thoreau: Philosopher of Freedom: Writings on Liberty by Henry David Thoreau* (New York: Vanguard Press, 1930), p. ix.

9. The average American's insecurity and concern about poverty, particularly in the early thirties, is demonstrated in a poll of "Public Opinion in the Thirties" reprinted in Daniel Aaron and Robert Bendiner, eds., *The Strenuous Decade: A Social and Intellectual Record of the 1930's* (New York: Anchor Books, 1970), pp. 62-64.

10. Russell Blankenship, *American Literature as an Expression of the National Mind*, rev. ed. (New York: Henry Holt and Co., 1931), p. 307.

11. Stanley T. Williams, *American Literature* (Philadelphia: J.B. Lippincott Co., 1933), p. 76.

12. *Native American Anarchism: A Study of Left-Wing American Individualism*, Smith College Studies in History, 17 (Northhampton, Mass.: Department of History of Smith College, 1932), pp. 46-51.

13. Max Lerner, "Thoreau: No Hermit," *Ideas Are Weapons: The History and Uses of Ideas* (New York: Viking Press, 1939), p. 45. This article is a slightly revised version that appeared earlier in the *Encyclopaedia of Social Science* (New York: Macmillan Co., 1934), XIV, 621-622. The fact that Thoreau was included in an encyclopedia of this kind is significant (the entry begins: "American philosopher"); it suggests how different the predominant view of the thirties was toward Thoreau in comparison to the twenties.

14. Odell Shepard describes his contemporaries in a review of Canby's biography of Thoreau: ". . . like most Thoreauvians, all of whom belong to the left wing of a minority, Mr. Canby writes as an enthusiastic advocate", *Nation* (October 7, 1939, p. 388).

15. With the exception of only a few articles such as Austin Warren, "Lowell on Thoreau," *Studies in Philology*, 27 (July 1930), 442-462; James Playsted Wood, "English and American Criticism of Thoreau," *New England Quarterly*, 6 (December 1933), 733-746; and F.W. Lorch, "Thoreau and the Organic Principle in Poetry," *PMLA*, 53 (March 1938), 286-302, the major portion of the academic criticism that did appear in scholarly journals of the thirties failed to make a significant contribution to Thoreau scholarship. See, for example, Fred DeArmond, "Thoreau and Schopenhauer: An Imaginary Conversation," *New England Quarterly*, 5 (January 1932), 55-64; J.B. Moore, "Thoreau Rejects Emerson," *American Literature*, 4 (November 1932), 241-256; E.J. Nichols, "Identification of Characters in Lowell's *A Fable for Critics*," *American Literature*, 4 (May 1932), 191-194; W.D. Templeman, "Thoreau, Moralist of the Picturesque," *PMLA*, 47 (September 1932), 864-889; J.G. Southworth, "Reply to W.D. Templeman, 'Thoreau, Moralist of the Picturesque,' " *PMLA*, 49 (September 1934), 971-974; A.W. Kelley, "Literary Theories About Program Music," *PMLA*, 52 (June 1937), 581-595; Grant Loomis, "Thoreau and Zimmermann," *New England Quarterly*, 10 (December 1937),

789-792; and Edith Peairs, "The Hound, the Bay Horse, and the Turtle Dove: A Study of Thoreau and Voltaire," *PMLA*, 52 (September 1937), 863-869. Academic criticism of Thoreau in the thirties had little to say about any important aspect of Thoreau and his work.

16. "Thoreau, the Rebel Idealist," *Americana*, 30 (January and April 1936), 89-118, 286-323. The quotation is on p. 92.

17. For an overview of the history and principles of Marxist criticism in the United States see Walter Sutton, *Modern American Criticism* (Englewood Cliffs, N.J.: Prentice-Hall, 1963), pp. 51-97.

18. "Parrington's *Main Currents*," *New Republic*, February 15, 1939, pp. 41-42.

19. "The Critical Principles of V.L. Parrington," *Science and Society: A Marxian Quarterly*, 3 (Fall 1939), 446-447.

20. V.F. Calverton, *The Liberation of American Literature* (New York: Charles Scribner's Sons, 1932), pp. 261-271.

21. Granville Hicks, *The Great Tradition*, rev. ed. (1935; rpt. New York: Biblo and Tannen, 1967), p. 10. Calverton's Marxist spade work in 1932 was enough to bury Thoreau in the past for most other Marxist commentators, who either generally ignored Thoreau or dispensed with him in a few pages. *The Great Tradition* and Bernard Smith's *Forces in American Criticism: A Study of the History of American Literary Thought* (New York: Harcourt, Brace, 1939), pp. 91-95, discuss Thoreau only briefly. Hicks, when he mentions Thoreau, agrees with Calverton point for point. Smith, however, because he deals with Thoreau in a critical context does not concern himself, in detail, with the problem of Thoreau's individualism being antithetical to Marxist collectivistic politics.

22. For a discussion of Calverton's and Gold's views on the Southern agrarian writers see Daniel Aaron, *Writers on the Left: Episodes in American Literary Communism* (New York: Harcourt, Brace & World, 1961), pp. 237-243. Gold is quoted on p. 327.

23. The few psychological approaches to Thoreau in the twenties and thirties were not particularly fruitful. Predictably, they focused upon his preference for nature over women. In 1925 Joseph Collins suggested that "Some day an interpreter of behavior will explain the man who wrote, 'For joy I could embrace the earth, I shall delight to be buried in it' " (*The Doctor Looks at Biography: Psychological Studies of Life and Letters* [New York: George H. Doran, 1925], p. 87). Collins' title promises more than the book offers; all he does is raise the question of Thoreau's psychological status. Many commentators in the twenties and thirties mentioned something in passing about Thoreau's "sublimations," but Ludwig Lewisohn was the first to deal with Thoreau's sexuality — or lack of it — in any depth from a self-described Freudian point of view in his *Expression in*

America ([New York: Harper & Brothers, 1932], pp. 136-152). Lewisohn says of Thoreau that "He was intellectually one of the bravest men that ever lived and also a clammy prig" (p. 136). Lewisohn has trouble maintaining the former though, because he seizes upon the latter and continually accents Thoreau's aversion to sex. Out of twenty volumes of writings, Lewisohn manages to find all eight or nine of Thoreau's specific references to sex and women; he concludes that Thoreau was "hopelessly inhibited, probably to the point of psychical impotence or else physiologically hopelessly undersexed and simply on this subject made the conventional pseudo-idealistic noise" (p. 139). Lewisohn is not clear in his own mind if Thoreau's social thought was generated by the independence of a brave intellectual or the "defective nature" (p. 151) of a solitary bachelor who did not realize that he was lonely. Though Lewisohn argues that Thoreau's social thought can be useful to us if abstracted from his personality and his "limited experience," he does not explain how — except to note that Thoreau's "great doctrine of civil disobedience, a doctrine that has in fact been practiced by all the highest spirits in human history, by all redeeming personalities" is currently (1932) being used in America "in connection with the Eighteenth Amendment" (p. 146). Of all the contemporary examples Lewisohn might have come up with, this is without question the most inappropriate. Apparently Lewisohn's own Dionysian spirit leads him astray from the spirit of Thoreau.

In a sense it is unfortunate that there are not more psychological approaches to Thoreau and his social thought in the twenties and thirties; perhaps then it would be possible to determine whether there was a pattern of minimizing Thoreau's ideas in such studies. But since there are no others, one can only say of Lewisohn's study what he says of Thoreau's politics — "queer but not dangerous" (p. 140).

24. Max Lerner, a sociologist of Marxist sensibilities, is an exception to the rule; he finds Thoreau's social thought in line with Marxist ideology, because he does not focus upon his "hermit-like individualism" which "may easily be overemphasized" (*Ideas Are Weapons*, p. 46). Instead he offers a Thoreau who wrote in *Walden* that "To act collectively is according to the spirit of our institutions" (quoted on p. 47). Lerner's approach to Thoreau seems to be a direct refutation of Calverton; he wants to redeem the "real force" of Thoreau's social thought for the twentieth century. It is interesting that Lerner accuses Emerson of what many commentators say of Thoreau: ". . . his chief weakness as a social thinker lay in his overestimate of the role of the individual in the social process and his underestimate of the place of the instituton" (p. 41). It is difficult to understand how Lerner can make this statement about Emerson but not Thoreau. Surely Emerson was more compatible with institutions than Thoreau, especially

SEVERAL MORE LIVES TO LIVE

in Emerson's later years (see George M. Fredrickson, *The Inner Civil War: Northern Intellectuals and the Crisis of the Union* [New York: Harper Torchbooks, 1968], pp. 176-180). Lerner glosses over Thoreau's individualism in order to welcome him into the Marxist camp.

25. Morton J. Frisch describes more fully the differences between New Deal liberalism and what Frisch calls the "older liberalism," which stressed individual rather than governmental action: "The Welfare State as a Departure from the Older Liberalism," in *The Thirties: A Reconsideration in the Light of the American Political Tradition*, eds. Morton J. Frisch and Martin Diamond (DeKalb: Northern Illinois University Press, 1968), pp. 68-83. For a contemporary distinction see Walter Lippman, *The Good Society* (Boston: Little, Brown & Co., 1937). Lippman's point of view is that of the older liberalism when he insists that "In the social discipline of all collectivists the inviolability of men is somewhere denied" (p. 209).

26. Quoted in Aaron, *Writers on the Left*, p. 259.

27. "Walden Revisited," *Nation*, May 3, 1933, p. 506.

28. Considerably more pessimistic than Krutch is George Shelton Hubbell's earlier article: "Walden Revisited: A Grammar of Dissent," *Sewanee Review*, 37 (July 1929), 283-294. Hubbell applies Thoreau's economy to a modern urban setting. In order to be an "urban Waldenite" one must resist the harmful pressures from advertising, technology, and materialism (285-288). Using Thoreau's simplified "regimen" applied to modern conditions, our "declining" culture is made more bearable for the individual but neither is finally saved from meaninglessness, because we are too distant and too alienated from the simplicity of Walden Pond. Ours is a "decaying social order," and even Hubbell's own "resort to urban solitude is but a retreating compromise, to render the inevitable as innocuous as it may be" (p. 294). Apparently, Hubbell read more of Henry Adams than Henry Thoreau.

29. Marxist thought was unfavorably compared with Thoreau's individualism several times in the thirties; see Henry Seidel Canby, ed., "Introduction," *The Works of Thoreau* (Boston: Houghton Mifflin Co., 1937), pp. 772-773; *New York Times*, June 25, 1938, sec. 1, p. 14; November 12, 1939, sec. 4, p. 8, and John T. Flanagan, "Emerson and Communism," *New England Quarterly*, 10 (June 1937), 243-261.

30. Henry Seidel Canby, "A Marxist America," *Saturday Review*, September 17, 1932, pp. 101-102.

31. Henry Seidel Canby, "Henry David Thoreau," in *Classic Americans: A Study of Eminent American Writers from Irving to Whitman* (1931; rpt., New York: Russell & Russell, 1959), pp. 207-208. Canby was extremely influential in keeping Thoreau before the American public of the 1930s. He wrote several articles, an anthology, and a biography of Thoreau, and as

editor of the *Saturday Review of Literature* he frequently mentioned him in its columns. Canby also reprinted many of his pieces on Thoreau; this further enhanced both their reputations. The chapter in *Classic Americans* (184-225), for example, was pared down — eliminating Canby's comments on Thoreau's style and nature writing — and reprinted in the *Yale Review*, 20 (March 1931), 517-531; and in Theodore Sizer, ed., *Aspects of the Social History of America* (1931; rpt. Freeport, N.Y.: Books for Libraries Press, 1969), pp. 95-115. The chapter was retitled in both as "Thoreau in the Machine Age" thereby accenting the relevance of Thoreau's social thought to the thirties. One year later three pages from the chapter appeared in *Catholic World*, 134 (January 1932), 478-480. As Canby said in *Classic Americans*, "We are ripe for a dose of Thoreau" (p. 225), and he made sure that the medicine was delivered.

32. Canby, anticipating critics of Thoreau who might ask what his solution was to *society's* ills, writes somewhat defensively that "If Thoreau provided no technique by which society as a whole could escape from wage slavery [and other injustices], at least his challenge to Americans did not imply a dictatorship" (*Thoreau* [Boston: Houghton Mifflin, 1939], p. 286). The quality of this argument is reminiscent of the student who presents his parents with a failing report card and assures them that everything is really all right after all, because at least he did not cheat. There was a minority of dissenters who were not convinced by this kind of defense; see Gilbert Seldes, "Thoreau" in *American Writers on American Literature*, ed. John Macy (New York: Liveright, 1931), pp. 164-176; Walter F. Taylor, *A History of American Letters* (New York: American Book Co., 1936), pp. 159-167; and Donald Cross Peattie, "Is Thoreau a Modern?" *North American Review*, 245 (Spring 1938), 159-169. Each of these writers finds Thoreau's social thought and politics dated because he does not address himself to the complexities of modern society. Thoreau may be important to the individual who seeks self-development, but his individualism, to "a nation struggling to control the billion-horsepower forces of the machine age," now "sounds somewhat beside the point" (Taylor, p. 166).

33. "Realometer," *Time*, October 16, 1939, p. 110. *Time's* assertion that Thoreau was the "most read" writer of the nineteenth century seems to contradict the *Reader's Digest* assessment that "few now read" Thoreau. The difference can be explained by noting that *Time*, unlike the *Reader's Digest*, was aimed at a college-educated audience (Peterson, *Magazines in the Twentieth Century*, p. 328), an audience that was more aware of Thoreau than the general public due to the anthologies that appeared in the thirties. Each of the three notable collections of Thoreau's writings produced in the thirties that would have been used in college curriculums

pointed to Thoreau's social relevance; see Bartholow V. Crawford, *Henry David Thoreau: Representative Selections, with Introduction, Bibliography, and Notes* (New York: American Book Company, 1934); Henry Seidel Canby, *The Works of Thoreau* (Boston: Houghton Mifflin, 1937), the "Introduction" to this anthology, which strongly emphasized Thoreau's social relevance, was printed earlier in the *Saturday Review of Literature*, December 26, 1936, pp. 3-4, 15, under the title of "The Man Who Did What He Wanted: A Proposed Definition of Thoreau"; and Brooks Atkinson, *Walden and Other Writings of Henry David Thoreau* (New York: Random House, 1937). It is noteworthy that Atkinson is much more tolerant of Thoreau's social thought and politics in the thirties than he had been in the previous decade. In a review of Canby's *Thoreau*, he implicitly recants his earlier condemnation of Thoreau in *Cosmic Yankee* (*New York Times*, October 8, 1939, sec. 6, pp. 1, 16).

34. Raymond B. Fosdick, "The Individual's Place in the Age of Machines," *New York Times*, June 22, 1930, sec. 3, p. 4. American reactions to modern industrialization in the twenties and thirties are succinctly discussed in Hoffman, *The Twenties*, pp. 285-306; and Curti, *Growth of American Thought*, pp. 688-690. In addition to Canby, who introduced this theme early in his treatments of Thoreau (e.g. "Thoreau, the Great Eccentric," *Saturday Review of Literature*, November 26, 1927, pp. 337-339, which was later reprinted in his *American Estimates* [New York: Harcourt, Brace, 1929], pp. 97-109, there were also many others who alluded to Thoreau's usefulness in the machine age; among them were Lewis Mumford, *The Brown Decades: A Study of the Arts in America, 1865-1895* (New York: Dover, 1931); and Randall Stewart, "The Concord Group," *Sewanee Review*, 44 (October-December 1936), 434-446. Also, see note 35.

35. See E.B. White, "One Man's Meat," *Harper's*, 179 (August 1939), 329-332; Robert Whitcomb, "The Thoreau Country," *Bookman*, 73 (July 1931), 458-461; and H. Brickell, "A Thoreau Pilgrimage," *North American Review*, 238 (October 1934), 376-377. Even Canby, in the most ambitious work on Thoreau of the decade, complains that Thoreau's "crystal-clear lake, wood-surrounded" has been reduced to "a railroad amusement park . . . where the memory of the poet-naturalist is celebrated by public baths, water slides, and boats for amorous couples" (*Thoreau*, p. 204).

36. "One Man Revolution," *Newsweek*, November 22, 1937, p. 33.

37. *Babbitt* (New York: Grosset & Dunlap, 1922), p. 294.

38. *The Living Thoughts of Thoreau* (New York: Longmans, Green and Co., 1939), p. 11.

chapter 3

THE WAR YEARS

Synchronize your watches, gentlemen.

If a man does not keep pace with his companions, perhaps it is because he hears a different drummer.

Any American who has made it through high school and spent a few Saturday afternoons at the movies (or evenings before his television) does not require identifications for the preceding quotations. He knows that the second quotation is from Thoreau because his teachers were fond of quoting it and because it has been used as a caption on everything from greeting cards to wall posters. It succinctly summarizes the individualistic and extravagant gait of that Concord saunterer. And he remembers the first quotation because it was almost an obligatory line for the John Waynes and Clark Gables of World War II films. The intense, square-jawed, authoritative hero who wound up his dangerous battle plans with the order to "synchronize your watches, gentlemen" spoke not only to the men in his command; he spoke to an entire nation at war.[1]

Naturally, Henry Thoreau would have had a difficult time in John Wayne's platoon.

America's anticipation of war resulted in a partial dim-out of Thoreau's reputation. The national mood was constrictive and disciplined rather than expansive and free. America was in the business of putting together a national army and had no time for a one-man revolution like Thoreau's. After witnessing the successes of Hitler's blitzkrieg in Europe, President Roosevelt in 1940 initiated preparedness measures which mobilized the country for an all-out war. The nation's first peacetime draft ordered Americans to get ready for war, and though no one wanted war, nearly everyone felt the pressure to keep pace with the same military beat. It was no saunterer's gait that Americans adopted; it was a synchronized march, and Thoreau was conspicuously out of step.

In 1940 an editorial in the *New York Times* suggested how the social and political climate of the war affected Thoreau's reputation. The editorial commented on Thoreau's failure to be elected to the Hall of Fame for outstanding Americans. It already included such writers as Emerson, Longfellow, Irving, and Lowell.

If today Thoreau fell short by five votes of the required sixty-five, it may well be that the moment is inauspicious for a man who preached civil disobedience; a bit of an anarchist one might call Thoreau. Today the nation demands civil obedience for national defense to the point of actual conscription in peace time. [2]

The author who did muster enough votes to be elected was an eminently safe one for the 1940s. Thoreau lost to Stephen Collins Foster, a writer whose melancholy songs satisfied a unifying, national nostalgia and helped to reinforce the popular view of the sad but somehow contented plantation "darky." The *Times* rightly described Foster's election as "a victory for the Sewanee River over Walden Pond." Everyone in his place and a place for everyone was the way to win the imminent war. The tone of the editorial makes clear that the *Times* thought it unfortunate that the national consciousness was predominantly in favor of safe, conformist behavior. The country's mobilization for war signaled a tightening on the reigns of individual freedom, but not everyone was eager to become a working part of the war machinery if it meant giving up that freedom. This was especially true of Thoreauvians who followed the libertarians of the 1930s in emphasizing Thoreau's individualism as an answer to modern encroachments upon personal freedom.

Writing eleven months before Pearl Harbor, Thomas Lyle Collins commented upon "Thoreau's Coming of Age" in reference to his reputation in the United States.[3] Following Canby, whose then recent biography he views as the climax of "interest in Thoreau as a critic of values," Collins asserts that Thoreau's relevance to the contemporary scene is based upon his setting forth and embodying "a true ideal of individualism which has not yet been extinguished, but which only grows brighter as the night draws on" (p. 58). Collins does not locate the source of darkness that threatens to eclipse individualism in the war in Europe; instead, he locates the threat in America itself as it prepares for the impending war:

The greatest enemy of America today is not fascism, not Nazi-ism, not communism — it is "Americanism." Our government is becoming divine, a thing in itself. This tendency is intensified by the recent renewal of hostilities in Europe; in contrast America is made to seem a paradise. The chamber-of-commerce-God's-country brand of nationalism . . . is once more in full cry. The next decade bids fair to transform America into "God's Country" in earnest. If ever we needed Thoreau, we need him now. (p. 59)

History has proved that Collins underestimated the fascist threat to America; however, history has also validated his fear that "God's Country" is always a dangerous place in which to live, but more on that later. Collins' warning that "If ever we needed Thoreau, we need him now" is a commonplace in Thoreau criticism; it is the imprimatur of the true Thoreauvian, who more often than not has an evangelical streak in him. Thoreau's orphic sayings have attracted many critic-priests lusting after a text. Consequently, Thoreau has something of a promiscuous reputation; like ladies of easy virtue, his politics have comforted whoever has bothered to pick them up. World War II provides a theater in which this theme can again be dramatized, and Collins, though he plays a relatively minor role, is an important element in the plot.

The objections that the libertarians voiced in the thirties about communism, socialism, and the welfare state were, in the forties, applied to the warfare state. Collins, like Krutch and Canby before him, argues that Thoreau is "more realistic" than social reformers because "each individual must work out his own individual problems" (p. 61). True individual freedom cannot be provided by the state; "The entire intellectual movement of the last decade bears evidence: from the beginning the assumption was that external political and economic reform would suffice" (p. 65). He judges the New Deal to be a failure. Meaningful change can come only from within. According to Collins, social reformers are deluded in thinking that true reform can be legislated or achieved collectively.

Obliquely, Collins hints that Thoreau (and Collins) would not be in favor of the United States entering the war in Europe — one of the vital issues of the period until the morning of December 7. He argues that noninvolvement does not necessarily mean social irresponsibility. Though he does not couch his discussion of an individual's moral responsibility to his fellowman and society within the context of the war, it is difficult to imagine his readers being able to divorce his comments from the war, particularly since he had asserted only three pages earlier that "Nazi-ism" was not the greatest threat that Americans had to face. Collins argues that if a person can live his life without supporting injustice in the modern world — a task much more difficult and "doubtful than it would have been a hundred years ago" — if he can, "or if he chooses to emigrate to Alaska or the South Seas [history has a way of being both rude and ironic], he is not thereby guilty of moral evasion." Collins quickly passes over the problem of directly or indirectly "supporting injustice," so that he can make his point: "Indeed," writes Collins, "reformers who refuse to live richly [in a spiritual sense], who sacrifice concern with the 'res privita' for concern with the 'res publica' are much less *moral* (i.e., less *good*) than a happy-go-lucky beachcomber" (p. 62). Unless one is willing to accept the politics implicit in a Simeon Stylites, this is nonsense. If Collins had made no claim of moral and *social* responsibility for this isolationist position, it could have been defended, perhaps, without the speciousness exhibited here, but in attempting to claim moral and social responsibility for being good rather than doing good, Collins has written himself up a pillar.

Although he goes on to support the efficacy of Thoreau's "principle of civil disobedience" and revels in calling it "un-American" because its "supercharged political dynamite" is "so radical as to make the reddest red look anemic" (p. 62), Collins is not really convinced by his own rhetoric. His concluding paragraph is written from the point of view atop the lofty pillar, not from the plains below. He reiterates his belief that the "ultimate problem . . . is individual," a problem that can be solved only from within when one is unencumbered by external concerns:

Only when we weary of complexity can we work towards simplicity. Only when we tire of attachment can we strive for freedom. It may be that Thoreau's increasing popularity bears this out. Because, as a matter of fact, more and more people *are* tiring of complexity and attachment. (p. 66)

Again, Collins does not refer explicitly to the impending war, but he voices the anxiety of most Americans who did not want to get dragged into Europe's problems. [4] "Complexity and attachment" meant war in 1941. Implicitly, Collins uses Thoreau as a rationale for American isolationism and noninterventionism. Thoreau may have lost the election to the Hall of Fame owing to his unwillingness to be conscripted into any cause, but his reputation did not suffer significantly — if at all — if Collins is correct in assessing his "increasing popularity." For some readers Thoreau provided an escape from history in 1940. There was an ocean of solitude separating the shores of Walden Pond from the white cliffs of Dover, and apparently some Americans were tempted to wash their hands clean in it.

With the exception of one commentator during the the war years, Thoreau did not go to war. Essentially he had a reputation as a passive resister, a noncombatant, and this seems to have disqualified him for battle. The single article of any significant length in which Thoreau was used unequivocally to justify the violence of the Allies appeared well into the war in 1944. "Thoreau Faced War" according to Max Cosman; he did not turn his back on it and rule it out as a means of achieving desirable, moral ends.[5] Cosman argues that Thoreau was against the Mexican War because he believed it to be an unjust war, not because he rejected war in principle. Thoreau realized when he championed John Brown that it was "madness for any one to think menacing evil could be dispersed with the reed of non-resistance" in lieu of a sword (p. 75). Cosman quotes Thoreau's famous statement in "A Plea for Captain John Brown" in which he says "I do not wish to kill or to be killed, but I can foresee circumstances in which both these things would be by me unavoidable" (quoted on p. 76). He calls attention to this passage in order to conclude with the major point of his article, which is that Thoreau speaks to Americans in 1944: "The circumstances which bedeviled his days are still with ours, and for us as for him, to kill or be killed is still unavoidable" (p. 76). Most Americans already knew that war and killing were necessary if they were to defeat the "menacing evil" which the Axis represented. Cosman's article is not aimed at them so much as it is aimed at commentators who disarmed Thoreau as early as the late thirties when the threat of war began.

It seems that several of the commentators who did not want Thoreau going off to war accented the passive resistance in his essay on civil disobedience while muting the violence of Thoreau's later comments on slavery and John Brown, because they themselves did not want America fighting a war. Canby's 1939 biography of Thoreau, which set the tone for much subsequent criticism, is a case in point.

Canby quotes the same passages from John Brown that Cosman was to refer to in 1944, but he does not apply them to his own time — when the war in Europe began to boil. Canby does point out that Thoreau moved to a position where he was willing to accept violence in support of a just cause, because Thoreau felt that passive resistance "was not enough in a state that had ceased to recognize human rights and was overriding personal integrity."[6] Canby notes this, but he does not approve: "Subtly, slowly, *as is happen-*

ing with so many idealists in the twentieth century [my emphasis],
the belief in justified violence had been capturing Thoreau's mind"
(p. 391). The diction here suggests that Thoreau was falling into a
trap — that he had made a mistake. Yet, Canby, though he abhors
violence and the justification of it "by moral necessity," excuses it
in Thoreau; he writes that the moral argument for violence is a
"dangerous thesis which may be used to justify the wildest fanaticism, but Thoreau makes it credible for John Brown" (p. 393). Canby shifts his readers' attention away from Thoreau's support of violence to Thoreau's commitment to principle. This emphasis is a just
one — it was Thoreau's — but Canby goes further. Every effort is
made gently but firmly to remove Brown's Sharps' rifle from Thoreau's hands. He speculates that even if Thoreau had been well and
younger when the Civil War broke out, "I doubt whether he would
have enlisted," because Thoreau would not have involved himself
in a war "fought by institutions" (p. 396). Moreover, he speculates
on what Thoreau's attitude would have been on a more recent developing war. This time, however, Canby chooses to remember
only the author of "Civil Disobedience," not the Thoreau of "A
Plea for Captain John Brown" or "Slavery in Massachusetts."

Canby asks the reader how Thoreau would act if he were living
today in a "dictatorial state, with torture at its command, and a
fanaticism as strong and far less reasonable than Thoreau's." No,
Thoreau would not pick up a gun; he would say, according to Canby that

The citizen will have to step back and, protecting integrity by
any concessions possible to it, endeavor to make the nobler
moral fervor prevail. But he would disobey rather than rebel,
and wrestle with weakness in himself [my emphasis] rather
than use violence against the despot in the enemy. (p. 238)

No doubt Thoreau had an extremely self-conscious strain in him,
but Canby casts him in the role of a long-suffering Hamlet. Thoreau was not one to suffer too long, however. Canby might have
avoided this distortion if he had devoted as much discussion to
"Slavery in Massachusetts" as he did to "Civil Disobedience." In
the former essay Thoreau repudiates Canby's notion that he would

have "wrestled with the weakness in himself" instead of the "despot." Thoreau is discussing slavery in the following passage, but in keeping with Canby's own extrapolations it might as well be directed to forced-labor camps in Europe. With sarcasm and militant conviction, he addresses all totalitarian governments:

Do what you will, O Government! with my wife and children, my mother and brother, my father and sister, I will obey your commands to the letter. It will indeed grieve me if you hurt them, if you deliver them to overseers to be hunted by hounds or to be whipped to death; but nevertheless, I will peaceably pursue my chosen calling on this fair earth, until perchance, one day, when I have put on mourning for them dead, I shall have persuaded you to relent. Such is the attitude, such are the words of Massachusetts.

Rather than do thus, I need not say what match I would touch, what system endeavor to blow up. . . .[7]

This passage antedates Canby's by almost eighty-five years, but Thoreau's words can, I think, be rightly considered a parody of Canby, who, apparently, did not hear this speech in "Slavery in Massachusetts."

My purpose here is not to transform Thoreau into a militant advocate of violence; my intention is to demonstrate, once again, that critics, in using Thoreau, are frequently compelled to perform a scissors-and-paste operation on the complete works. I do not believe that Canby purposely distorted Thoreau in order to present him as a pacifist who deserved emulation in 1939. Very likely, he simply found what he wanted to find and what others before him had found. Perhaps because Gandhi had seen in Thoreau's "Civil Disobedience" a confirmation of his own principles, principles that proved highly successful for Gandhi in India, critics were inclined to focus upon that aspect of Thoreau, because it seemed more significant and was associated more with his stay at Walden than with the later "Slavery in Massachusetts" and the John Brown episode. Certainly, the major portion of writing about Thoreau has always focused upon the Walden years, for they produced his most popular essay and book, "Civil Disobedience" and *Walden*.

Even a writer who was extremely hostile to pacifism and civil disobedience during World War II assumed that Thoreau was a thoroughgoing pacifist. Arthur M. Schlesinger, Jr., ignored the later essays and in discussing Thoreau's thought in terms of Jacksonian democracy, warned of the dangers of his moral stand in "Civil Disobedience" because it is "justified only by the sternest private obedience, and the angels are all too likely to turn into brutes."[8] Schlesinger does not have Thoreau in mind as one of those brutes — Thoreau "earned his beliefs and his immunities." What Schlesinger does not have in mind are contemporary pacifists:

Little men covering cowardice with a veil of self-righteousness, lay claim to the exemptions of a Thoreau with the most intolerable pretense. The camp followers of a war which he fought, they are presently the camp followers of a war fought by the rest of society, accepting the protection of the state but disclaiming any obligations. Their performance should not compromise his case. (p. 388)

It is surprising that Schlesinger does not use Thoreau's later essays in order to show that even Thoreau was willing to fight and die for a moral cause. The fact that Schlesinger does not use them suggests that either he was not very familiar with them or they did not conform to his conception and use of Thoreau. Schlesinger was not alone in this.[9]

After the war there was a more embarrassing example of a myopic view and use of Thoreau offered by Henry Miller in his 1946 preface to *Life Without Principle: Three Essays by Henry David Thoreau*.[10] Miller reprints "Civil Disobedience," "Life Without Principle" and "A Plea for Captain John Brown." He describes Thoreau as one of the "half-dozen names in the history of America which have meaning for me" (p. 162). His courage and conviction — his civil disobedience — set him apart from the America of 1946 which Miller sees as conservative and oppressive. "In these last hundred years the State has come to be a Frankenstein" (p. 166), and the chief manifestation of this monster is the atomic bomb. Miller's preface was written during the debates that immediately followed the bombing of Hiroshima and Nagasaki. To Miller, Thoreau is a steady voice from the revered past who speaks out against the use of the bomb:

He would not have rejoiced that the secret of its manufacture was in the hands of the righteous ones. He would have asked immediately: "Who is righteous enough to employ such a diabolical instrument destructively?" He would have had no more faith in the wisdom and sanctity of this present government of the United States than he had of our government in the days of slavery. (p. 164)

Perhaps, but Miller's ally is a dubious one. In "A Plea for Captain John Brown," one of the essays that Miller reprints but which he barely mentions in the preface, Thoreau says about Brown's use of violence: "I think that for once the Sharps' rifles and the revolvers were employed in a righteous cause. The tools were in the hands of one who could use them" (*Reform Papers*, p. 133). Miller's assertion that Thoreau would have categorically rejected the use of such a "diabolical instrument" as an atomic bomb is called into doubt. Indeed, it is refuted in Thoreau's next paragraph: "The question is not about the weapon, but the spirit in which you use it." In effect this was precisely the argument that the Truman administration used to justify the bombing of Hiroshima and Nagasaki. Henry L. Stimson, Secretary of War when the bombs were dropped, described them as "great new instrument[s] ["tools"?] for shortening the war and minimizing destruction."[11] Consider Thoreau again: "I shall not be forward to think him mistaken in his method who quickest succeeds to liberate the slave." Thoreau might not have used the bomb on Japan, but would he have used it on Harpers Ferry?

Absurd as it seems (and is) the question cannot be dismissed too quickly. Since Thoreau commentators project him into the future, it is not unreasonable to reverse the process in order to illustrate a point. If Henry Stimson used Henry Thoreau's argument, then it is possible that Thoreau might also have used Stimson's weapon. These Henrys have more in common than just their first names. Put bluntly: Right Makes Might Right. This is an argument that is beautifully symmetrical but awkward to pronounce. For commentators like Miller it is easier to leave such things unsaid, because it is disarming and, much worse, it arms Thoreau. As Miller said of contemporary Americans who are afraid publicly to echo Thoreau's ideas: ". . . how impossible it would be today to give public utterance to such sentiments" (p. 163). After all, almost everyone knew that Thoreau was a pacifist — or at least he was unwilling to be conscripted into anything but a private individual war. Such was the prevailing attitude during the war. But not everyone was charmed by this as the war proceeded. The *New York Times*, which in 1940 lamented Thoreau's failure to be elected to the Hall of Fame, shifted its opinion of Thoreau in 1945.

By the close of the war the *New York Times* editorial page had allied itself less with Thoreau and more with the necessity for total mobilization and the collective commitment necessary to defeat the Axis. It had become clear that the only way to win the war was by international cooperation; Pearl Harbor had demonstrated that isolationism and aloofness from vital world issues were impossible. America stumbled into the war with its head buried in the sand and emerged from the conflict a champion of internationalism. In a centennial editorial marking Thoreau's retreat to Walden Pond, the *Times* found praiseworthy his devotion to "the highest laws of moral consciousness" and his spiritual aspirations, but unlike the editorial five years earlier, written one full year before the United Stated entered the war, the *Times* in 1945 rejected Thoreau's individualism:

is there anything in his philosophy that would have corrected the isolationism of the Thirties when, like Thoreau, we withdrew from the society of nations and tried to preserve our freedoms by living to ourselves? At a terrible cost we have learned, and shall try to remember always, that we cannot be free by trying to live alone. Normally, man is a social animal; and to be normal, the world must be a society of nations.[12]

In a very real sense, the *New York Times* blamed the Thoreaus of America for World War II. Thoreau, the left-handed hero of 1940 who, owing to the conservative national mood, was not granted the public recognition that was due him, had become by 1945 one of the reasons why the age was inauspicious for liberal democratic politics. Isolationism—practiced either in a hut or on a continent—was dangerous. Thoreau's individualism applied on a national scale was perceived by the *Times* as a potential enemy of freedom because it provided no safeguards to preserve individual freedom. This objection to Thoreau was not a new one; it had been voiced thirteen years earlier by Marxist critics who argued that Thoreau's individualism had no "practical value" because he was "not interested in individualists who organized themselves socially in order to defend their individual freedom." [13]

The individual that the *Times* considered to be dangerously isolationist on a political level was for a devoted Thoreauvian like Henry Miller the solution to America's postwar problems. Writing in his 1946 preface, Miller argues that

The problem of power, an obsessive one with Americans, is now at the crux. Instead of *working* for peace, men ought to be urged to relax, to stop work, to take it easy, to dream and idle away their time for a change. Retire to the woods! if you can find any nearby. (p. 165)

This same mood was expressed before the war by Thomas Lyle Collins, who believed that Americans felt the need to unburden themselves of "complexity and attachment." The desire to light out for the woods is an understandable one and perhaps a useful means of establishing and preserving one's own integrity. That same desire when pursued on a national level, however, is, according to the *Times*, politically naive and socially destructive. The newspaper was concerned with reading the times, not the eternities, and so it could not share the enthusiasm expressed by one Thoreauvian who proudly declared that "Thoreau was concerned only with the Orphic politics of the soul, the only politics for man — no politics." [14] The *Times* conceded that it might be all right for an individual to take such a stand, but to turn this into a national policy would be to endanger both the nation and the individual.

Thoreauvians were not bothered, apparently, by the type of criticism that the *Times* leveled at them. They praised Thoreau throughout the war years as an exemplary model for individuals disillusioned with the oppressiveness of big government, machines (both industrial and political), and any other aspects of American life that called for the subservience of the individual. Essentially, the writers who held this view restated for an ever-widening audience the same ideas that were written by the libertarians of the thirties.[15] Walter Harding, Thoreau's most prolific and devoted critic since the 1940s, sums up the libertarian view of Thoreau during the war:

Thoreau is a philosopher of freedom. I can think of no other so completely unmitigatedly opposed to the ever-growing dominance of the centralized state of today over the individual and his conscience. There is no better antidote for "Mein Kampf" than "Walden."[16]

In this passage Harding encapsules the sensibilities of many Thoreauvians.

The term *Thoreauvian* gained currency in the thirties. One of the first writers to define the term in print was Canby in 1931: "There is still a minority determined to live their own best lives, at Walden or elsewhere, which is what one has to do in order to become a Thoreauvian."[17] The cardinal principle to be observed in living one's best life was a staunch individualism, a principle that verged on dogma. This individualism, was, in a sense, institutionalized with the founding of the Thoreau Society in 1941. The Thoreau Society has been a significant force in establishing and furthering Thoreau's reputation in the United States.

In the summer of 1941 Harding mailed a letter to people interested in Thoreau. The letter called for a "Thoreau Birthday Mecca" at Concord. The subsequent pilgrimage on July 12 marked the beginning of the society. The meeting featured a talk by Raymond Adams, H.W. Gleason's slides on Thoreau country, and "a tour of several of the Thoreau shrines."[18] The purpose of the society was to "honor" Thoreau, generate a wider interest in his writing, "coordinate research in his life and writings, and to act as a repository for Thoreauana."[19] The *Thoreau Society Bulletin* chronicles in its valuable continuing bibliography Thoreau's ever-growing popularity in the academy and in popular culture at large. Its readers are kept abreast of the latest scholarly approaches to Thoreau while at the same time being informed of things of a more ephemeral nature: they learned in 1947, for example, that "Rose Wilder Lane, the novelist, has named her dog 'Henry David Thoreau.' " [20]

The society has also served as a repository of libertarian sensibilities. Occasionally, short pieces on Thoreau were reproduced from other sources and mailed to members. One such piece was written in 1945 by Frank Chodorov, who touted Thoreau's no-organization position in *Analysis*, a periodical which replaced editorial notes and copyright information with this: "PLEASE COPY — Nothing in this paper is copyrighted. Readers are invited to lift whatever suits their purpose."[21] Like Thoreau, he too wanted to be used to further the cause of individualism.

Chodorov's view of Thoreau as a libertarian seems to have been basically the same as that of the secretary of the society, Walter Harding, who has for all practical purposes been the backbone of the society and its publications since its inception. The same year that Harding had forwarded Chodorov's article to members, he wrote that Thoreau is of especial use now that "people have forsaken the individual within them and have rushed towards a cure-all collectivism."[22] Harding's influence on Thoreau's reputation — his numerous reviews, articles, books, and activities — can hardly be overemphasized. His view of Thoreau's social thought and politics was allied with that of the predominant view of the forties; like Canby and Miller he tended to remember the Thoreau of "Civil Disobedience" rather than the supporter of John Brown's violence. Thoreau was not a dangerous isolationist but an exemplary individual.

Harding was a conscientious objector during World War II.[23] This position, which required enormous courage in the forties, seems to have influenced what he chose to emphasize in Thoreau. In a review of Henry Miller's *Life Without Principle: Three Essays by Henry David Thoreau*, Harding writes that the " 'Preface' is one of the most penetrating analyses of Thoreau that I have seen." He wishes that "every student of Thoreau" and "every citizen of the world would pay it heed" because "It might bring back the revival of the individual spirit that Thoreau himself so wanted."[24] Harding had not changed his opinion eight years later when he reprinted the preface in *Thoreau: A Century of Criticism*, in which he describes it as "one of the most cogent and understanding interpretations of the politically-minded Thoreau to reach print" (p. 162). Miller's analysis is not penetrating. What Harding seems actually to praise is Miller's presentation of Thoreau as an individualist who was essentially nonviolent. Without question, Thoreau was an individualist, but, as the *New York Times* pointed out, it was highly questionable if "every citizen" ought to "pay it heed." And as Thoreau himself pointed out in "A Plea for Captain John Brown," he was, at least in theory, ready to kill or be killed for what he considered to be a just cause.

As will be demonstrated in subsequent chapters, Harding was influential in keeping these views in the forefront of commentary on Thoreau into the fifties and sixties. Like many other Thoreauvians, it seems that Harding saw too much in Thoreau that he personally valued to see objectively some of the implications of his politics. Harding described the problem himself in 1945: "We [Thoreauvians] admit that we are hero-worshipers, but we hope that we retain at least an iota of objectivity about our hero. The last thing we would want to see would be Henry Thoreau enshrined as a sacrosanct little white God."[25]

Harding's sincerity makes it all the more unfortunate that during the war Thoreau was enshrined by most commentators. Even F.O. Matthiessen, a non-Thoreauvian who was extremely sensitive to politics and whose politics were very different from Thoreau's, made a pilgrimage to the mecca in his *American Renaissance*. He traveled a route very different from the libertarians, but he arrived, nevertheless, at the same shrine to be charmed by Thoreau's flute. A detailed tour of Matthiessen's route is necessary in order to appreciate the detours he had to make around Thoreau's politics so that he could revere Thoreau as politically relevant to the twentieth century.

Matthiessen's *American Renaissance* (1941) has been justly called a "landmark" in American criticism. In 1950 Henry Nash Smith compared its importance to that of Vernon L. Parrington's *Main Currents in American Thought*:

Each of these books set the tone for a decade of scholarship
and criticism. Parrington's emphasis on Jeffersonian liberalism forecast the predominantly social criticism of literature
during the thirties. Matthiessen's quite different emphasis on
tragic insight and his insistence that the content of literature
cannot be understood apart from its form define the main
lines of approach to American literature during the decade
just past. [26]

Though *American Renaissance* charted a course for American
criticism different from that of *Main Currents*, there was still some
continuity in the flow of ideas between the two. Matthiessen
greatly admired Parrington's treatment of the liberal tradition in
American literature because he shared his loyalty to liberal principles. Matthiessen, however, also felt a strong loyalty to art. Where
Parrington had emphasized the social and political backgrounds
contemporary to the writers he examined, Matthiessen "concen-
trated entirely on the foreground, on the writing itself." He did not
believe, as did some of Parrington's disciples, that criticism which
focused on books as works of art was merely "belletristic trifling."
Unlike Parrington, Matthiessen had an abiding interest in and respect for the text itself. He did not repudiate Parrington; he simply
went beyond him. Matthiessen insisted that critical interpretations
of a work must be based upon "close analysis" and hard evidence
from the text: ". . . you cannot 'use' a work of art unless you have
comprehended its meaning." [27] He made clear that his method of
close textual reading, used in order to evaluate the fusion of a
work's form and content, was not simply criticism for criticism's
sake. He did not consider true scholarship the work of a leisure
class "lackey" if it was performed with a democratic faith. Quoting
Louis Sullivan, Matthiessen asked of himself and all scholars what
he considered to be the ultimate question, a question that serves as
the bedrock of standards for a scholar in a democracy: "Are you
using such gifts as you possess for or against the people?" (p. xvi).
In his emphasis upon the integrity of the text Matthiessen reflects
the forties' growing acceptance of New Critical methodology, and
in his recognition that literary critics have professional responsibilities that go beyond the text he demonstrated his own integrity. This

dual sensibility — the recognition of the value of formalistic methods while at the same time rejecting the conservative politics usually aligned with the formalists — permitted Matthiessen to see the importance of not only Henry James and T.S. Eliot but also Sherwood Anderson and Theodore Dreiser. Matthiessen was interested in both what a writer had to say and how he said it.

Of the five major writers dealt with in *American Renaissance*, Matthiessen has less to say about Thoreau than any of the other four (Emerson, Hawthorne, Melville, and Whitman). Nevertheless, there are many pages devoted to discussions of Thoreau's writing and thought; of these, however, there are only three pages set aside for his politics. As the subtitle of the book indicates, the subject at hand is *Art and Expression in the Age of Emerson and Whitman*, not politics; therefore, it is understandable that Matthiessen did not want to be "deflected any further" than three pages in assessing Thoreau's politics, because he wanted to get on with Thoreau's writing (p. 79). And he does. Matthiessen's brilliant analysis of *Walden's* organic symbolic structure (pp. 153-175) not only placed Thoreau in a literary tradition, it became a tradition in itself. His strong influence on Thoreau criticism has for its monument the many subsequent studies that developed and refined his suggestions. [28]

Matthiessen's contention is that Thoreau's "particular value to our culture" can best be determined by focusing upon *"what* he created through examining his own *process of creation"* (pp. 79-80) rather than his politics. This emphasis is consistent with his intentions as he expresses them in his opening remarks ("Method and Scope," pp. vii-xvi), but it is curious that he chooses to discuss the achievement of Thoreau's art and expression without reference to his politically oriented essays, since Matthiessen himself was very concerned about politics.

Matthiessen made no secret of his own politics; he was a committed man who described himself as a Christian and a Socialist. [29] The common denominator of his Christianity and socialism was a strong sense of brotherhood, a sense that a person's true identity is achieved through his relationship to his fellowman. An attitude of aloofness from society harmed an individual because it robbed him of a meaningful identity, and it harmed society because it robbed the world of the individual's potential contribution to it. He viewed the individual from a Christian perspective and society from a socialist perspective: although man had fallen, society could be improved through democratic, collective action. As much as Matthiessen insisted that American *Renaissance* was a book about art and expression, when the opportunity presented itself — organically — he made quite clear that he was not like James Joyce's God of the Creation who was beyond and above his creation, refined out of existence, indifferently paring his fingernails. Matthiessen had no qualms about broadening the scope of *American Renaissance* when he could relate a writer's mode of expression to what he considered to be a useful political tradition. In Chapter 7, "Hawthorne's Politics, with the Economic Structure of *The Seven Gables*" (pp. 316-337), Matthiessen discusses more than just art and expression in the age of Emerson and Whitman; he finds a writer whose politics are very close to his own. He describes Hawthorne's politics as paradoxical, because he was both a conservative and a member of the Democratic party. Hawthorne was conservative because he was intensely aware of the dark side of man's nature and did not, like Emerson, have a romantic belief in the "infinitude" of man. Yet he belonged to the Democratic party, because he had an abiding faith in democracy and man's potentiality even though man was limited. Matthiessen finds in Hawthorne's response to society's economic ills "at least a faint perception of the need for collectivism" (p. 336). These happen to be Matthiessen's own attitudes toward the nature of man and the necessary mode of societal reform, and these attitudes inform his view of Thoreau's ideas concerning man and his relationship to society; however, they inform his view in an unexpected way.

Matthiessen's conception of the nature of man is antithetical to Thoreau's. Discussing his Christian beliefs in *From the Heart of Europe*, Matthiessen wrote that he "accepted the doctrine of original sin, in the sense that man is fallible and limited, no matter what his social system. . . ." He therefore "rejected the nineteenth-century belief in every man as his own Messiah, along with the other aberrations of that century's individualism. . . ."[30] There are numerous passages that might be quoted from Thoreau's writings to illustrate how different from Matthiessen his views on the nature of man are, but one brief poem establishes the difference clearly enough:

> In Adam's fall
> We sinned all.
> In the new Adam's rise
> We shall all reach the skies.
>
> *(Journal*, II, 153)

Matthiessen does not mention this poem, but if he had it is likely that he would have clipped Thoreau's wings by reminding him of Icarus who fell into the sea, metaphorically if not geographically close to the *Pequod*. Like Melville he might have issued the warning to "Heed it well, ye Pantheists." The Adamic Emersonian hero who was a system unto himself was not Matthiessen's hero; his hero was "The hero of tragedy" who "is never merely an individual, he is a man in action, in conflict with other individuals in a definite social order" (p. 179). He is the hero in history. Matthiessen describes his hero in aesthetic terms, but his hero is, nevertheless, of political significance in that he is more "mature" in his understanding of the web of relations that bind the individual to society than either Thoreau or Emerson.

Because Hawthorne and Melville have this "mature" view of society, of humanity, and the good *and* evil that characterize human life, Matthiessen finds more breadth and complexity in their ideas and expression. Throughout the book their sensibilities are juxtaposed to Emerson's and Thoreau's, and the latter's are found shallow by comparison. Matthiessen begins *American Renaissance* with two quotations, one of which is a passage from *King Lear* marked by Melville in his copy of the play: "Men must endure / Their going hence even as their coming hither: / Ripeness is all" (p. vi). When Matthiessen gets to Thoreau's politics, he begins his discussion with the following line from Thoreau: "Methinks my own soul must be a bright invisible *green* [my emphasis]" (p. 76). Matthiessen has in mind Thoreau's own sense of hopeful expectation, but he could have had in mind Thoreau's immaturity, his greenness, in comparison with Melville's lesson in *Moby Dick* (pp.

445-459). The irony would certainly be in keeping with Matthiessen's sympathies, which are with the democratic mass of humanity, the brotherhood of people, not the "self-appointed Messiah" like Ahab, whose "self-enclosed individualism . . . carried to its furthest extreme, brings disaster both upon itself and upon the groups of which it is part" (459).

It is a misrepresentation to suggest that Matthiessen even hinted that Thoreau was akin to Ahab, but I have implied it because I think it is a logical extension of Matthiessen's values and his reading of Ahab, whose messianic impulse he views as more ungodly than godlike. Thoreau's individualism has in it the potentialities for an Ahab from Matthiessen's point of view, except that Thoreau seemed to be benign and content to be the captain of a huckleberry party; hence Matthiessen lets him off rather easily: "So far as there was a defect in his valiant self-reliance, it emerged when he turned his back on other men, and sought for truth not in the great and common world but exclusively within himself" (p. 653). This is precisely what Ahab does when he launches himself after the white whale, and the same strain is found by Matthiessen in a more recent "Superman" — in "the voice of Hitler's megalomania" (p. 546). But Matthiessen does not explore the politics of Thoreau's individualism in any detail. Instead, when he does comment upon them, he relies upon earlier commentaries and chooses from them a Thoreau that is compatible with his own politics.

Given Matthiessen's socialism and his view of the nature of man, one would think that he would reject the politics of Thoreau's Transcendental individualism, but he does not. Rather, he rejects the idea that Thoreau's politics are those of a Transcendental individualist who denied the efficacy of collective action. Matthiessen notes that Thoreau is too often "remembered for his two most extreme acts" of individualism: his going to Walden Pond and his refusal to pay his poll tax. He argues that they have been blown out of proportion:

Thoreau's radical value does not lie in his gestures of protest, the shock of both of which, incidentally, was cushioned by his curcumstances, since he could build his hut on land borrowed from Emerson, and friends saw to it that his tax was

paid and so got him out of jail after one night. His contribution to our social thought lies in his thoroughgoing criticism
of the narrow materialism of his day. (pp. 77-78)

In this passage Matthiessen emphasizes two of his own prime beliefs: the inevitable interrelatedness of human beings and the
writer's significance to the life of the community by providing it
with his insights. Thoreau's "proletarian" point of view was in reaction to the "mercantilism" and the deadening "standardization"
of his times which limited a person's freedom, and according to
Matthiessen, "He did not want that freedom for his private self
alone. His deepest reason for disliking the pinched Yankee standardization was its starvation of the minds and spirits of the citizens"
(p. 79). Following Max Lerner, Matthiessen writes that Thoreau's
commitment to collective action has not been emphasized enough,
and he quotes a line from *Walden* which all such commentators
cite, because it is one of the few sentences like it in Thoreau's complete works: "To act collectively is according to the spirit of our institutions" (p. 79). Matthiessen is aware of the "vigorous paradoxes" of Thoreau's social thought (he cites Schuster's study of his
"left-wing individualism," [p. 77]) but he chooses to accent a more
useful Thoreau who is compatible with his own collectivistic
politics.

Matthiessen allows his enthusiasm and appreciation for Thoreau's art to interfere with a view of his politics that would be more
in keeping with his own values, values which were highly suspicious of Transcendental individualism. In effect, he ignores Thoreau's individualistic politics because he wants to find collectivistic
principles in a writer he admires; otherwise he would have to rele-
gate Thoreau to a historical junk heap, where the Marxists of the
thirties had dumped him. He would have to reduce Thoreau "to the
position that Whitehead has described: 'The self-sufficing independent man, with his peculiar property which concerns no one else, is
a concept without any validity for modern civilization' " (p. 77).
Matthiessen wanted to establish Thoreau's validity.

Thoreau was not the only vigorous paradox in *American Renaissance*; Matthiessen was as well. He used New Critical principles at
a time when they were practiced largely by conservatives, but he

had the liberal social consciousness of a Parrington. He frequently expressed reservations about writing criticism in a political and social vacuum, and yet he had misgivings about critics who accepted "the current simplified conception of 'the usable past.' "[31] Moreover, Matthiessen himself seems to have simplified Thoreau in search of a usable past that conforms to his stated aim to present a "literature for our democracy" (p. xv).

Matthiessen's approach to Thoreau is Janus-like. His treatment of Thoreau's art looks forward to the mythic and symbolic readings that have been a staple item in Thoreau criticism since the forties. Yet Matthiessen's overview of Thoreau's politics looks back to the commentators of the thirties, who duly noted his paradoxes but then promptly either rejected his politics or called for their revival. Both approaches to Thoreau's politics were strong on conviction but weak on supporting evidence. Indeed, the latter approach was institutionalized in a book that has been, since 1946, a guide for students of American literature making their way from survey courses to comprehensive doctoral exams. In the *Literary History of the United States* Townsend Scudder follows Matthiessen in one of the most widely read chapters on Thoreau ever written. After noting Thoreau's insistence on the "individual's right to self-determination," Scudder asserts that Thoreau "never denied the value of enlightened communal action."[32] Though Scudder, like Matthiessen, does not discuss Thoreau's politics in any detail, he too places him within a liberal collective tradition without attempting to explain why he belongs in it.

American Renaissance is a transitional point in Thoreau criticism. Despite Matthiessen's attempt to salvage Thoreau's relevance for modern civilization, most commentators who followed Matthiessen refined and elaborated upon Thoreau's art, but they did not try to prove the timeliness of Thoreau's social and political thought. That was left to the Thoreauvians. Academic criticism tended to shy away from Thoreau's politics, and instead it took up the cause of Art. After World War II, when the country gradually slipped into the conservative 1950s, and when academic criticism began to rival General Motors in production, there was a shift in Thoreau criticism from reform to form. The social and political thinker was transmogrified into the mythic and symbolic writer.

The effects of this shift upon Thoreau's reputation and the
American response to his social and political thought are described
in the next chapter.

NOTES

1. The line is quoted in Richard R. Lingeman's *Don't You Know There's
a War On? The American Home Front, 1941-1945* (New York: G.P. Put-
nam's Sons, 1970), p. 219. Lingeman's study is a popular history that is
well documented and invaluable in re-creating the effects of the war upon
the average American who did not go off to fight.

2. *New York Times*, November 19, 1940, p. 22.

3. "Thoreau's Coming of Age," *Sewanee Review*, 49 (January 1941),
57-66.

4. See Merle Curti, *The Growth of American Thought*, 3rd ed. (New
York: Harper & Row, 1964), pp. 727-729.

5. "Thoreau Faced War," *Personalist*, 25 (Winter 1944), 73-76. Another
article published in the same year as Cosman's also goes beyond passive resistance in attributing a response to Thoreau if he were alive to confront
the authoritarianism of the forties. But the author, when he raises the
problem on the last page, says that Thoreau "would have suffered martyr-
dom rather than compromise his conscience." He does not mention violent
resistance; see C.A. Madison, "Henry David Thoreau: Transcendental Individualist," *Ethics*, 54 (January 1944), 110-123. For Madison, Thoreau's
"accentuated individualism" is unrealistic "now that we are in the grief of a
total war" (p. 121).

6. Henry Seidel Canby, *Thoreau* (Boston: Houghton Mifflin, 1939), p.
391.

7. *Reform Papers*, ed. Wendell Glick (Princeton, N.J.: Princeton University Press, 1973), p. 102. Subsequent references to the essays collected in
Reform Papers will be cited within parentheses in the text.

8. *The Age of Jackson* (Boston: Little, Brown, 1945), p. 388.

9. There are several commentators who describe Thoreau as a pacifist
just before and during the war: Charles Child Walcutt, "Thoreau in the
Twentieth Century," *South Atlantic Quarterly*, 39 (April 1940), 168-184;
Edward Dahlberg, "Thoreau and Walden," *Can These Bones Live?* rev. ed.
(1941; rpt. New York: New Directions, 1960), pp. 13-25 (this was originally published under the title *Do These Bones Live?*); and James R. Robinson, "Civil Disobedience," *Conscientious Objector*, 4 (February 1942), 5. It

is noteworthy that a 1941 chapter that focused on Thoreau's support of
John Brown minimized, like Canby, Thoreau's support of violence. There
is only one study of Thoreau cited in the bibliography, and that is Canby's
Thoreau. See Hope Holway, *Radicals of Yesterday: Great American
Tradition* (Norman, Oka.: Cooperative Books, 1941), pp. 24-31.

Thoreau was vaguely — and occasionally only very vaguely — associated in most Americans' minds with the quietude of Walden Pond and the
passive resistance of Gandhi. A popular syndicated cartoon entitled "This
Curious World" published in the August 30, 1945, *San Francisco News*
featured a sketch of the hut at Walden Pond and its caption read: "Mohan-
das Gandhi derived the idea of non-violent resistance from reading Henry
Thoreau's 'On the Duty of Civil Disobedience,' written when the latter was
jailed for non-payment of taxes on his cabin at Walden Pond." Quoted in
TSB, 14 (January 1946), 4.

10. This preface is reprinted in Walter Harding, ed., *Thoreau: A Century of Criticism* (Dallas, Tex.: Southern Methodist University Press,
1954), pp. 162-170. The page numbers in the text refer to Harding's reprint
of the preface.

11. Henry L. Stimson, "The Decision to Use the Bomb," *Harper's Magazine*, 194 (February 1947), 97-107, rpt. in Paul R. Baker, ed., *The Atomic
Bomb: The Great Decision* (New York: Holt, Rinehart and Winston,
1968), pp. 9-21. The quotation is on p. 10 in Baker. Baker's collection is extremely useful in understanding the political and moral dimensions of the
debate.

12. "Walden Ideals," *New York Times*, June 17, 1945, sec. 4, p. 8.

13. V.F. Calverton, *The Liberation of American Literature* (New York:
Charles Scribner's Sons, 1932), p. 269.

14. Dahlberg, *Can These Bones Live?* pp. 17-18. Just as there were extreme advocates of individual isolationism modeled after Thoreau's retreat
to Walden Pond, there were also extreme denunciations of Thoreau's philosophy. Its present-day supporters were seen by one writer as members of
an "escapist cult" who, in turning away from the actualities of history,
demonstrated that they were "vaguely disturbed." See Kelsey Guilford,
"The Thoreau Cultists—Are They Insane?" *Chicago Tribune*, December
1, 1946, sec. 4, p. 48. "A Defense of Thoreau" by Walter Harding will be
found on the same page as Guilford's article.

15. A few representative examples are: Ralph H. Gabriel, *The Course of
American Democratic Thought* (New York: Ronald Press, 1940), pp.
47-51; Irwin Edwin, *Fountain Heads of Freedom: The Growth of the
Democratic Idea* (New York: Reynal and Hitchcock, 1941), pp. 149-153; Jo
Ann Wheeler, "Reflections on an Early American Anarchist," *Why?* 2 (July

1943), 2-3; Walter Harding, "A Thoreau Evening at Cooper Union," *TSB*, 11 (April 1945), 2; Benson Y. Landis, "The Squatter's Hut at Walden," *American Journal of Economics and Sociology*, 4 (April 1945), 327-332; and Walter Harding, "A Century of Thoreau," *Audubon Magazine*, 47 (March-April 1945), 80-84.

With the forties, published material on Thoreau becomes ubiquitous. He is found in books, journals, magazines, newspapers, cartoons, and advertisements of every sort. Since there are literally hundreds of items, it would be impractical and pointless to list these for the forties or the subsequent decades. I have made no attempt to list them all because two noteworthy attempts have already been made, though even they are not complete. The continuing bibliography of the *Thoreau Society Bulletin* is a cornucopia of writing on Thoreau; it has been edited in a convenient form by Walter Harding, *A Bibliography of the Thoreau Society Bulletin Bibliographies, 1941-1969* (New York: Whitston Publishing Co., 1971). Supplementing this to 1967 is Christopher A. Hildenbrand, *A Bibliography of Scholarship About Henry David Thoreau: 1940-67* (Hays: Fort Hays Kansas State College, 1967). In the forties academic interest in Thoreau branched out to cover a broad number of topics ranging from source studies to analyses of his poetry. The major portion of them tended to be limited in scope, more concerned with examining some specific aspect of Thoreau and his writing — for example, a fragment of Jacobean song in *Walden* or his view of the Irish — and less concerned with using him. Articles of this type account for a large percentage of Thoreau criticism since the forties. My emphasis is, of course, on those remaining commentaries which implicitly or explicitly use Thoreau for the purpose of primarily making a political point rather than uncovering an unknown fact.

16. "The Significance of Thoreau's *Walden*," *Humanist*, 5 (August 1945), 120.

17. *Classic Americans* (1931; rpt. New York: Russell & Russell, 1959), p. 225.

18. A copy of one of these letters is in The Beinecke Rare Book and Manuscript Library at Yale University: Za, T391, 1, pamphlets on Thoreau.

19. A statement of purpose of the adopted bylaws of 1948 will be found in *TSB*, 24 (July 1948), 3. The early *TSB* numbers have no pagination; I have added them for convenience. The Thoreau Society has, at times, actively engaged in lobbying in order to further its namesake's reputation. In 1945, for example, the society urged its members to assure Thoreau's election to the Hall of Fame (in 1940 he had lost by "only two or three votes of the necessary three-fifths") by writing to the electors of the electoral

board and/or to their "favorite magazine or newspaper." Despite their collective efforts, Thoreau lost yet once more; see *TSB*, 11 (April 1945), 1.
The society also asked its members to write to Houghton Mifflin in 1948 to
persuade the company to republish Thoreau's *Journals*. See *TSB*, 23 (April
1948), 4.

20. *TSB*, 18 (January 1947), 1.

21. Frank Chodorov, "Henry David Thoreau," *Analysis*, 2 (November
1945), 1-2. *TSB*, 14 (January 1946), 4, indicates that a copy was sent to
each member. In 1954 Chodorov was to become editor of *The Freeman: A
Monthly for Libertarians*, which was a self-described champion of "rights
of the individual, the free market, private property, and limited government" (quoted in Susan J. Turner, *A History of The Freeman* [New York:
Columbia University Press, 1963], p. 182). This magazine was a
descendant of the liberal *Freeman* of the twenties but in name only. The
later magazine's politics were avowedly conservative; it included writers
such as Max Eastman and William F. Buckley. Chodorov later contributed
to Buckley's *National Review*. Chodorov's use of Thoreau suggests the
often noted fact that the laissez-faire liberalism of the nineteenth century
has been welcomed by conservatives of the twentieth century; it also
suggests that when Thoreau's individualism is uprooted from the nineteenth century, his individualism may lose its liberal tone in a modern context. This shift in tone is discussed in Chapter 4.

22. Harding, "The Significance of Thoreau's *Walden*," p. 121.

23. See "News Notes About Members," *TSB*, 3 (April 1942), 1.

24. *TSB*, 16 (July 1946), 2.

25. *TSB*, 12 (July 1945), 2:

26. Henry Nash Smith, "American Renaissance," *Monthly Review*, 2
(October 1950), 223. Smith's article appeared in a memorial issue devoted
entirely to Matthiessen and published not long after his death. For other
discussions of him see Richard Ruland, *The Rediscovery of American
Literature*, pp. 209-273; Giles B. Gunn, "Criticism as Repossession and Responsibility: F.O. Matthiessen and the Ideal Critic," *American Quarterly*,
22 (Fall 1970), 629-648; and George Abbott White, "Ideology and Literature: *American Renaissance* and F.O. Matthiessen," *TriQuarterly*, 23/24
(Winter/Spring 1972), 430-500.

27. F.O. Matthiessen, *American Renaissance: Art and Expression in the
Age of Emerson and Whitman* (New York: Oxford University Press, 1941),
pp. ix-xi. For further discussion of Matthiessen's critical "Method and
Scope" see his *The Responsibility of the Critic* (New York: Oxford University Press, 1952), pp. 3-18.

28. The increasing critical interest after Matthiessen in Thoreau as a

literary artist who consciously used symbol and myth is described in Theo-
dore Haddin's unpublished dissertation (University of Michigan, 1968),
"The Changing Image of Henry Thoreau: The Emergence of the Literary
Artist," pp. 88-168.

29. I am indebted to Ruland's discussion of Matthiessen's Christian and
socialist convictions in *The Rediscovery of American Literature*, pp.
213-222.

30. F.O. Matthiessen, *From the Heart of Europe* (New York: Oxford
University Press, 1948), p. 82. Ruland discusses this passage on pp.
218-219.

31. The quotation is from a review of Newton Arvin's *Whitman*. Matthiessen takes Arvin to task for attempting to make Whitman out to be a
socialist (*The Responsibilities of the Critic*, pp. 215-217). Similarly, in a review of Canby's *Thoreau*, Matthiessen criticizes Canby's treatment of
"Civil Disobedience" and "Life Without Principle" in his attempt "to try to
prophesy what Thoreau's attitude would have been toward 'dictatorship'
and 'the totalitarian state.' Such isolation of Thoreau's ideas from their
original context obscures any chance of getting at their real meaning." This
does not prevent Matthiessen, however, from arguing toward the end of
the review that Thoreau was more of a collectivist than the total
individualist that Canby presents (*The Responsibilities of the Critic*, pp.
212-214). Oddly enough, Arvin's review of Canby's *Thoreau* complained
that Canby neglected to use Thoreau sufficiently; he did not do justice to
Thoreau's "bearing on the needs of our time." Arvin's prose gives one a
sense of how important this issue was to the critics of the thirties: "Mr.
Canby writes as an eclectic, editorial, rather conservative liberal; but that
position is no more a point of view than the Gothic of the Yale Library is a
style of architecture. A better book about Thoreau might be written by a
vegetarian, an anarchist or an Anglo-Catholic" (*New Republic*, October
18, 1939, p. 308).

32. "Henry David Thoreau," *Literary History of the United States*, ed.
Robert E. Spiller et al., 3rd. ed., rev. (New York: Macmillan, 1963), p.
414.

chapter 4

INTO THE FIFTIES: THOREAU AS MYTHMAKER AND TROUBLEMAKER

As a political warrior, Thoreau was a comic little figure with a receding chin, and not enough
high style to carry off a gesture. As a political
writer, he was the most ringing and magnificent
polemicist America has ever produced.

Stanley Edgar Hyman, 1946

There are orators, politicians, and eloquent
men, by the thousand; but the speaker has not
yet opened his mouth to speak, who is capable
of settling the much-vexed questions of the day.
We love eloquence for its own sake, and not for
any truth which it may utter, or any heroism it
may inspire.

Thoreau, "Civil Disobedience"

In 1941 F.O. Matthiessen's *American Renaissance* surveyed the
ground in which Thoreau's reputation as a literary artist would
eventually flourish. Matthiessen's influential work discussed Thoreau's social and political thought only in passing because Mat-

thiessen centered his attention on Thoreau's craftsmanship and technique rather than on his social thought and political activity. However, *American Renaissance* influenced not only Thoreau's literary reputation but also his political reputation as well. As subsequent critics of the forties increasingly focused upon Thoreau's art as their primary field of interest, his social and political thought diminished in importance. Thoreau's politics were mentioned only in passing. Commentaries on Thoreau tended to be about how he expressed his ideas rather than about what his ideas were. Unlike the thirties there was considerably more attention devoted to form rather than content. This was not the intention of Matthiessen, who was a man of strong social and political convictions; it was, however, implicit in his treatment of Thoreau. After World War II the seeds that Matthiessen had sown in 1941 began to grow, but the field of Thoreau's reputation yielded a different crop from the 1930s. There were still some patches of social and political thought, mostly cultivated and harvested by Thoreauvians, but the primary crop was Thoreau as the flower of American prose who, according to Stanley Edgar Hyman, "wrote the only really first-rate prose ever written by an American, with the possible exception of Abraham Lincoln." [1]

The pen proved to be a good deal mightier than the Sharps' rifle for the critics who followed Matthiessen in the late forties and fifties. Thoreau the reformer seems to have been a casualty of the war years, and, like his own death, there is not much of a struggle to report; he simply faded away. A form of him did return, though, in the figure of the literary artist. Taking one world at a time, this chapter first examines the postwar decline of Thoreau's social and political reputation along with the attending growth of his literary reputation in the late forties and fifties, and then — lest reports of the death of Thoreau the reformer be greatly exaggerated — the chapter describes the patches of Thoreau's social and political thought that persisted during the same period.

An influential essay by Stanley Edgar Hyman entitled "Henry Thoreau in Our Time," which followed *American Renaissance* and was strongly influenced by Matthiessen, provided the direction and tone for much postwar criticism on Thoreau. Hyman's essay has been read by nearly all students of Thoreau; indeed, it would be difficult to avoid the essay, since it appears in each of five of the most widely used collections of critical essays on Thoreau.[2] Certainly one reason for the popularity of the essay is its engaging style. In addition, it consciously sets itself apart from much previous criticism, with the exception of Matthiessen's. From the vantage point of 1946, Hyman looks back on Thoreau commentaries and calls for a new emphasis in Thoreau criticism which takes into account his complexities and insists upon viewing him chiefly as a writer, a literary artist.

Following Matthiessen, Hyman argues that "Thoreau's power lies precisely in his re-creation of basic myth, in his role as the protagonist in a great cyclic ritual of drama" (p. 175). *Walden* is a "vast rebirth ritual" (p. 176). The significance of this ritual on an abstract political level — one of several levels operating simultaneously — is that the protagonist of *Walden* moves "from individual isolation to collective action" (p. 178). Hyman discusses in some detail how "Thoreau's political value, for us, is largely in terms of this transition from philosophical aloofness" (pp. 179-182). A significant portion of his essay is devoted to what Hyman considers Thoreau's movement toward a position of social responsibility. He treats not only *Walden* but "Civil Disobedience" and "A Plea for Captain John Brown." But when he begins the final section of the essay in which Thoreau's style is discussed, Hyman turns his readers away from Thoreau's politics, because "All of this [Thoreau's social criticism and his active commitment to "principle"] takes us far afield from what must be Thoreau's chief importance to us, his writing" (p. 182). It is the "resources of his craft that warrant our study" (pp. 182-183), not his politics.

Despite Hyman's treatment of Thoreau's politics, he makes clear that they are secondary in importance to his style. It may not be an exaggeration to suggest that Hyman goes so far as to depoliticize Thoreau in his emphasis on Thoreau as a writer. He suggests that one of the primary reasons for Thoreau's attraction to John Brown — two men "as different as any two personalities can be" — was that in addition to sharing Brown's principles and perceiving him as a redemptive force in American life, Thoreau found particularly effective his "literary style." Hyman points out that "Just as writers in our own day were drawn to Sacco and Vanzetti perhaps as much

for the majesty of Vanzetti's untutored prose as for the obvious
justice of their case, Thoreau somehow found the most convincing
thing about Brown to be his speech to the court" (pp. 185-186). Although it is true that Thoreau was attracted to Brown's eloquence,
it was for him *a sign* of Brown's redemptive power for Americans,
not a reason for it. Hyman's emphasis on Brown's speech in ac-
counting for Thoreau's attraction to him places an extraordinary
premium on style. This emphasis tends to minimize political issues
and place Thoreau in an almost aloof position, a position more
concerned with art as it is made than with life as it is lived. This
seems to be Hyman's position too.

Early in his essay Hyman offers his view of the artist's relationship to politics. He describes Thoreau's refusal to pay his poll tax as
a futile act, and he sees the only importance of the entire episode in
Thoreau's "political essay based on it." In pairing the futile act with
the effectively written essay, "we have," according to Hyman, "an
allegory for our time on the artist as politician":

the artist [is] as strong and serviceable in the earnest practice
of his art as he is weak and faintly comic in direct political
action. In a day when the pressure on the artist to forsake his
art for his duties as a citizen is almost irresistible, when every
painter is making posters on nutrition, when every composer
is founding a society devoted to doing something about the
atom bomb, when every writer is spending more time on
committees than on the typewriter, we can use Henry Thoreau's example. (p. 173)

Although Hyman does not deny that an artist can have a political
function in society, he limits the artist's role to his specialty. Looking back on this essay in 1962, "in a world of space travel and Freedom Riders," Hyman reaffirmed his belief that Thoreau's chief
"message" continued to be relevant to a "young literary generation"
which had experienced the politics of the 1930s and then World
War II with its subsequent threat of nuclear annihilation. Hyman,
"a member of no incorporated body but the American Numismatic
Society and the human race," insisted that writers could learn from
Thoreau that a "writer's place is not on the picket line nor even on

the Admirable Cause Committee, but at his desk, writing the truth as he sees it."[3] The tone of Hyman's assessment of the role of the artist in society suggests a frustration with causes and the vagaries of mundane, expedient politics. Leave politics to the politicians and truth to the artists. This is a sentiment with which Thoreau sympathized and that he often shared ("The poet must keep himself unstained and aloof" [*Journal*, III, 5]). This sentiment is also a retreat from politics, but whereas Thoreau more often than not slipped off into the underbrush, Hyman closes his study door behind him. Hyman cites both the ineptness of Thoreau as a "political warrior" and the art of Thoreau's prose so that Hyman can use both to admonish his fellow artists to make art, not politics.

It is noteworthy that in the context of Hyman's 1946 discussion of Thoreau's treatment of John Brown, Thoreau is described as "not only [primarily] a writer, but a writer in the great stream of the American tradition, the mythic and non-realist writers" (p. 174). Despite the fact that he earlier referred to Thoreau as a "political writer" (p. 172), his main effort is to place Thoreau in a literary rather than a political tradition. Hyman takes Thoreau's "Plea for Captain John Brown" and rarefies it into myth. Thoreau was concerned with immortalizing Brown, but his attempt to invest Brown with a heroic mythology was essentially a deliberate political action, a fact which Hyman avoids. When Hyman sets Thoreau and Lincoln apart as great American prose writers, he dismisses the fact that often great art is created as a political act and becomes an artistic act after the event. Hyman asserts that art is created from artistic acts only; this oversimplifies the multiple kinds of feelings, attitudes, and activities that may turn out to be art. In order to unseat Thoreau from Hyman's "Admirable Cause Committee" one has to imagine that the crowd which listened to Thoreau's plea for Brown in Concord's town hall thought of the speech as a literary event. America, however, simply has never produced that many Norman Mailers. Hyman prefers his Thoreau in a symbolic context rather than in a political, historical context. He perceives Thoreau from an artistic point of view; as Hyman wrote in 1962 confirming his earlier view of Thoreau, "I must report that I find no images of Thoreau more attractive than my own, and that some are considerably less attractive" (p. 169).

In Hyman's distribution of functions the writer is relegated to be an artist. If he engages in "direct political action," the artist not only weakens his true identity, but he also seems "faintly comic." Hence one aspect of Hyman's argument is that if a writer does not wish to take the risk of looking foolish, then he ought to remain in his study. A century before Hyman's essay, Emerson pointed out in "The American Scholar" that this exclusiveness leads to a society of compartmentalized functionaries: "The priest becomes a form; the attorney a statute-book; the mechanic a machine; the sailor a rope of the ship." And, one might add, the writer a pen. This kind of specialization is essentially conservative; it makes one's life neatly patterned, precisioned, controlled, and predictable. Once one's pattern has been clearly established and, as Hyman phrased it in 1962, one is consistently "faithful to that image" (p. 169), there is no danger of appearing as a "comic little figure." A writer who does not stray from his life's pattern — from his role as artist — and who invests himself with that pattern need not fear that he might come unbuttoned while engaging in direct political action outside his study. The pattern precludes the engagement. Hyman's Thoreau, the "revolutionary of absolute truth" (p. 176) at work in the study, is considerably less vulnerable than the revolutionary in history. Given the influence that Hyman's essay was to have on subsequent critics who also patterned Thoreau as a literary artist whose politics served merely as an occasional framework for his art, it is not unreasonable to ask: what are patterns for? The postwar tendency to minimize Thoreau's politics in favor of formalistic and mythic readings of his prose is related to the predominant politics of the period.

There is general agreement among historians of the recent past in the United States that during the decade which followed World War II the country's prevailing mood was conservative.[4] The tensions produced by the cold war made atheistic communism look worse than ever, and the weapons technology that developed during the war made the Soviet Union seem more dangerous than the Axis had been. To Americans the cold war denied that the United States had won an unconditional victory in 1945. The land of the free and home of the brave was not secure after all. Concern for external and internal security became a national pastime; indeed, a senator from Wisconsin built his entire career around the average citizen's fear of communist subversion and un-American activities. The anxiety aroused by alleged communists spilled over into many areas of American life. Liberals and liberal causes were also suspected of subverting the American way of life if communists happened to share their views on a particular issue. Predictably, McCarthyism turned into a witchhunt with its investigating committees rivaling the inanities of Cotton Mather's *Wonders of the Invisible World*. The search was on for "reds" and "pinkos" and, it seems, any other color that deviated from the norm. Sitting before one of these inquisitional outings one might be asked: "Do you ever entertain Negroes in your home?"[5] A tough question for a black man, that. Despite the successes of organizations such as the American Civil Liberties Union and the American Association of University Professors, these tactics of intimidation worked to the extent that criticism and dissent were frequently associated in the public mind with disloyalty. During the past decade, this sensibility found its way onto automobile bumper stickers with the motto: "America: Love It or Leave It." Unlike the forties and fifties, however, the late sixties and early seventies witnessed a strong unintimidated countermovement, and so one was just as likely to stop at a red light and read on the car ahead: "Viet Nam: Love It or Leave It." Not so nearly thirty years ago when Henry F. May noted in an article describing "The End of American Radicalism" that "Almost never in this country's history have there been so few bold and vigorous critics of the social order." [6]

Orthodoxy was officially valued in nearly every phase of American life, and in the face of the communist threat, nuclear war, and muddled national goals, Americans were nonetheless optimistic and affirmative. One aspect of this affirmative impulse was a revival of religion. An index to the pervasiveness of this return to a belief in absolutes can be found in a song that was a strong popular success in 1953. The title: "I Believe." Yes, there is Someone in the Great Somewhere who listens to our prayers and watches over us.[7] If Americans lost the Soviet Union as an ally at the end of the war, they compensated for that loss by rediscovering an ally in the sky in the early fifties. Although academicians may not have been as enthralled as the average American during the period with this dogged kind of optimism, and although it is unlikely that they fell asleep counting their blessings, they were not known for their negative vigilance. American scholars may have been as skeptical as Emerson's Montaigne, but there were very few Napoleons among them. In the context of this conservative political atmosphere, Hyman's insistence upon viewing Thoreau first and foremost as a literary artist takes on additional meaning. The period's emphasis on Thoreau as an artist had some political threads in its pattern.

Yet the emergence of Thoreau as a literary artist in the late forties and fifties can be accounted for, in part, by pointing to the increased interest among critics of the period in myth and symbol. Critics after Matthiessen discovered that Thoreau's art was heavily mythic and symbolic. Unlike Matthiessen, critics were not interested in Thoreau and his contemporaries because they shared a manifest "devotion to the possibilities of democracy"; instead, critics found them interesting because they shared, in Charles Feidelson's words, a "devotion to the possibilities of symbolism."[8] Hence Thoreau attracted much attention because he was, from a critical point of view, in vogue. It is also possible, however, to trace the rise of Thoreau's literary reputation from a political and social perspective.

The increased interest in Thoreau as a literary artist at the expense of his social and political reputation coincides with a general tendency among critics to avoid questions of politics. Fixing Thoreau in a pattern that accented the literary artist allowed a critic to concentrate more on matters of form than content. The focus of attention was on safe matters of form which could be skillfully examined by objective scholarship in the study. A writer with a challenging style was for many critics more interesting than a writer with challenging ideas, ideas that might require some work outside the study. Most critics, either by preference or by fate, confined themselves to the limitations that the conservatism of the period imposed upon them. It was not expected of them that they would leave their desks for active political involvement, and most did not. Like the world outside the study, the majority of Thoreau critics of the late forties and fifties pursued a policy of containment. In 1953 Leo Marx noted this proclivity among critics of *The Adventures of Huckleberry Finn* who substituted "considerations of technique for considerations of truth." Marx speculated on the reasons

for this: "It seems not unlikely . . . that the current preoccupation
with matters of form is bound up with a tendency, by no means
confined to literary quarters, to shy away from painful answers to
complex questions of political morality." [9] If Marx did not have in
mind the 1949 Bollingen Prize for Poetry in the preceding passage,
the award for Ezra Pound's *Pisan Cantos* is, nevertheless, a dramatic example of the period's critical emphasis upon formal concerns
in literature. Marx conjectured that the "mechanical sociological
criticism of the thirties" was, perhaps, one reason why critics contemporary to him were "less sensitive to questions of what might be
called social or political morality" in literature. Accompanying this
lack of interest was an increased concern with "moral problems
which arise in the sphere of individual behavior" rather than in a
social sphere (p. 236).

By the close of the 1950s Leo Marx's conjecture was shared by a
number of intellectuals who looked back upon the postwar period
in an attempt to account for the decade's conservatism. William G.
Carleton, writing in 1959 about "American Intellectuals and
American Democracy," found that most postwar intellectuals
"have surrendered to non-involvement or non-commitment, or re-
tired into formalism, or become obsessed with techniques. . . ."[10]
Unfortunately, they have, according to Carleton, abandoned their
commitment to the liberalism which characterized the work of a
writer like Parrington for a nearly valueless conservatism that is
not based upon any recognizable ideology but upon a withdrawal
from politics. This escape from commitment is called by such intellectuals "objectivity or sophistication or wisdom," while moral
judgments are considered to be "hortatory" and "evangelistic" and
unprofessional. Echoing Leo Marx, Carleton argues:

One way of escaping commitment in subject matter is to concentrate on form. In all the intellectual disciplines today, even
in the humanities and the social sciences, there is a growing
concentration on forging methods and techniques that will
make the discipline truly "scientific." Now, of course, nobody
objects to sharpening the tools of investigation and research,
but an excessive concern for methodology may also be a way
of avoiding all substantive import. (pp. 189-190)

And when "substantive" matters are treated, according to Carleton, they are devoid of any social and political considerations, because many writers and critics have turned their backs on man's "social environment" in their pursuit of the "individual psyche." They ignore the historical and social dimensions of life by cultivating a preoccupation for an "individual man's motivations, love life, sex drive, frustrations, complexes, and neuroses; and there is a neglect . . . not only of social considerations and problems but even of the impact of society and environment on individual man himself" (p. 190).

To point out this retreat from social and political life is not to say that those critics who wrote criticism that had nothing overtly to do with politics were secreting in their manuscript pages a subtext of conservative ideology. Indeed, probably most were or considered themselves to be of a liberal political persuasion. Nor does it mean that a critic has an obligation to run a security check on the political thought of a writer. The point is that such criticism when released to the world outside the study has political implications insofar as it reflects the attitudes of the historical moment that provides the context for intellectual activity. Even though literary criticism may overtly avoid politics and history in its method and scope, there is no guarantee that such criticism is written free from the influences of politics and history. The questions that were raised about Thoreau during the late forties and fifties were compatible with the predominantly conservative politics of the postwar era, an era in which President Eisenhower complained in 1954 that the country had too many "wisecracking so-called intellectuals going around and showing how wrong was everybody who don't happen to agree with them."[11]

Wisecracking was nearly regarded as an un-American activity in the fifties. And, of course, if ever there was a wisecracker in American literature it was Henry David Thoreau. Significantly, critics of the fifties reacted to Thoreau in much the same way that the majority of commentators of the conservative 1920s responded to Thoreau's politics. Just as the "stupendous radical" of the twenties was largely ignored in favor of the benign nature writer, so was the stupendous wisecracker of the fifties subordinated to the eloquent artist and mythmaker. But the criticism of the fifties was not so green as to take Thoreau for a simple nature walk; its critical path was an inward exploration.

Sherman Paul's *The Shores of America* has been widely regarded as the major study of Thoreau in the 1950s. Paul's close reading of Thoreau is an attempt to chart in detail the development of his inner life and art so that the modern reader might better understand Thoreau and know "what it meant to live a Transcendental life," a life style which Paul finds interesting and compelling owing to its intense concern for integrity and authenticity. Directing his study on an "inner stage," Paul tries "to get inside" Thoreau in order to produce what "might be called a spiritual biography or a biography of vocation."[12] Unquestionably, Paul's study is an important contribution to the writing of Thoreau's spiritual biography. Reviewing *The Shores of America* in 1959, Walter Harding wrote that the "important fact about this book is that in it Thoreau criticism has at long last reached maturity" (which is to say that Paul's book was the first book-length study of Thoreau using new critical techniques in order to deal with Thoreau as a mythmaker). After praising the book, Harding also notes "one strange lacuna" in what is otherwise a comprehensive study: the political essays are nearly ignored in a book that has more than 400 pages.[13] Paul's index, which runs for 15 pages, does not include a listing for politics. There are the same number of references (five) listed for Lucy Jackson Brown, Emerson's sister-in-law, as for John Brown, and twice as many more for Sir Thomas Browne. As Harding points out, Paul hurries through a discussion of "Civil Disobedience" in only a handful of pages and barely mentions "Slavery in Massachusetts" or the John Brown essays.

Paul does not explain why he avoids Thoreau's political essays; it is only evident that he does. The care, the time, and the meticulous explanation which Paul extends to nearly every other aspect of Thoreau — from his college essays to "Wild Apples" — is noticeably absent from his cursory treatment of the political essays. Paul seems to be considerably less compelled by Thoreau's politics than by his Transcendentalism. Short of some obligatory remarks on Thoreau's commitment to "higher law" and a summary of Theodore Parker's discussion of Transcendental assumptions related to politics, Paul has little to say about any of the issues that critics have raised concerning Thoreau's politics. All except one.

Taking up the problem of how a Transcendentalist can know that his commitment to a higher law is not simply a personal whim or a delusion, Paul sets out to distinguish Thoreau from the "Ethan Brands, Ahabs, and Hollingsworths who act rashly" and risk destroying society. Paul, citing Parker, briefly outlines the problem which the Transcendentalist presents in a political context: the danger is that the " 'transcendental moralist' might 'abhor the actual rules of morality,' that in his impatience with the necessity of compromise and the tardiness of social change might resort to absolutism in practice as well as in idea." Like Parker, Paul is well aware of how potentially dangerous Transcendental morality can be when it crosses over that mortal bridge from the world of idea to the world of history: "There were Ahabs by the score at the Chardon Street conventions, few Captain Veres." Lest his reader think that there might be something fatally wrong with Thoreau's Transcendental politics, Paul pays careful attention to the hint of his reader's hitching tiller and places a firm grip upon it to steer the reader away from too closely identifying Thoreau with Ahab:

As far as other reformers went Thoreau was aware of the danger of legislating one's dyspepsia into law, and what saved Thoreau from this predicament was his refusal to use coercion in behalf of his ideas. He was not a reformer in this sense; persuasion and example were his only weapons. For him good government, like Paradise, began at home; social ethics were personal ethics, and the only valuable reform was self-reform. One could avoid the dangers of transcendental madness by limiting reform to oneself. (p. 246)

Paul attempts to eliminate any doubts or reservations about Thoreau's politics by assuring his reader that Thoreau never dreamed with his hand on the helm and never used "coercion in behalf of his ideas." And besides, neither Thoreau's hut nor his rowboat accommodated more than two or three people. Paul implies that even if Thoreau's Transcendental politics were a form of "dyspepsia." it represented no "predicament" for Thoreau because Thoreau's self-imposed quarantine meant that his politics would never be organized into group action. By avoiding crowds, "by limiting reform to oneself," Thoreau's case of absolutism was no threat to community health. Indeed, the Thoreau that Paul describes is positively good for community health precisely because he did go it alone and create in *Walden* "a fable of the renewal of life" (p. 293) for his fellowman. For Paul, Thoreau is a mythmaker but not a troublemaker; and although *The Shores of America* brilliantly establishes and demonstrates the former, it avoids and glosses over the latter.

Three pages before he writes that "persuasion and example were" Thoreau's "only weapons," Paul nevertheless notes that Thoreau "championed the bloody ways by which John Brown upheld the law." He writes of Thoreau who repudiated "coercion" as a mode of reform, that

Blood was a price he was willing to pay: he was not speaking entirely metaphorically when he said, "But even suppose blood should flow. Is there not a sort of blood shed when a man's conscience is wounded?" A stickler for complicity, he knew that by aiding Brown he was helping him to shed it. (p. 242)

Paul is no stickler for consistency here. If Thoreau's only weapons were persuasion and example, then they were of a very high caliber indeed. It is not a Thoreau pencil but a Sharps' rifle that speaks out most forcefully in "A Plea for Captain John Brown." Yet Paul does not reconcile this with his assertion that Thoreau's version of reform skirts coercion; it does not become clear how Thoreau differs from "other reformers" or from Ahab. For whatever reasons, Paul's own unwillingness to subject Thoreau's politics to a close scrutiny commensurate with the rest of his study is representative of the ahistorical and apolitical bias of many critics concerned with form, myth, and the individual psyche in the fifties. Such critics tended to limit their professional interests in Thoreau to his art and mythmaking to the exclusion of his social and political thought.[14]

Of course, not all critics of the late forties and fifties were interested solely in Thoreau's art. Many addressed themselves to the issues implicit in his politics, and although their opinions were by no means unanimous, they tended to challenge Thoreau's political thought more often than they advocated it. Writing in 1949, C. Carroll Hollis flatly stated in a brief treatment of "Civil Disobedience" that the major thrust of the essay — the idea that an individual's conscience takes precedence over the authority of the state — is not a useful "guide to political action."[15] In judging Thoreau's politics inadequate as they are expressed in "Civil Disobedience," Hollis finds him "guilty" of "the romantic heresy." Thoreau, according to Hollis, fails "to recognize the primacy of the state" (p. 531). By failing to understand that the authority of the state is based, at least in the United States, upon democratic majority rule rather than sheer brute power, Thoreau falls into his "central error" in "Civil Disobedience." Thoreau's error is the "Rousseauistic idea that consent on the part of the citizen constitutes the state's authority and refusal dissolves it" (p. 531). Hollis signs on the dissenter of "Civil Disobedience" whether Thoreau likes it or not. Thoreau's refusal to pledge allegiance to the state does not, for Hollis, deny the authority of the state. Thoreau's rejection of the state demonstrates only his own political irrelevance.

Hollis' emphasis upon the integrity and preservation of organized society and government over the individual reflects the period's general concern for public rather than private welfare and national rather than individual security. His is a conservative sentiment, and the term *conservative* is particularly appropriate here, because Hollis does not describe Thoreau's position as the politics of anarchism (as many previous commentators had), but rather as the politics of a "complete or absolute liberalism" which offers no means of preserving the institutional resources of society. Clearly, Hollis places his faith in the authority of institutions rather than in the self-expression of individuals. His view of liberalism is cautious; he does not want to sound like a Joseph McCarthy, but neither does he want to sound like a Vernon Parrington:

I fancy myself as a liberal of sorts, and many of my friends are more liberal still, but I know of no one who is an absolute liberal in Thoreau's sense except Thoreau. By absolute liberalism, in the extreme and reprehensible sense in which I use the term here, I mean the exaltation of the privilege of freedom of will so as to justify its independence of authority. (p. 532)

Although Hollis fancies himself a "liberal of sorts," in associating the anarchistic streak in Thoreau with liberalism, he discredits liberalism by linking it to what he considers to be an extremist position.[16] Thoreau's individualism — what Parrington called his "potent liberalisms" — is worthless on a political level, according to Hollis, but useful and "significant" for Thoreau as a "mystical poet" because it is necessary for a writer's "mystical awareness" (pp. 532-533). Hollis does not clarify what he means by this assertion, but his point is that Thoreau's politics are acceptable when they are removed from a political context and safely placed in an aesthetic context. There the "central error" perpetuated by the romantic heretic is aesthetically pleasing rather than socially dangerous. If the postwar era could accommodate Ezra Pound's politics in the name of art, it is not so surprising that Hollis could find Thoreau's politics acceptable on the same level.

A more detailed consideration of Thoreau's politics — and liberalism — is found in Heinz Eulau's 1949 article, "Wayside Challenger: Some Remarks on the Politics of Henry David Thoreau."[17] This essay takes issue with earlier liberal readings of Thoreau which placed him in either a collectivistic or Jeffersonian tradition. Eulau, a political scientist rather than a literary critic, begins his discussion with a consideration of the failures of contemporary liberalism. He argues that modern American liberalism fails to live up to its own rhetoric. Despite its pride in being "critical in spirit and pragmatic in method," liberalism is guilty of "self-righteous indignation" owing to its tendency to perceive issues in a black-and-white perspective. This binary sensibility results in "ethical absolutism," an inability to recognize that other positions on an issue may incorporate values that are just as valuable as that of the liberal stand. The smugness that Eulau attributes to liberals is caused by liberalism's failure to distinguish between "morality" and "moral realism." With almost Hawthornesque or Melvillean logic, Eulau points out that "In contrast to morality, moral realism is aware of the possibility of good or bad consequences not as polar opposites, but of the possibility of 'good-and-bad' consequences as ambivalent unities." Eulau asserts that Thoreau's relevance to contemporary politics is not the result of his political usefulness. Thoreau is germane only because he is one of the sources of liberalism's failures, particularly the failure which allows itself to be challenged by the absolutist "metaphysical notion of individual moral conscience as a valid axiom of democratic politics" (pp. 117-118). Eulau rejects the idea that an individual can base his actions upon his own conscience. He considers it a "politically dangerous concept" because virtually anything can be done in the name of it (p. 119).

Eulau does not present Thoreau as a prototypical liberal of the twentieth century. Instead, he argues that modern American liberalism fails in its attempts to claim Thoreau as one of its own: "Some recent interpreters [Max Lerner, Townsend Scudder, and F.O. Matthiessen] have tried in vain I think, to make Thoreau palatable to liberalism by reading their own preferences [collectivism] into his writings." Eulau insists that Thoreau was not a collectivist; his "whole political philosophy was based on the theoretical premise of individual conscience as the only true criterion of what is politically right and just" (p. 118). He reasons that because liberals have convinced themselves that Thoreau was a liberal collectivist, they overlook his *self*-righteousness and fall into the same trap of "ethical absolutism" that he did. Hence liberalism "tends to become an affair of mere pronunciamento and simple magic formula" (p. 117), and in its extreme forms is capable of adopting a credo that amounts to little more than: We are right, therefore we do.

Pointing to the difference between Thoreau's peaceful "Civil Disobedience" and his later support of violence in "A Plea for Captain John Brown," Eulau finds Thoreau inconsistent, paradoxical, dangerous, and guilty of both "moral intransigence" and expediency (pp. 127-130). He believes Thoreau's arguments backing Brown betray a willingness to accept the argument that the end justifies the means — and this justification from a moralist who supposedly would have nothing to do with expediency. These problems are, again, generated by Thoreau's insistence upon the unyielding individual conscience as the bedrock of all action. His politics must be repudiated because "Thoreau's mind was totally closed to the democratic conception of politics as a never-ending process of compromise and adjustment" (p. 127). This refusal to accept the necessity for compromise in politics suggests to Eulau that despite Thoreau's interest in political issues, he was "unpolitical"; his unwillingness to concern himself with the workings of government renders futile any efforts (such as Parrington's) to place him in a

Jeffersonian political tradition (pp. 119-120). And to the extent that modern American liberalism is also intransigent and unrealistic, it too must be seen as divorced from a useful political tradition.[18]

Eulau's article is important for several reasons. His essay is the first lengthy detailed effort to examine critically Thoreau's politics. His linking Thoreau's politics to contemporary liberalism is an attempt to illuminate what he considers to be the dark errors committed by both Thoreau and contemporary liberals in the name of enlightened thought. Eulau, like Hollis, places his faith in institutional modes of change, which for him are more predictable, reliable, and useful than the politics of the individual zealot. Eulau's position, however, is more carefully reasoned than Hollis'. Anyone who claims to have God on his side is not for Eulau, as it was for Thoreau, "a majority of one already." Rather, he is singularly dangerous; he threatens not only institutions but lives.

For an American chilled by the exigencies of the cold war, Eulau's plea for "compromise and adjustment" was especially meaningful. Without "compromise and adjustment" individuals and institutions, even the world, might self-destruct. On an international level this fear was the result of the insecurity generated by the sudden mushrooming of the atomic age. On an individual level — which goes beyond the scope of Eulau's article — "compromise and adjustment" were one way to avoid possibly damaging frustrations on a psychological level.

During this period happiness became synonymous with stability — as it usually does following a war — and stability became synonymous with mental health. One student of Thoreau, Walter Scott Houston, who viewed Thoreau's relationship to society very differently from Eulau's, perceived Thoreau as a useful model for contemporary Americans precisely because he was willing to engage in the kind of compromise which Eulau believed Thoreau was incapable of tolerating. Houston finds that Thoreau is modern in his attitudes toward reform because instead of trying to alter the world he adjusts himself to the world while compromising as little as possible. This position, according to Houston, is recommended by contemporary psychiatrists. Houston's assumption seems to be that society at large is fundamentally healthy and needs little adjustment; it is the individual who requires analysis more than any institution.[19] These values are in marked contrast to Parrington's earlier comment upon the same problem concerning the relationship of the individual reformer to society: "To the inmates of Bedlam a sane man will appear queer." Although Houston and Eulau disagree over Thoreau's willingness and ability to compromise, there is no question that they both agree that compromise and adjustment are desirable virtues; the agreement may constitute good advice, but their agreement is a sign of their times also. The more consensus and continuity an individual might share with society, the better off he was. Despite the differences in their assessment of Thoreau's usefulness to moderns, both Eulau and Houston premised their respective views of Thoreau upon the belief that American society and its institutions were basically good and deserved to remain stable. One does not hear from them any howl of protest that America has gone wrong. That would have to wait until the 1960s.

The majority of Americans after World War II believed that the most threatening challenge to the stability of American society and its institutions was communism. When Thoreau's social and political thought was not condemned for being self-righteously opposed to institutional authority, Thoreau was occasionally used to combat communists. Thoreau's individualism, condemned by Hollis and Eulau as a vice, was praised as a virtue by Joseph Wood Krutch. Krutch, nature lover and staunch individualist, continued in 1948 the battle he had begun in the early thirties by using Thoreau's individualism to fend off Marxist solutions to contemporary American problems. His book-length study, *Henry David Thoreau*, may be considered an exposition and evaluation of Thoreau's lifelong attempt to "Simplify!" This single word sums up for Krutch Thoreau's "lesson" for Americans. [20]

Early in the book Krutch assesses Thoreau's reputation and places a heavier emphasis on the content of Thoreau's writings than on its form. In contrast to Hyman, Krutch believes that it is not the "sheer brilliance" of Thoreau's writing that is "chiefly responsible" for his fame (p. 5). As great as his prose style is, his

most ardent admirers are those who have accepted him as some kind of teacher, who cherish his writings almost as though they were sacred books, and who feel with him a communion of spirit often personal and almost secret. (p. 7)

Krutch divides Thoreau's "disciples" into two distinct groups: (1) those who admire him primarily because they too are "nature lovers and solitaries" and (2) those followers, like Mahatma Gandhi and some leaders of the British Labour party, who have seen him as a social reformer (p. 7). Of these two groups Krutch seems to prefer the former, because he minimizes the latter by stressing Thoreau's "conviction that reform is possible only insofar as each man reforms himself, and that all attempts to save mankind through concerted effort are vicious and self-destructive." Simplification, not industrialization or a redistribution of wealth — or any other material mode of amelioration — is the most direct, and only, route to meaningful reform. "Most reformers" from Krutch's point of view are, if not frightening, worthy of little more than contempt, because they ignore the "fundamental good" that Thoreau championed: ". . . a life devoted to contemplation in close contact with the phenomena of nature and relieved only by the simple activities attendant upon providing for himself the simplest necessities of life." For Krutch this is not an invitation to escape from reality. Thoreau's refusal to concern himself with material matters (such as a redistribution of wealth and resources) is, of course, uncharacteristic of "most current social philosophies," but this refusal does not mean that he was a selfish escapist. Rather, Krutch argues, Thoreau was more responsible than "most proponents of social change" because his verson of self-reform went beyond a call for a "society so organized that everyone may ride somewhere in next to no time and for next to nothing" (p. 8). The implication is that it is the social reformer who is fundamentally irresponsible and "escapist," because such a reformer treats only symptoms rather than causes. [21]

Krutch's treatment of contemporary reformers is couched in broad and general terms; he makes no specific charges against any particular movement, only "most" of them. It is not until nearly the end of his study that Krutch mentions communism as one of the movements he has in mind (pp. 255-260). His strategy is to allow the reader to think the evil. By allowing the reader to think it for himself, Krutch, like Henry James, releases himself from any weak specifications. This technique can be an effective and aesthetically satisfying method when employed in writing fiction, but when used in a critical essay it subtly substitutes a reader's imagination for what should be a writer's discourse. Even Henry James admitted that there were some good ghosts, but Krutch does not explicitly admit to the efficacy of any organized reform movement because it would weaken the theme of his story. It would spoil his attempt to prove that Thoreau's self-reliant individualism is the untried solution to contemporary problems. Krutch's description of Thoreau's rhetorical technique in *Walden* describes Krutch's own forays against organized collective reform movements: "He discharges a shaft, and is gone again before we can object or challenge" (p. 110).

In order to convince his reader that individual reform is more important than organized societal reform, Krutch emphasizes that when Thoreau occasionally deviated from his usual concern for his own salvation, he was more confused than committed. As an example of this shift in consciousness from an individual to a social level, Krutch chooses Thoreau's support of John Brown, which he sees as inconsistent with "Civil Disobedience," because the earlier essay was nonviolent and because it was an attempt by Thoreau to disengage himself from complicity in slavery in the United States. With the Brown episode however, Thoreau did advocate violence and could not "wash his hands" of the problem of slavery. Krutch does not, like Hyman, celebrate this shift as a movement toward social responsibility; instead, he notes that Thoreau's inability to reconcile his attitude toward Brown with his earlier views as expressed in "Civil Disobedience" was one of "several factors which disturbed the happy confidence of *Walden* and to some extent poisoned the paradise which he thought he had found" (p. 133). Krutch does not present this frequently noted fact as a laudable personal sacrifice to the altar of social responsibility, or as a painful necessary step for an artist with a moral vision, or even as only a momentary burst of emotion in response to a man who seemed to be a Transcendental hero. Krutch is not concerned with the problem of whether Thoreau was wrong or right about defending Brown or responding to a burning social issue. What Krutch is more interested in is that Thoreau's defense of Brown not be interpreted as a repudiation of the importance of individual self-reform. Immediately after pointing out the contradiction between Thoreau's support of Brown and his earlier position, Krutch writes that "it is nevertheless a mistake to suppose, as present-day radicals are always tempted to assume, that he ever gave up one philosophy for another or ever became converted heart and soul to any religion of social responsibility" (p. 133). This is correct, but the facts here carry a heavier burden than scholarly truth. Krutch wants no more to have his reader converted by some "present-day radicals" to a "religion of social responsibility" than he will allow those same radicals — whoever they are — to claim Thoreau. Such social movements, if one is sensitive to Krutch's diction, are populated by fanatics and evangelists, not individualists. Thoreau may have conducted one revival meeting in behalf of Brown, but Thoreau himself was not converted "heart and soul," nor did he turn it into a movement, and so he saved himself. Krutch is careful to point out that Thoreau was only "a very reluctant crusader" (p. 239). As Thoreau recognized, he was by temperament more inclined to "wash his hands" of such matters, and Krutch calls attention to that phrase from "Civil Disobedience" in order to give social reformers a reason to disassociate themselves from Thoreau: ". . . if the present-day revolutionists were anxious to repudiate rather than to claim him they would certainly call attention to the usual associations of that phrase: 'wash his hands of it' " (p. 135). The revolutionaries can have Freud and Marx but not Thoreau (p. 257).

The inadequacy of the concept of individual self-reform for providing a realistic and responsible means of reform on any level — whether for the individual or for society — can be seen in one of its more negative manifestations in its approach to the problem of slavery in the nineteenth century. Krutch describes Thoreau's thrust in the first chapter of *Walden* against reformers who sought to liberate the slaves from physical bondage but who failed to recognize the necessity of freeing themselves from a materialistic society that makes slaves of all people. The abolitionists did not go far enough; instead of merely "tinkering with the details," writes Krutch (summarizing Thoreau with approval), they should have been concerned with the "whole conception of what men should live for." Krutch asks rhetorically: "Was the freedom his fellow townsmen enjoyed itself so noble and so happy that Negroes should be promised ultimately something like it? Would it not be better if the New Englanders should first heal themselves?" (p. 150). At best, the questions raised here are remarkably innocent; at worst, they suggest a condescending doctrine of stewardship. If Krutch had imagined himself or Thoreau actually addressing these questions to a slave — say a Frederick Douglass — the naive quality of the questions would have been immediately apparent. There can be little doubt that most slaves would have somehow freely endured the imperfections of New Englanders if offered the opportunity. This total, "radical" view of self-reform leads, in effect, to no reform at all.

On an individual level Krutch's questions are important to the extent that they guard against a person's fashioning any human activity into an instrument with which to suppress a fear of living a meaningless life. Reforming others probably will always be a means by which some people avoid self-reform, but seen from a point of view a little higher, a perspective that includes the inescapable reality and power of society to shape the quality of an individual's life, the spiritual injunction to Heal Thyself becomes, when translated into the language of history, Ignore Thy Neighbor. To be accurate and fair it must be emphasized that this is not the intention of such individualism; it is, rather, the effect of the politics built into it: Thoreau "went off to Walden to demonstrate that if you do not like the world you find yourself in and do not think you can change it very soon, you can at least move away from it" (p. 258). Any pilgrim's progress is predicated upon his turning his back on the world's work so that he can devote his energy and attention to the spiritual road ahead. If an individual is not to become a victim of the world's complex deficiencies, then he must therefore build his own simpler world; "any real improvement must proceed from within outward" (p. 259). Krutch seems to place responsibility for living a meaningful life squarely on the individual rather than on the society in which he lives and his relationship to it. [22]

Although Krutch is certainly aware of the historical, political, and socioeconomic forces that influence the quality of an individual's life, he, like Thoreau, perceives them as symptoms rather than causes of humanity's ills (pp. 259-260). This perception of symptoms rather than causes is significant, for in spite of Krutch's not sharing Hollis' or Eulau's confidence and faith in society's institutions, his insistence upon individual reform may in actual practice produce the same results.

From Thoreau's perspective, if an individual feels frustrated, trapped, and unhappy, it is not so much society's failure but his own. The individual must renovate himself instead of merely condemning society. True meaningful change — radical reform — must be initiated and achieved by individuals, since the only worthwhile reform proceeds from within outward. This mode of problem solving tends, however, to support the status quo in a society, because it removes pressure from institutions and shifts pressure to the individual, who is seen as responsible for his own condition. This emphasis on individual responsibility rather than social or institutional responsibility has a conservative tone to it because change is measured on an individual, internal, spiritual scale rather than on an observable quantitative social scale. There is little or no institutional accountability, since institutions are perceived as a relatively ineffectual means of reform anyway. In addition, faith in individual reform is predicated upon the idea that a person's problems are such that they can be solved by that person. Poverty, for example, is not poverty if an individual can convince himself that it is not. (Krutch applauds the "psychological advantage" of this faith in "purely individual action," but he does not mention its social consequences [p. 10].) Thus poverty is not so much the result of historical and economic forces, lack of training or education — or whatever — rather, it is essentially a state of mind. Since the individual in the right state of mind can transcend his circumstances, the power of the individual is far greater than the magnitude of his problems. This of course minimizes the importance and complexity of problems that are experienced by individuals but which are generated by social, economic and institutional conditions. In this scheme of things even if an individual believes that society and its institutions are *not* essentially sound (Thoreau's and Krutch's position), his relationship to it — his ignoring them — lends support to society and its institutions in that the effect of the individual's position is identical to that of those who believe all is well.

Thoreau's individualism is considerably less radical in a political and historical context than Krutch supposes. In the world of politics the dissenting individual *self*-reformer is, more often than not, easily absorbed into the silent majority; and even eccentricity, when it does not generate too much suspicion, is usually a welcomed relief, because it need not be taken seriously. If Thoreau's readers enjoy the rhetorical jokes that resulted from his unwillingness to take seriously the bustling nineteenth century, it should also be remembered that probably only a handful of his contemporaries could mention his name without smiling (or frowning). There are many Concord jokes in *Walden*, but it is likely that as many Walden jokes circulated in Concord. In signing off, Thoreau risked being written off, and he was in his own time.[23]

Thoreau's achievements clearly do not rest solely upon his social and political thought (nor, it must be emphasized, does the value of Krutch's book), and he should not be judged from that perspective alone, but in judging his ideas from such a perspective, it should be recognized that his mode of self-reform, when he was true to it, did nothing to change the world in which Thoreau and his fellowman lived. Thoreau would argue that he made no attempt to change the world and that he attempted to keep the world from changing him, but such a defense does not make his political posture any less conservative in its effects. His is a passive, inadvertent conservatism.

Krutch's use of Thoreau's individualism to combat Marxism and collectivism in America did not blind him to the problems that the United States faced as a nation and a society. Like Thoreau, and like the Marxists, Krutch was very much aware of many of the country's shortcomings in the late forties and fifties. His quarrel with the Marxists was based on how the United States was to be changed, not on the necessity for that change, but in 1949 several commentators discussed the differences between Thoreau and Marx for a somewhat different purpose. They sought to boost Thoreau and America and to discredit Marx and the Soviet Union. Communism was perceived as a direct threat to American ideas about democratic government and the individual. By having Thoreau and Marx confront each other in a comparative essay, some commentators were able to subject Marx ("an egoist with a weak stomach and a taste for caviar and pickles")[24] to a public dunking in Walden's distinctly American waters. Thoreau's individualism

— or at least the use to which it was put — is presented in all its
complacency in the following passage by C.R.B. Combellack:

We Americans may be reactionary swimmers against the current of our time, but it is nevertheless our glory that we do
really — we hope really — believe in individualism, in people
not as members of a class or state or ant heap but as men. It is
important that almost all Americans think that they are members of the middle class. The hatred between classes which
Marx saw so clearly we do not see . . . simply because by and
large the class distinctions do not exist here. [25]

One need not be a Marxist to wince at a statement so remarkably
naive. Combellack's response to Marxism is not the same as
Krutch's. She does not refute the Marxist approach to reform; in
place of that argument she denies the need for reform, because, in
the United States, "We live in a society of such classlessness as is a
Marxist dream of the distant future" (p. 445). Krutch was not content to play the role of a Mr. Smooth-It-Away; in 1951 he noted as
one of the reasons for the steady fascination with Thoreau in
American life an "increased comprehension of his social criticism."
Thoreau "is read in an age when the gloomiest see a future darker
than he did and even the more optimistic are beset by doubts and
fears." [26]

Among those who were gloomy and beset by doubts and fears
were Marxists and liberals. Despite a 1949 *New Yorker* complaint
that some "hard-working, Johnnies-come-lately" Marxists were
trying to claim Thoreau as one of their own owing to "a few
crotchety remarks he made about the factory system and because
of his essay on civil disobedience," there were actually few Marxists
who expressed in print interest in Thoreau. [27] The only significant
Marxist treatment of Thoreau of article length which appeared during the period was written by Samuel Sillen and published in
Masses & Mainstream in 1954. [28] Sillen is attracted to him because
he finds that Thoreau's "pages crackle with dissenting opinions" (p.
1), and given Sillen's perception of America in the early fifties, that
makes Thoreau important. Thoreau's outspoken dissent "summons
us to resist the assault on reason and conscience which demogogi-

cally presents itself today as Americanism" (p. 9). Pointing to the
political apathy and conformity of Americans, Sillen particularly
criticizes intellectuals for not having the backbone to stand up and
be counted on the side of America's "democratic heritage" as did
Thoreau. Like many commentators before him, Sillen uses Thoreau
as a touchstone for individual courage; his peroration encapsules a
number of the unpopular Marxist and liberal causes with which
Thoreau was associated in the years following World War II:

> The crises in which we find ourselves has this distinctive fea-
> ture: that so many of the most influential American writers
> have persuaded themselves, or rather been coerced or cor-
> rupted into pretending, that they have no responsibility for
> all that; they will tend their own gardens and cultivate the
> religion of art; not theirs the fault if the Rosenbergs are mur-
> dered, or fellow-writers put under the ban, or teachers and
> clergymen bludgeoned by the modern Know-Nothings, or
> Communists thrown into jail because they protest against un-
> just and unnecessary wars, Jim Crow, and indeed the defile-
> ment of American literature.
>
> "O for a man who is a *man*," said Thoreau, "and, as my
> neighbor says, has a bone in his back which you cannot put
> your hand through!" He was himself such a man. And he bids
> us, at this fateful hour for our country, not to compromise for
> less. (p. 9)

Sillen's primary purpose is to invoke Thoreau and only secondarily
to explain him.

The "crisis" to which Sillen refers was felt by many intellectuals
in the fifties, and though most Marxists left Thoreau pretty much to
himself, a number of liberals turned to the spirit of Thoreau for a
solution to the crabbed bad faith created by McCarthyism. In 1951
a paid political advertisement appeared in the *New York Times*
signed by seventeen artists, writers, and scholars (among them,
Louis Adamic, Mark Van Doren, Arthur Miller, Louis Untermeyer,
A.B. Guthrie, and Nelson Algren) urging Americans to reject "self
appointed judges" who find citizens "subversive" because they refuse to take loyalty oaths or abandon their own political convic-

tions. Their position was that unless Americans "like Thoreau in his Concord jail" spoke out against the "voices of bigotry and aggressive intimidation" loose in the United States, liberty would be only a memory in this country. The same appeal which Sillen later made to American intellectuals was made by these concerned liberals to the general public. [29]

A more lighthearted, but no less serious, manifestation of the ways the hut at Walden Pond and its owner were used to expose the dangers of the House Un-American Activities Committee and its owner, McCarthy, was presented by E.B. White in the pages of the *New Yorker*. Neither the man nor the magazine was any more enamored of McCarthyism than of Marxism. In a delightful farce White has McCarthy go to Walden Pond to investigate Thoreau, who, given the senator's nebulous and ridiculous criteria, is found to be subversive and un-American. By accenting Thoreau's self-reliance, his simplicity, and his independence — characteristics valued by most Americans — and allowing McCarthy to turn them into something un-American, White exposes how thoroughly benighted McCarthy's crusade for red-blooded American patriotism was.[30] Thoreau was useful to White and to those who refused to knuckle under to McCarthyism because the author of "Civil Disobedience" claimed that it was not only a right but a duty to say no in thunder. Perceived as a means by which Americans might be convinced that dissent was not automatically to be equated with communism, Thoreau was held in high esteem by those who would not accept a Sears Roebuck catalog as a substitute for the Bill of Rights.

On the occasion of the *Walden* centennial, the Thoreau Society's 1954 presidential address delivered by Raymond Adams extends further the "evils" of America life that ran counter to the spirit of Thoreau. [31] Among other things, Adams cites ecological waste, the growth of cities, the power of the military, a false sense of "progress," and rampant materialism as indications that the American character has gone "soft": Americans have "electric blankets because we lack the vitality to keep ourselves warm, bubble baths that are symbolic in that they are tepid, perfumed and bubbly like the physical lives of the bathers." Adams does not limit himself, however, to what may sound like a pitch for cold showers and an athletic morality; he also indicts the American political morality that causes us to "think our teachers are subversive and our scientists are traitors." Adams does not mince words; he has no use for the "weaseling and diversionary tactics of a McCarthy" (p. 3). His presidential address delivered on a quiet summer's day in Concord must have seemed very strong to his mixed audience of college professors, high school teachers, nature buffs, and local antiquarians. The United States, suggested Adams, desperately needed Thoreau, because "the years between 1945 and 1954 have shown us a harvest of falsity and fear and fascism in America such as Thoreau never saw between 1845 and 1854" (p. 4).

Considering that Adams' speech was delivered in the early fifties, not the late sixties, and the setting a literary society, not a political rally, and the speaker a scholar from the English department of the University of North Carolina, not a Louis Kampf from the Massachusetts Institute of Technology, Adams' speech was very strong indeed. There is, however, a distinct difference between Adams' historical moment and his approach to what he perceives as America's malaise, and the activism of the late 1960s. He concludes his summary of the country's ills with a charge to his audience that they not simply slip into pessimism and despair over the state of the nation or merely wistfully admire *Walden* and its author. Rather than resorting to gloom or nostalgia, "Nothing will do except to witness *Walden* in the way a few people have witnessed it during its first century by having their very lives cleansed and emboldened by the brave book" (p. 4). Adams' solution is not expressed in the language of politics; his is the language of evangelism. There is no mention of any form of direct social or political action to eliminate the "falsity and fear and fascism in America." Adams asks his audience to "witness" *Walden*, to undergo some form of self-conversion; but he has already established that it is American society and its politics which need converting, and so it is not at all clear how a rededication by the members of the Thoreau Society to the principles expressed in *Walden* would change anything. Adams' approach to Thoreau seems to be the society's version of the fifties' popular song "I Believe," but here the faith is not predicated on the notion that everything is basically all right; here is a belief that self-reform is somehow contagious, a belief which Thoreau shared. With this abiding faith, the college professors, the high school teachers, the nature buffs, and the local antiquarians can all go home and meditate upon Thoreau, confident that by witnessing *Walden* they have made the world a better place. And if they are wise, they will follow Thoreau's periodic advice to stay away from the newspapers, unless they, like Thoreau, are willing to have their nature walks spoiled by the *Times* and one of its occasional advertisements for freedom in America.

If this treatment of Adams' speech seems excessively severe, it is in response to the excessive claims that are made for self-reform as a means of ameliorating social conditions. Using Thoreau's insights to describe what is wrong with America, they inadvertently help to perpetuate those wrongs by attempting to use Thoreau's nineteenth-century faith in the power of individual reform as a means to correct those wrongs. Although unintentional, this breeds self-righteousness (and the language of the evangelist), and, unfortunately, it is difficult to respond to self-righteousness without seeming to be righteous oneself. This was Thoreau's dilemma too.[32]

Like Joseph Wood Krutch, Adams urges his countrymen to view contemporary America with the acuteness of Thoreau's critical perception and to transform one's inner self in response to that perception. Both critics stress Thoreau's relevance; they make every effort to ensure that Thoreau is not written off by a modern technological corporate America, but it would take the 1960s to transform Thoreau into an activist reformer of any wide reputation. Critics of the fifties were willing to sit down and think about what was wrong about America, but rarely did they sit-in about those same conditions.

As in previous decades there was in the postwar decade a litany of commentaries which turned to Thoreau's life and writings as a New Gospel capable of saving America. Some of these commentators were more extravagant than others in their assessment of the efficacy of Thoreau's thought. Willard Thorp, for example, suggested that if the world were populated by Thoreaus, mankind would regain a lost pastoral innocence: "If that happy day should ever come, we should have no need for engineers, certainly for atomic engineers, and we could all go huckleberrying in Thoreau's party."[33] This image of simple innocence was attractive to those Thoreauvians who "wanted out" of a world that seemed unresponsive to their idealism. Prescribed as good medicine for "tired nerves and disturbing emotions," Thoreau was taken for the common gloom almost as frequently as aspirin was for the common cold. The causes of the illness for which he was prescribed were little different from the same conditions which prompted earlier commentators to turn to Thoreau for "a sense of peace and security":

The failure of material success to produce happiness has brought a new appraisal of values that is turning more people to those of Thoreau. Increasingly in our industrial and mechanized society, men recognize that he speaks directly to the conditions of everyday living and that more and more he becomes their encourager and helper in their efforts to disentangle themselves from the trappings and encumbrances of our complex, highly organized society. While growing collectivism and the increasing demands of the state continuously encroach upon personal freedom and threaten to remove it, Thoreau helps an individual to remain a person and not merely a belt-driven wheel in a machine. [35]

The typical Thoreauvian's reaction to oppressive societal machinery in the fifties was to escape it rather than to attempt to humanize it or shut it down. The focus of attention was upon the pastoral retreat offered by *Walden*. "Slavery in Massachusetts" and the John Brown episode were scarcely mentioned in the 1950s, and until the late fifties "Civil Disobedience" was more frequently discussed out of politeness to its influence abroad (particularly in terms of Gandhi) than in the context of American life.   Thoreauvians seemed to want nothing to do with the nuts and bolts of social and political machinery, and although they deplored the main drift of the fifties, their rejection of social and political problems in favor of the quietude of *Walden* conformed neatly to the conservative mood of the period.

There were even some few efforts to include Thoreau in the predominantly corporate temperament of the postwar decade. In these attempts to shift attention away from the anarchical side of Thoreau's thought, there was the faintest suggestion that Thoreau was not radically different from the socially responsible citizen of the late forties and fifties. John C. Broderick, examining Thoreau's journals for evidence that in some circumstances he did support the functions of government, challenged the stereotype of Thoreau as a "no-government" man. Broderick points out that there are many passages in Thoreau's writings in which he makes "specific proposals for legitimate governmental activity" in the areas of crime prevention, controlling stray animals, conservation, and laws for taxes in support of education, roads, and lighthouses. [37] Quick to note that this in itself does not make Thoreau a member of the Concord Jaycees, Broderick argues that although an awareness of these proposals does not vitiate Thoreau's philosophical anarchism, it "may soften the lines somewhat" of that image (p. 285). Near the end of his article Broderick makes clear that his reason for citing evidence that Thoreau advocated certain governmental activities is to make Thoreau appear more socially responsible in the eyes of Americans. He quotes Reginald L. Cook, another student of Thoreau, in order to frame the question which Broderick's article attempts to answer. The question deals with the problem presented by Thoreau's moral individualism and its relationship to civil law. Cook, though sympathetic to Thoreau's individualism, believes that the robber barons of the late nineteenth century demonstrate that "unless ethical idealism is implemented by restrictive legislation to curb rapacious aggressiveness it is ineffectual. A body of just and enforced laws is the chief realistic implementation which is required to make any idealism — Concord or otherwise — effective." After presenting Thoreau's specific proposals for government, Broderick concludes that "Thoreau's proposals in his journal, if not in his political essays, imply his own partial acceptance of that point of view." (p. 289).

No attempt is made by Broderick to judge the practicability of Thoreau's call for a blend of individual and institutional action; the "question of whether Thoreau's ideal of individual action supported and fostered by government can be effected without a strong central authority, though engaging, is one beyond the scope of this brief note" (p. 289). Rather than discussing one of the central problems associated with Thoreau's individualism, his concern is focused upon correcting Thoreau's image, and that aspect of his image with which Broderick concerns himself makes Thoreau more acceptable to the predominant values of the readers of the fifties. Broderick stresses what Thoreau has in common with the fifties by citing his concern for stray animals, crime prevention, roads, and lighthouses, rather than Thoreau's concern for moral and political issues. [38]

The most lengthy study of the 1950s that does examine Thoreau's social and political concerns is Leo Stoller's *After Walden* (1957). Stoller goes beyond the scope of Broderick's brief note and deals with the problem of the practicability of Thoreau's call for a type of reform that blends individual and institutional action. In a decade when American life continued to become more and more institutionalized while the individual seemed to matter less and less, Stoller's treatment of Thoreau's attempt to deal with the same problem was timely.

Focusing his attention upon Thoreau's later years, Stoller argues that Thoreau softened his intensely individualistic attitude toward reform because Thoreau began to recognize that "the protection of the spiritual interest of the many might require curtailment of the material interest of the few." [39] Unless some restrictions were placed upon individual freedom, the materialist who grew wild according to his own nature could, through poor forest management or irresponsible industrial planning, replace the spiritual signs latent in nature with the sign of the dollar:

In his approach to both industry and agriculture, Thoreau was being compelled . . . not only to accept a union between principle and expediency but to recognize that the success of the single man in his private life was dependent on the success of the community of men in their social life. He was moving toward the point at which he could no longer argue as in "Civil Disobedience" that government "can have no pure right over my person and property but what I concede to it" (IV, 387). (pp. 128-129)

But Stoller sees this shifting attitude toward the need for collective, social reform as incomplete on a political level in terms of Thoreau's involvement in the struggle to abolish slavery. Stoller points out that Thoreau always remained outside any of the organized movements to end slavery. Even

Thoreau's "Plea for Captain John Brown" is still, on the level
of doctrine, the statement of a thinker who is outside parties
and organizations and who has no grasp of the impulses that
govern politics in men built differently from himself. He no
longer speaks of boycotting conservative newspapers, the day
for so timid a blow having presumably passed. But he is still a
disunionist . . . he still derides politics, and he still measures
political acts only with the ruler of principle, careless of consequences. (p. 143)

Although Stoller notes the apolitical quality of Thoreau's response
to the issue of slavery, he defends Thoreau by suggesting that
"every political coalition needs its radical catalysts." Thoreau's
"speeches on slavery paid the debt" owed by his unwillingness to
become more actively involved on a political level (pp. 142-143).
Stoller does not attack Thoreau for his unconcern regarding movements and effective action, but he makes clear that he does not find
efficacious Thoreau's "unwilling[ness] to take the steps that would
have placed him more firmly and *significantly* [my emphasis]
among the people whom he had helped and spoken for" (p. 147).
Stoller's own faith in collective movements (a faith which manifested itself in his interest in the civil rights and peace movements of
the sixties) does not allow him to respond with enthusiasm to
Joseph Krutch's reluctant crusader because, despite Thoreau's support of the Union in the Civil War and his "recognition that the
achievement of correspondence with higher law is not a matter
solely for the individual but for society as well," Thoreau never
was able to recognize the necessity for "organized political action"
(pp. 152-153).

Just as Stoller's study of Thoreau described Thoreau's union of
principle and expediency in his later life, so was Stoller's later use of
Thoreau a combination of principle and expediency. Writing in
1962 on the relevancy of Thoreau's politics, Stoller argued:

It is not strategies, after all, that keep his words alive, it is the
Prometheus in them, Shelley's Prometheus, who will never
make peace with an overlord. As long as we can hear this
voice, which is timeless, we shall be certain to discover its appropriate tactics, which are of the hour. [40]

This assessment of Thoreau is similar to what Stoller writes in *After Walden* (for example, see p. 10), but here is more of an insistence on Thoreau's relevance. What is interesting about the passage written in 1962 is that the controversy that was associated with Thoreau's reputation in the 1960s was not about the "Prometheus who will never make peace with an overlord" but about the tactics of the hour, a problem which Stoller — like Thoreau — minimizes. Stoller makes a distinction between the usefulness of Thoreau's ideals and his "strategies," but some who were contemporary to him and who were to follow did not make the same distinction; they used as their precedent Thoreau and what they assumed were his "strategies," not Stoller. The tactics of the hour were to become the concern of the decade of the sixties.

NOTES

1. "Henry Thoreau in Our Time," *Atlantic Monthly*, 178 (November 1946), rpt. in Walter Harding, ed., *Thoreau: A Century of Criticism* (Dallas, Tex.: Southern Methodist University Press, 1954), p. 174. The Hyman quotation with which this chapter begins is on p. 172.

2. In addition to Harding's 1954 collection of essays, versions of Hyman's essay are reprinted in: Lauriat Lane, Jr., ed., *Approaches to Walden* (Belmont, Calif.: Wadsworth Publishing Co., 1961), pp. 49-56; Sherman Paul, ed., *Thoreau: A Collection of Critical Essays*, Twentieth Century Views (Englewood Cliffs, N.J.: Prentice-Hall, 1962), pp. 23-36; Owen Thomas, ed., *Walden and Civil Disobedience*, Norton Critical Edition (New York: Norton, 1966), pp. 314-326; and Wendell Glick, ed., *The Recognition of Henry David Thoreau: Selected Criticism Since 1848* (Ann Arbor: University of Michigan Press, 1969), pp. 334-351.

3. "Henry Thoreau Once More," *Thoreau in Our Season*, ed., John H. Hicks (Amherst: University of Massachusetts Press, 1966), p. 169. This article originally appeared in the *Massachusetts Review*, 4 (Autumn 1962), 163-170.

4. See, for example: Merle Curti, *The Growth of American Thought*, 3rd ed. (New York: Harper & Row, 1964), pp. 752-764; Daniel Snowman, *America Since 1920* (New York: Harper & Row, 1968), pp. 116-130; and Franklin D. Mitchell and Richard O. Daires, eds., *America's Recent Past* (New York: John Wiley & Sons, 1969), pp. 339-348. My discussion of the

postwar conservative mood in the United States draws upon these overviews.

5. A. Powell Davies, "Loyalty Needs Better Friends," *New Republic*, February 4, 1952, p. 11. Quoted in Curti, p. 757.

6. "The End of American Radicalism," *American Quarterly*, 2 (Winter 1950), 291. For confirmation of the prevailing belief in the fifties that "there are hardly any radicals of any sort left," see Richard Hofstadter's "The Pseudo-Conservative Revolt," *The American Scholar*, 24 (Winter 1954-1955), 9-27. An indication of the complacency of the period can be conveniently found in an article in the same issue of *American Scholar*, entitled "The True Face of Our Country" (pp. 28-34), in which a 1954 Phi Beta Kappa oration delivered at Harvard University by John La Farge, S.J., "communicate[s] to the entire world the news of our recent great liberating achievement: the unanimous decision of the Supreme Court of the United States on May 17, outlawing the principle of racial segregation in the nation's public schools." There was cause for celebration, but not to the extent that La Farge hoped and believed. He wanted to persuade himself and others that everything was really all right with America: ". . . we want to continue telling this event, because we believe it removes a painful blemish from the true face of our country. This decisive step refutes the gross caricatures which have been spread so widely by Communist propaganda; it corrects unduly pessimistic ideas as to the racial situation in the United States which are currently accepted even in friendly nations abroad. It is quite characteristic that the Soviet press has abstained from mentioning it at all" (p. 128). History — notably the race riots of the sixties — did not share his faith and enthusiasm.

7. Two useful articles which examine the relationship between American popular music and society are both to be found in *American Quarterly*, and both are written by the same author, Hughson F. Mooney: "Songs, Singers and Society, 1890-1954," 6 (Fall 1954), 221-232; and "Popular Music Since the 1920's: The Significance of Shifting Taste," 20 (Spring 1968), 67-85. Music is not the only indication that suggests a postwar religious revival in the United States. One might also point to the fact that at President Eisenhower's first inauguration leading the parade was none other than "God's Float" (Curti, *The Growth of American Thought*, p. 771), and, of course, it is well known that under Eisenhower's administration the United States became one nation "under God."

8. *Symbolism and American Literature* (Chicago: University of Chicago Press, 1953), p. 4.

9. "Mr. Eliot, Mr. Trilling, and Huckleberry Finn," *The American Scholar*, 22 (Autumn 1953), 423-440, rpt. in Thomas D. Young and Ronald

E. Fine, eds., *American Literture: A Critical Survey* (New York: American Book Co., 1968), II, 240-241. Robert Gorham Davis had earlier made the connection between formalistic methodology and conservative politics in a much more explicit way in "The New Criticism and the Democratic Tradition," *The American Scholar*, 19 (Winter 1949-1950), 9-19. See also Daniel Aaron, "Conservatism, Old and New," *American Quarterly*, 6 (Summer 1954), 99-110.

10. "American Intellectuals and American Democracy," *Antioch Review*, 19 (Summer 1959), 188. Some of the causes for the decline in liberal activity and writing are presented in Earl H. Rovit, "The Lost Criticism," *AAUP Bulletin*, 45 (December 1959), 543-549; and Allen Angoff, "Protest in American Literature Since the End of World War II," *CLA Journal*, 4 (March 1961), 31-40.

11. Quoted in Richard Hofstadter, *Anti-Intellectualism in American Life* (New York: Alfred A. Knopf, 1966), p. 10.

12. *The Shores of America: Thoreau's Inward Exploration* (Urbana: University of Illinois Press, 1958), pp. vii-viii.

13. *TSB*, 66 (Winter 1959), 3-4.

14. The following list of articles and books is a representative list of works written in the fifties which examine Thoreau's art and/or myth-making. Some are more valuable to Thoreau studies than others, but all of them avoid discussing his politics in any detail: Charles Feidleson, *Symbolism and American Literature* (Chicago: University of Chicago Press, 1953), pp. 135-142; John C. Broderick, "Imagery in *Walden*," *University of Texas Studies in English*, 33 (1954), 80-89; Frank Davidson, "Thoreau's Hound, Bay Horse, and Turtle Dove," *New England Quarterly*, 27 (December 1954), 521-524; R.W.B. Lewis, *The American Adam* (Chicago: University of Chicago Press, 1955), pp. 20-27; Richard S. Kennedy et al., "The Theme of the Quest," *English Record*, 8 (Winter 1957), 2-17; Wright Morris, *The Territory Ahead* (New York: Harcourt, Brace & World, 1957), pp. 39-50; J. Lyndon Shanley, *The Making of Walden* (Chicago : University of Chicago Press, 1957); Carl Hovde, "Nature into Art: Thoreau's Use of His Journals in *A Week*," *American Literature*, 30 (May 1958), 165-184; William Bysshe Stein, "*Walden*: The Wisdom of the Centaur," *Journal of English Literary History*, 25 (September 1958), 194-215; Joseph J. Moldenhauer, "Images of Circularity in Thoreau's Prose," *Texas Studies in Literature and Language*, 1 (Summer 1959), 245-263; Delmar Rodabaugh, "Thoreau's 'Smoke,' " *Explicator*, 17 (April 1959), item 47; and David Skwire, "A Check List of Wordplays in *Walden*," *American Literature*, 31 (November 1959), 282-289.

Although Walter Harding notes the political "lacuna" in *The Shores of*

America, and although his interest in Thoreau is not chiefly mythic or formalistic, his own treatment of Thoreau's support of Brown is equally brief. In *A Thoreau Handbook* (New York: New York University Press, 1959), he reports on some of the various critical responses to the John Brown episode and concludes by writing that "The fundamental distinction of the John Brown essays is that they apply the principles of the earlier essays to a particular man and a particular situation, even though some aspects of that man's character and action were at variance with some of Thoreau's principles" (p. 67). Harding, no more than Paul, examines in detail those "aspects" of Thoreau and his politics that might expose some serious blemishes in his social thought. In effect both use a transcendental airbrush on Thoreau in order to preserve a positive image of his politics.

15. "Thoreau and the State," *Commonweal*, September 9, 1949, pp. 530-533.

16. Robert Ludlow, an associate editor of *The Catholic Worker*, replied to Hollis' article and found him to be the antithesis of "liberalism." Ludlow charged that in making "the state the determiner of morality, and the majority supreme his [Hollis'] view nowise differs from the fascists . . ." (*Commonweal*, September 23, 1949, p. 582).

17. *Antioch Review*, 9 (Winter 1949-1950), rpt. in Sherman Paul, ed., *Thoreau: A Collection of Critical Essays, Twentieth Century Views* (Englewood Cliffs, N.J.: Prentice-Hall, 1962), pp. 117-130.

18. For a more complete (and less partisan) assessment of Thoreau's support of Brown see Wendell Glick's unpublished doctoral dissertation: "Thoreau and Radical Abolitionism: A Study of the Native Background of Thoreau's Social Philosophy" (Northwestern University, 1950).

19. "An Analysis of Some of the Criticism of Henry David Thoreau," unpublished master's thesis (University of Alabama, 1948), p. 165. See also the conclusion to Francis B. Dedmond's unpublished master's thesis, "Thoreau as a Critic of Society" (Duke University, 1950), in which Dedmond agrees with Thoreau that the answer to society's problems consists of reforming oneself (p. 64).

20. *Henry David Thoreau* (New York: William Sloane Associates, 1948), p. 3.

21. An equally positive view of Thoreau's individualism will be found in Reginald L. Cook's *Passage to Walden* (Boston: Alfred A. Knopf, 1949). Cook does not express, however, the same animus to collective reform as Krutch. Cook simply chooses not to deal with the issue in his study; he writes that the purpose of his book is that it "attempts neither to tell the story of Henry Thoreau's life, nor to evaluate his relationship to the "golden day" and the era of atomic energy. Its chief aim is to penetrate the

essential quality and evoke the richness of his correspondence with nature. The source of his vitality was nature; the ultimate end of this vitality was the cultivation of the human spirit" (p. xv). Although Cook laments and deplores the "age of Fordissimus" (p. 118), his primary interest in Thoreau is his relationship to nature rather than society.

22. A latter-day example of the political results of this insistence upon individual responsibility can be seen in a statement by Senator Byrd of West Virginia explaining why he voted against President Johnson's rent-supplement bill designed to get the poor out of the ghettos: "Wherever some people go, the rat holes will follow. Wherever some people go, the slums will follow. People first have to clean up inside themselves." Quoted in Robert Sherrill, "The Embodiment of Poor White Power," *New York Times*, February 28, 1971, sec. 6, pp. 48-49.

23. For a discussion of this see Raymond Adams, "Thoreau and His Neighbors," *TSB*, 44 (Summer 1953), 1-4.

24. C.R.B. Combellack, "Two Critics of Society," *Pacific Spectator*, 3 (Autumn 1949), 442.

25. Ibid., p. 444. In addition to Combellack's treatment of Marx and Thoreau see also E.B. White, "Henry Thoreau," *New Yorker*, May 7, 1949, p. 23; and R.N. Stromberg, "Thoreau and Marx: A Century After," *Social Studies*, 40 (February 1949), 53-56. Both pieces attack Marx and defend Thoreau's individualism.

26. "The Steady Fascination of Thoreau," *New York Times*, May 20, 1951, sec. 7, p. 28.

27. E.B. White, "Henry Thoreau," *New Yorker*, May 7, 1949, p. 23. Certainly one explanation for the scarcity of Marxist treatments of Thoreau is that the Marxists of the thirties had already strongly rejected his individualism.

28. "Thoreau in Today's America," *Masses & Mainstream*, 7 (December 1954), 1-9. This article is a reprint from *Looking Forward* (New York: International Publishers, 1954), pp. 153-164. Like the Marxists of the thirties, Sillen cites Thoreau's deficiencies from a Marxist point of view, but he maintains that "Thoreau's sense of social responsibility may well be emulated today, whatever the specific fallacies of his solutions" (p. 5). See also Adam Lapin, "On the 135th Anniversary of Henry Thoreau," *The Worker*, January 27, 1952, p. 7.

29. Louis Adamic et al., "What Are You Doing Out There?" *New York Times*, January 15, 1951, p. 9. One mild example of the kind of suppression feared by the signers of the *Times* ad concerned Thoreau's reputation and occurred several years after the ad had appeared. Several congressmen objected to having a popular anthology, *Profile of America*, translated for

use abroad by the U.S. Information Service, because the book was "objectionable," "obnoxious" and "not representative of American life and ideals." The evidence offered, among other reasons, was that the anthology contained a passage from *Walden* which was "damaging" and that a photograph of a little red schoolhouse built in 1750 "should not have been included because the communists might say this represents the American school system." The *New York Times* reported and condemned this nonsense on its editorial pages for June 19, 1955, p. 8; and July 8, 1955, p. 22.

30. E.B. White, "Visitors to the Pond," *New Yorker*, May 23, 1953, pp. 28-31.

31. Raymond Adams, "Witnessing *Walden*," *TSB*, 48 (Summer 1954), 1-4.

32. Fourteen years later Adams would discuss direct action when he once again addressed the Thoreau Society concerning, among other topics, civil disobedience and sit-ins in "Thoreau's Return to Concord," *TSB*, 96 (Summer 1966), 1-4. In addition to noting the contribution to justice that civil disobedience had made, Adams warned against the excesses of sit-ins because they are "more active, even aggressive," than Thoreau's version of civil disobedience. His treatment of the topic seems to be more the result of his times than a personal identification with protesters: "I wish sometimes that they [protesters] would read more of Thoreau than the essay on civil disobedience. If they would read *Walden* until they get well into the second chapter, they would come upon this sentence which I warmly recommend to them — and the warmer the more I recommend it: 'I got up early and bathed in the pond; that was a religious exercise, and one of the best things which I did' " (p. 1). Although Adams discusses civil disobedience as a strategy, it is evident that, basically, he would prefer — as he did in 1954 — that protesters have "their very lives cleansed and emboldened" by *Walden* and the pond.

33. Willard Thorp, "Thoreau's Huckleberry Party," *TSB*, 40 (Summer 1952), 4.

34. Edyth Walker, "Walden — A Calming Influence," *TSB*, 42 (Winter 1953), 1-2.

35. Leonard Gray, "The Growth of Thoreau's Reputation," *TSB*, 42 (Winter 1953), 4. For similar representative views of Thoreau as a useful answer to the problem of the individual's relationship to society during the period see: Joseph Ishill et al., *Thoreau: "The Cosmic Yankee": Centennial Appreciations* (Los Angeles: Rocker Publications, 1946); Reginald Cook, "Thoreau in Perspective," *University of Kansas City Review*, 14 (Winter 1947), 117-125. John Haynes Holmes, "Thoreau's 'Civil Disobedience,' " *Christian Century*, June 29, 1949, pp. 787-789; Simeon Stylites, "Paging

Mr. Thoreau," *Christian Century*, December 26, 1951, p. 1505; Rella
Ritchell, "Thoreau: Poet and Philosopher," *TSB*, 41 (Fall 1952), 2-3; William Chapman White, "Get Moving Thoreau!" *New York Herald Tribune*,
July 21, 1953, p. 22; Lewis Leary, "A Century of *Walden*," *Nation*, August
7, 1954, pp. 114-115; E.B. White, "Walden — 1954," *Yale Review*, 44
(Autumn 1954), 13-22; Henry Beetle Hough, *Thoreau of Walden: The Man
and His Eventful Life* (New York: Simon and Schuster, 1956); Samuel Mid-
dlebrook, "Henry David Thoreau," in *Great American Liberals*, ed.
Gabriel R. Mason (Boston: Starr King Press, 1956), pp. 69-79; and, somewhat more skeptically, Albert Roland, "Do-It-Yourself: A Walden for the
Millons? " *American Quarterly*, 10 (Summer 1958), 154-164.

The extent to which Thoreau's reputation — his usefulness — was
jealously guarded by one Thoreauvian can be seen in a seven-page review
by Odell Shepard of Perry Miller's *Consciousness in Concord: The Text of
Thoreau's Hitherto "Lost Journal" (1840-1841) Together with Notes and a
Commentary* (Boston: Houghton Mifflin, 1958). Miller is extremely critical
of what he considers to be Thoreau's egotistical personality and pontifical
way of dealing with people and issues. Shepard is even more critical of
Miller in his bitterly entitled review: "Unconsciousness in Cambridge,"
Emerson Society Quarterly, 13 (Fourth Quarter 1958), 13-19. Shepard
writes that Miller's lengthy review is characterized "by frequent inaccuracies of statement, by assertions unproved and unprovable, by confusions
and inconsistencies of thought, by the dragging-in of matters wholly ad-
ventitious, and by the use and abuse of violent language in a prose style
habitually feeble, fumbling, slovenly and dull" (p. 14). Shepard does not
like Miller's book, and he does not like Miller either: ". . . himself [Miller]
unremarkable as an exemplar of certain Christian virtues, he brings the
charge of 'blasphemy' against" Thoreau (p. 15). Miller may be off the
mark, but Shepard hits low.

36. Carl Bode notes this tendency in "Thoreau the Actor," *American
Quarterly*, 5 (Fall 1953), 247-252. For discussions of Thoreau's reception
outside the United States see Eugene F. Timpe, ed., *Thoreau Abroad:
Twelve Bibliographical Essays* (Hamden, Conn.: Archon Books, 1971).
The essays deal with Thoreau's influence in England, France, the
Netherlands, Germany, Switzerland, Italy, Bohemia, Russia, Israel, India,
Japan, and Austria.

37. "Thoreau's Proposals for Legislation," *American Quarterly*, 7 (Fall
1955), 285-290.

38. Another brief treatment which tends to homogenize Thoreau for the
fifties will be found in Louis B. Salomon's "Practical Thoreau," *College
English*, 17 (January 1956), 229-232. Salomon argues against what he re-

gards as the popular misconception that Thoreau was a smug impractical hermit who did not recognize the value of organized society and government or the benefits of commerce and machinery. For a discussion of Salomon's article, a discussion which does not so much refute him as agree with him from a different perspective, see Wade C. Thompson, "The Impractical Thoreau," *College English*, 19 (November 1957), 67-70. The way to defend Thoreau's individualism, writes Thompson, is "not to present Thoreau as 'practical,' but to present Thoreau as an exaggerator" (p. 69).

On a less academic level, two representative examples of Thoreau being absorbed into the period can be seen in editorial comments in "Management Man," *Nation's Business* (February 1949), which describes Thoreau as having "the mind of a man who makes a good management engineer," because he "abhorred waste of time and energy"; and in "Freedom and the Individual," *Christian Science Monitor* (October 28, 1952), which argues that Thoreau would have paid his taxes to support the Korean War. Since 1941 the *Thoreau Society Bulletins* have diligently recorded many of the perverted distortions of Thoreau in American popular culture. An index to his popularity is that since the forties he has frequently appeared in advertisements (and with curious results): "A Revlon toiletries advertisement in *Business Week* for Aug. 12, 1950, says, 'Most women lead lives of dullness, quiet desperation, and I think cosmetics are a wonderful escape from it' " (cited in *TSB*, 33 [October 1950], 4).

39. *After Walden: Thoreau's Changing Views on Economic Man* (Stanford, Calif.: Stanford University Press, 1957), p. 128.

40. "Civil Disobedience: Principle and Politics," in Hicks, *Thoreau in Our Season*, p. 41.

chapter 5

THOREAU AND THE MOVEMENT TOWARD A NEW AMERICA

If you want to say something hip, turn to Henry
Thoreau.
    From an ad for Bergen Evans' *Dictionary of Quotations* (1968)[1]

Contact! Contact!

Thoreau, *Maine Woods*

After the conservative politics of the 1950s came the deluge. Nearly one hundred years after Appomattox, the United States was again at war with itself. For a number of Americans in the 1960s, especially the young, the rediscovery of poverty and racism, coupled with an awareness that the war in Vietnam represented a travesty of American principles rather than a preservation of those principles, created an intellectual and social milieu geared for the writing of Henry David Thoreau, a milieu in which Thoreau was eagerly read and often quoted. Unlike World War II, the war in Vietnam did not generate a relatively solid conservative consensus among the public. Many refused to believe that the North Vietnamese represented a threat to national security. The Domino Theory used by the White House to justify the escalation of the war was perceived by a significant number of Americans as only a theory — and only a game. In the context of a decade of protestations against war, racism, poverty, materialism, and environmental pollution, Thoreau's social and political reputation rode the crest of wave upon wave of dissent. He had at one time or another said no to all of the right things; his everlasting nay affirmed his significance and relevance for many Americans in the 1960s. He seemed as 100 percent American as Ben Franklin had in previous decades.

Never before had Thoreau enjoyed such popularity. He became important to the reform impulse of the 1960s, and as that impulse spread so too did Thoreau's political reputation. *Walden*, addressed, in part, specifically to students, had finally found its readership. Moreover, Thoreau's attack on materialism in *Walden* was made doubly relevant by the Concord rebel's repudiation of unjust government in "Civil Disobedience," perhaps the most widely known American essay of the decade. These works may have elicited only a frown in his own time, but they would have projected him onto a television screen in the sixties. Thoreau was IN. This chapter examines how he arrived there and the social engagements arranged for him.

In 1955 Bruce E. Burdett, a student of Thoreau's reputation, could justly point out that although Thoreau's writings were relevant to mid-twentieth-century America, he would very likely remain an obscure writer in terms of popular culture.[2] Burdett could not have foreseen, of course, the events of the sixties that were to change the tone and style of American life. His perspective was necessarily informed by his own present moment, a moment in which relatively few Americans were interested in Thoreau's social and political thought, because as Burdett points out, they were too busy being abundant, prosperous, and fully employed (p. 86). As much as the man in the grey flannel suit living his orderly corporate life has become a cliché to describe the life style and the aspirations of the fifties, there is, nevertheless, an archetype behind the cliché. These values prevailed among the young as well as the middle aged.

At the 1956 annual meeting of the Thoreau Society, Herbert F.

West of Dartmouth College delivered an address on what he called the younger generation's response to Thoreau.[3] West polled his students on some of Thoreau's social and political ideas and found that most of them "agreed that individualism is on the wane and conformity is not only fashionable but almost a necessity if one is to get on." In addition to being concerned about themselves and their ability "to get on," the students also expressed an unwilling- ness to see the corporate, social fabric torn. Eighty percent of West's students felt that the "anarchistic attitude" expressed in "Civil Disobedience" was "harmful": "One must not, cannot, obey the 'moral law within' the students feel, but must make obeisance to the laws of the land, whether it concerns conscientious objection or any other moral decision." Although West's sampling was ex- tremely small, his findings were typical. Short-haired, clean- shaven, and tied and jacketed, most students of the fifties found Thoreau to be more of a threat to their values than an eloquent ex- pression of them. Dissension was not fashionable then.

That fashion began to change in 1956, however, the moment that Rosa Parks boarded a Cleveland Avenue bus in Montgomery, Ala- bama, and, obeying the moral law within, took a vacant seat in the front of the bus. She refused to give up her seat to a white man and was arrested. She said no, and her refusal generated the career of Martin Luther King, a movement, and, in a sense, the first page of a social history of the 1960s. Henry David Thoreau had a friend in Rosa Parks, and, more directly, a disciple in Martin Luther King.

The Montgomery bus boycott of 1956 was the first nationally significant direct action taken by American blacks. Recounting the episode in detail two years later, King wrote in *Stride Toward Free- dom* that initially he had doubts concerning the morality of the boycott, but after thinking about Thoreau's "Civil Disobedience" he "remembered how, as a college student, I had been moved when I first read this work. I became convinced that what we were pre- paring to do in Montgomery was related to what Thoreau had ex- pressed. We were simply saying to the white community, 'We can no longer lend our cooperation to an evil system.' "[4] Mentioning that he had reread "Civil Disobedience" several times, King de- scribed the essay as his "first intellectual contact with the theory of nonviolent resistance" (p. 91). King was one of the first members of the civil rights movement to cite Thoreau as an inspiration and an ally, and as King gradually gained prominence in the movement so did Thoreau. The man who spent a night in the Concord jail had earlier been linked to nonviolent resistance and the black person's struggle for freedom in the United States, but before King there had never been a highly visible popular movement to sustain the connection so that "Civil Disobedience" would be perceived as relevant to a large number of contemporary Americans. Indeed, even a writer who praised "Civil Disobedience" in the year of the Montgomery boycott did not perceive the relevance of nonviolent resistance in the United States, because the civil rights movement was barely underway; Thoreau's social and political thought was for exportation:

Undoubtedly, the future will witness further use of the principle of civil disobedience, as conceived by Thoreau and perfected by Gandhi. The power of oppressed peoples everywhere, even in the ruthless dictatorships of modern times, can make itself felt through these means. A current example is the fight of the colored races of South Africa against the Strijdorn government — a renewal of Gandhi's crusade. [5]

There is no mention of the United States. As an approving editorial in the *Nation's Business* made clear in the early fifties, Thoreau's popularity during the period was predicated on his relationship to nature, his desire to "transact some private business," and his escape from worrying about the uncertain "fate of the entire world."[6] Thoreau was popular in the United States during the 1950s largely because he was perceived as apolitical rather than political.

By the end of the 1950s, when Thoreau's "Civil Disobedience" was more widely known and associated with the civil rights movement, the debate concerning the efficacy of civil disobedience as a strategy for blacks naturally included discussions of the essay as well. Homage was not always paid to Thoreau; occasionally he was attacked. One such negative treatment by Ernest Earnest challenged the principle of an individual's moral conscience superseding the laws of the state, because the same argument could be used, according to Earnest, to support segregation. He particularly takes "college professors" to task for claiming Thoreau as a civil rights advocate, because

The intellectual who praises Thoreau as a political thinker is about as realistic as the exurbanite who believes himself to be a spiritual inhabitant of Walden. Both are victims of their own neurotic compulsions and of Thoreau's charming literary style. The fact remains that Henry Thoreau is the spiritual ancestor of Governor Orval Faubus. [7]

Earnest argues that Thoreau and Faubus are both wrong in principle, because neither would accept a "compromise between conflicting views." Earnest's critique of Thoreau is not significant because it contributes anything new to the issue; instead, it is important because it comes just before a moment in Thoreau criticism when Thoreau would be widely celebrated and elevated precisely because he would not *compromise*, a word that would become an epithet in the sixties. For Americans who had grown weary of the conventions and conformity of the fifties, Thoreau was a welcome relief.

As the fifties ended, Thoreau's name was more frequently linked to an American literary tradition of dissension and rebellion which placed him beside writers such as Dreiser, Steinbeck, Ginsberg, Kerouac, and Mailer. John P. Sisk, in an article tracing a subversive tradition in American literature that led up to the Beats, described Thoreau as an "ideal subversive," because Thoreau "both states and is civil disobedience" as a result of his life style and his writing. Sisk praised the Beats, Thoreau, and other writers in the subversive tradition, because they refused to compromise their principles. [8]

While the country moved toward the confrontations that would erupt at lunch counters, universities, and street demonstrations in the sixties, Thoreau criticism began to make efforts to place in focus King's use of "Civil Disobedience." In order to do that it was time, as Paul Lauter suggested in 1959, to shed new light on Thoreau. Lauter, in an essay review of several books on Thoreau (including Perry Miller's *Consciousness in Concord* and Sherman Paul's *The Shores of America*), complained that current criticism, typified by Paul and Miller, tended to overemphasize Thoreau's prose art and that Miller accented too heavily the "gloomy, morbid and perverse" in Thoreau's character. The attention paid to Thoreau's personality and his literary artistry "unwisely tended to neglect the Concord writer's concern with social action."[9] Lauter's point was that criticism ought to take into consideration a writer's intentions — and the tensions of the critic's own times. In the sixties there were many critics who did. This is not to say that there was a dearth of studies concerning Thoreau's literary artistry during the decade (indeed, one critic read his social criticism as lyric poetry), but there were many more discussions concerning the meaning and relevance of his social and political thought than there had been in the fifties.[10]

In 1960 the *Emerson Society Quarterly* invited a number of college professors to share briefly with their readers effective methods of teaching Thoreau to undergraduates. Of the ten or so articles offering approaches to Thoreau, there was nearly an even split in emphasizing either a formalistic approach or a content-oriented approach to his work. Although none of the professors denied the importance of either form or content in Thoreau's writing, there was a tendency to express a preference for one or the other. John C. Broderick, for example, placed his emphasis on the necessity for an "understanding of the *genre* in which Thoreau works":

Certainly the ideas of Thoreau must be understood and confronted, but only (or primarily) as they exist in a literary medium. My own conviction is that separate consideration of Thoreau's ideas should emerge at a very late stage in undergraduate study and that even graduate students should be taught to consider Thoreau primarily as a literary man, a craftsman working in a specific medium.[11]

Broderick represents the drift of Thoreau criticism since F.O. Matthiessen's *American Renaissance* (1941) and Stanley Edgar Hyman's 1946 essay, "Henry Thoreau in Our Time." The paramount issue in Thoreau's writings is perceived by Broderick to be the style, not the issues.

In contrast to Broderick's emphasis is Walter Harding's approach to Thoreau, an approach which accents the importance of what

Thoreau has to say rather than how he says it: ". . . while Thoreau is unquestionably eminently important as a stylist, he is far more important as a thinker. His primary appeal to the student should be (and usually is) as a philosopher rather than as an artist." [12] This statement is consistent with Harding's abiding interest (but not the sole interest) in Thoreau as part of a usable American past. He tends to use Thoreau in order to understand the present, whereas those primarily interested in Thoreau's art have a tendency to use the past in order to understand Thoreau's style by placing his style in a historical literary context. Neither approach is necessarily mutually exclusive, but the attitudes that Harding and Broderick express are, in a broad sense, indicative of two of the major approaches to Thoreau in the sixties. The formalistic approach was limited to academic treatments of Thoreau, but the concern with Thoreau's ideas went well beyond the walls of university classrooms and libraries. In a decade characterized by controversy, it is not surprising that Thoreau's social and political ideas fascinated the popular imagination and many an academic's too.

Brooks Atkinson, a columnist for the *New York Times* during the sixties, serves as a useful introduction to Thoreau's popular reputation. Atkinson, who had described Thoreau's politics thirty-three years earlier as "unworthy of the poet who sang of Nature in *Walden*," describes the relevance of "Civil Disobedience" without any disapproval; like Atkinson, the times had changed:

It [civil disobedience] is the technique of the sit-in demonstrations by Negroes in the South today. The pacifists who scramble aboard nuclear submarines are acting on the same principle; also the Quakers who defiantly sailed into the part of the Pacific isolated by the United States administrative order for the explosion of nuclear bombs. [13]

It would be difficult to overemphasize how much Thoreau's "Civil Disobedience" was in the air in the early sixties for those involved in protest groups or interested in them. In 1960 Thoreau's name was not only in the air but also on the sea — a rowboat used to picket nuclear submarines in Groton, Connecticut, was named *Henry David Thoreau*, a name which also made its way into a pri-

son by way of Reverend Willard Uphaus, who refused to provide
the state of New Hampshire's subversive activities investigators
with names; he went to jail with a volume of Thoreau's "Civil Disobedience" as a companion.[14] In addition, his name was enshrined
in New York City. Thoreau was finally elected to the New York
University Hall of Fame in 1960 after a successful campaign spon-
sored by the Thoreau Society. It was not necessary, as it had been
in 1945, for Walter Harding to defend Thoreau's eligibility for election when it had been challenged by someone who felt that Thoreau had wrongfully seceded from the Union by writing "Civil Disobedience." Harding aptly pointed out that Robert E. Lee had been
elected to the Hall of Fame in 1900 — in the first election.[15] Fifteen
years after Harding's witty reply, there was less of a need to defend
"Civil Disobedience" on so basic a level, for the nation was less in-
sistent on union than it had been in 1945 when unity was required
to meet the exigencies of the war.

The single most famous fact of Thoreau's life had once been perceived as his going off to Walden Pond in order to drive life into a
corner; in the sixties that was superseded by Thoreau's night spent
in jail in order to drive the government into a corner. For many, the
cell as much as the cabin represented the locus of Thoreau's values.
One critic neatly summed up the shift in perspective with the title of
his article on Thoreau: "Civil Disobedience: The Way to Walden."[16] This emphasis would have met with a cold reception during the 1920s, World War II, and the 1950s, when challenging the
government was frequently equated with disloyalty; but by 1962
there was enough interest in Thoreau's social and political thought
for the *Massachusetts Review* to devote almost an entire issue to
"what a Thoreau relevant to our day and predicament looks
like."[17] The interest in Thoreau's social and political thought can
be explained in broad terms: Americans were generally becoming
more sensitive to social and political problems; the Kennedy administration helped to quicken in many Americans the reformist
impulse that was mostly dormant in the fifties, and as Americans
looked to the future for new frontiers it was not surprising that
some were borne back into the past in search of a voice commensurate to the vision. Several of the pieces in the *Massachusetts Review*

attempt to measure how accurately Thoreau's voice matches the reformist vision of the sixties.

The collection is, according to its editor, John H. Hicks,

the first to have documented the immediacy of Thoreau's relevance for intellectuals and strategists of the Negro revolution in America; and for those — in South Africa, Denmark, America and elsewhere — committed to the cause of civil liberties in the twentieth century turmoil of war, of the superstate and police state, of vast changes social and political. (p. 1)

Included in the collection are personal statements which serve as testimonials on the relevancy of Thoreau's social and political thought and also critical discussions which either support or repudiate his relevance.

Hicks provides in his 1966 introduction a useful and succinct overview of the articles, and in doing so he notes the often discussed shift in Thoreau's position of passive nonresistance in "Civil Disobedience" to his later support of John Brown's violence. Although Hicks praises the collection for its balance and the place made in it for "substantial demurrer" among the contributors concerning the applicability of Thoreau's ideas (p. 9), it is clear, — given that "more Americans are finding sanction in Thoreau's 'Civil Disobedience' than ever before" (even more so in 1966 than in 1962, when the essays were first published), — that Hicks chooses to play down the problem of violence in his introduction by referring to the dualism in Thoreau which makes him appealing "to causes militant and pacifistic alike" as a "philosophical and tactical flexibility." This phrase is a euphemism for the contradiction that can be seen in Thoreau's vacillating movement from a firm belief in the efficacy of the moral law to his faith in John Brown's means. By minimizing this contradiction, indeed, by transforming it into a virtuous "flexibility," Hicks attempts to make Thoreau more appealing and relevant. In the next sentence it is suggested that Thoreau's "philosophical and tactical flexibility," his eventual championing of violence ʼs a means of reform, "may yet prove vital to inspiring the kind of moral resourcefulness men need for the unprecedented social problems they now face" (p. 7). Here is another euphemism. The phrase "moral resourcefulness" is used as a rhetorical cloak for violence. This use of language is surprising; it is more typical of the Department of Defense in the sixties (an arm of the government once called the War Department), but such usage is made no more acceptable because it comes from an academician rather than a general. What is called to question here is not the hint that violence may be one necessary mode of change for the United States in the sixties; instead, what is objected to is an apparent unwillingness to be forthright. Hicks refuses to declare outright that Thoreau ultimately did support violence (at one point Thoreau's attitude toward violence is described as "ambiguous" [p. 11]), and yet he uses it to reinforce Thoreau's relevance for those who would use violence in the 1960s. Hicks seems to want everyone to find Thoreau relevant. [18]

Had Hicks dealt more openly with the issue of violence, he might have found himself questioning Thoreau's relevance for some of the writers in the collection. He might have felt it necessary to point out that the first piece in the collection by Martin Luther King refers to only one aspect of Thoreau's approach to reform. King uses "Civil Disobedience" to characterize Thoreau and freedom rides and peaceful protests and bus boycotts, but he never mentions Thoreau's interest in John Brown. [19] His Thoreau is a mirror image of his own values. Thoreau was constant in his inability to endure injustices patiently, but he was not constant in his assessment of the way in which evil must be resisted. King was not alone in this assumption; it has always been assumed that Thoreau meant "Civil Disobedience" more than he did "A Plea for Captain John Brown" or "Slavery in Massachusetts." One reason for this is that nonviolent resistance is generally a more socially acceptable and assimilated mode of reform than violence; consequently, the image of Thoreau as a pacifist is more useful than his image as a reformer who is willing, at least on paper, not only to die but also to kill for a cause. Official sanction was awarded Thoreau as a pacifist, but his support of Brown's violence was officially ignored. It is necessary to go beyond the essays momentarily in *Thoreau in Our Season* in order to demonstrate this.

One of the greetings read to those who had gathered at the New York Hall of Fame in 1962 to unveil the Thoreau bust in commemoration of Thoreau's death was a brief telegram which praised the selection of Braj Kumar Nehru, ambassador to the United States from India, as the principal speaker, because Ambassador Nehru's presence reflected "Thoreau's pervasive and universal influence on social thinking and political action." The influence referred to, of course, is Gandhi's program of nonviolent resistance. The telegram was signed: "With all best wishes. John F. Kennedy." [20] Implicit in Nehru's presence was a perception of Thoreau's social thinking and political action that linked Thoreau to a commitment to both social justice and a peaceful approach to reform. A liberal president can afford to tolerate some nonviolent civil disobedience, but no president can endure a John Brown.

Thoreau's reputation as a pacifist was sustained throughout the decade, because few Americans wanted to entertain the notion that, as one black militant put it, violence was as American as cherry pie. Most reformers wanted a peaceful revolution. Many commentators on Thoreau were content to view his relationship to Brown as little more than eccentric. A summary statement by one critic, Herbert L. Carson, is fairly typical of the way in which Thoreau's support of violence is defused; Carson finds it merely "surprising" that "this sensitive exponent of non-violence spoke so directly and passionately in favor of the militant John Brown." [21] The word "surprising" is, in effect, an instrument used to dismiss the significance of Thoreau's action; it is no more adequate to describe Thoreau than it would be in reference to Martin Luther King if he had become an advocate of urban guerrilla warfare. Yet given the attention that the politics of the sixties focused upon the Thoreau of "Civil Disobedience" and despite Thoreau's own warning in the essay that "peaceable revolution" may not be "possible" (*Reform Papers*, p. 76), he was perceived by the majority of commentators as essentially nonviolent in his approach toward reform. Indeed, Lewis Leary has noted that in 1969 "Civil Disobedience" was reprinted as a "peace calendar" which included photographs of contemporary protest demonstrations. Thoreau was part of everyday life in the sixties for innumerable supporters of nonviolent reform. [22]

Another personal testimony in *Thoreau in Our Season* affirming
the relevance of "Civil Disobedience" for the 1960s immediately
follows King's, and it too discusses the debt that the civil rights
movement owes to Thoreau. William Stuart Nelson, then vice-
president of Howard University, explains, among other things,
what nonviolent resistance involves. He stresses nonviolence as a
strategy, and embedded in his discussion is a curious defense of
Thoreau's support of Brown. It is curious because instead of con-
fronting the dilemma that Thoreau's support represents in terms of
nonviolent resistance, Nelson raises the problem and then obfus-
cates the entire matter by seeming to address himself to the issue,
when in fact he turns his back on it. The following two paragraphs
are complete and represent Nelson's treatment of the dilemma:

Thoreau saw through the crust of John Brown's violence, a
violence which Brown had learned from thousands of years of
pagan and Christian history and the practice of his own time.
Thoreau, penetrating that crust, identified himself with the
spirit of the man which sought the overthrow of an evil system.

The lesson here is that in a movement motivated by genuine non-violence, such as inspires the current resistance to
racial injustice in America, men risk their lives not for beliefs
but for *passionate* beliefs, beliefs in which intellectual accord
has been deepened by spiritual identification. [23]

No justification can be made for violence simply because it is
"thousands of years" old, and Nelson, realizing this, only
half-heartedly offers it as an argument. The question for "a movement motivated by genuine non-violence" is not whether people
who spiritually identify with a passionate belief are willing to risk
their lives but whether or not such people should kill — or support
killing — for those beliefs. Nelson does not play very closely to the
horns of the dilemma. The second paragraph does not reconcile or
explain Thoreau's endorsement of Brown's violence; indeed, it
seems to have nothing to do with it at all. Possibly, Nelson sensed
this himself, for in an expanded version of this essay delivered two

years later as an address to the Thoreau Society he deleted the second paragraph. [24]

In the expanded and revised version, Nelson does not deal with the issue in any greater detail, but neither does he give the impression that he has resolved it. He omits speaking of an explicit "lesson" to be learned from Thoreau's support of Brown. Nelson flatly states that "Thoreau was not a pacifist" (p. 3), and he quotes Thoreau to the effect that he would, in certain circumstances, both die and kill for a cause. This seems to be offered simply as information, and yet Nelson, without reservation or qualification, places Thoreau, Gandhi, and King in the same tradition of nonviolent resistance (p. 2). This paradox makes no sense until Nelson's assessment of the black person's position in America is taken into account.

Throughout the address Nelson points out that blacks have already waited too long for full citizenship and equal human rights in the United States. Although he expresses hope and faith that the country will right these injustices, he ends with a warning that threads its way through the address when he says that America must soon meet its responsibilities to all people because the "gods of destruction . . . must not be tempted too often. It may be the fire next time" (p. 3). Nelson's point, though implicit, is clear enough: any man—even a Thoreau committed to the principles of civil disobedience — can be pushed too far. Two years earlier, Nelson had strongly emphasized Brown's willingness to die in behalf of a just cause; he did not at all accent Brown's readiness to kill for it. In 1964, after two more years of the civil rights movement, a euphoric March on Washington that produced more good feeling than genuine reform, and the assassination of President Kennedy, Nelson seems to suggest that it is America that must resolve the paradox of Thoreau's support of violence. While Nelson presents Thoreau as a voice that civil rights workers would do well to heed in their efforts to generate reform nonviolently, he also seems to offer Thoreau as an archetype of what they might ultimately have to resort to if the country is deaf to that voice. For Thoreau, "passive resistance was not enough where wrong was rampant" (p. 3), and since Thoreau is presented as worthy of emulation, there is, after all, an implicit lesson here for civil rights workers. But in 1962 Nelson's faith in the efficacy of nonviolent resistance was apparently firmer, and so he emphasized an image of Thoreau that was ready to be self-sacrificing in the name of justice rather than to make sacrifices of others in the name of righteousness. It was this self-sacrificing Thoreau who was most often invoked in the early sixties, and although many commentators depicted Thoreau as an advocate of nonviolent reform while a few others called attention to his interest in John Brown's methods, most commentators who used Thoreau agreed that he was an indigenous prototype for the contemporary activist committed to social change. Just as Thoreau had looked to the past and the Declaration of Independence for one of his precedents, so too did many dissenters of the sixties look to Thoreau for theirs.

Staughton Lynd, a well-known activist and historian who was deeply committed to the civil rights and antiwar movements of the sixties, furthered Thoreau's political reputation by stamping the New Left seal of approval upon him in an article published in *Liberation* several months after the *Massachusetts Review* had devoted almost an entire number to Thoreau's social thought. The 1963 article was entitled "Henry Thoreau: The Admirable Radical," and Lynd found him to be precisely that in a monthly magazine that has been described as primarily "pacifist, radical and libertarian in tone."[25]

Lynd begins his treatment of Thoreau's radicalism with a brief assessment of his reputation; he introduces Thoreau as one who "has become the patron saint of new radicals and of all unadjusted Americans" ("unadjusted" in the sense that they will not compromise their values). His aim, however, is not simply to cite the various individuals and groups that use Thoreau as a "Gospel and Baedeker" for reform; Lynd's purpose is to examine the "nature of Thoreau's dissent," because, from Lynd's point of view, it is still misunderstood, since Thoreau is often regarded as a pacifist and an anarchist. Lynd discusses Thoreau's support of Brown in order to demonstrate that he did not shun violence when employed in a just cause; "What Gandhi took from Thoreau was not pacifism . . . but the concept of civil disobedience" (p. 21). Thoreau's alleged anarchism is also refuted with references to his willingness to support better, more just governments. Rejecting Thoreau's popular image as either a pacifist or an anarchist, Lynd offers him to his readers as a "revolutionary" activist who must be perceived "whole" in order to be understood and, it is implied, used. If Thoreau is seen as a whole, his life at the pond is not antithetical to his political life. His "passion for the water-lily and his concern for the auction block" are then perceived as complementary rather than contradictory (pp. 22-23). What unifies the naturalist and the reformer in Thoreau is his insistence on direct action. [26]

Lynd argues that "what was central for Thoreau was neither nonviolence nor civil disobedience but direct action: the absolute demand that one practice — right now, and all alone if necessary — what one preaches" (pp. 25-26). Going to the pond was as much an act of social rebellion as civil disobedience or John Brown's raid. Lynd does not make an issue of the means of reform, because he is interested in gathering "non-aligned individuals" of the new radicalism under one umbrella in order that they might discover what unites them — their insistence on direct action as a response to injustice. Lynd sees this insistence as "the essential quality of the new radicalism"; the rest is peripheral: "Would it not be more truthful for the young radicals [of today] to say that they believe in nonviolence when possible, civil disobedience if necessary, but direct personal action in all cases whatsoever? That was Thoreau's view . . ." (p. 26). Lynd sees no "inconsistency" or "hypocrisy" in Thoreau's writing on these matters, but that is because he flattens the landscape of Thoreau's thinking and emotions. If Thoreau was anything, he was radically inconsistent. Taking his support of Brown in 1859 as an example — particularly appropriate here — it is possible for one to look back to a younger Thoreau who confidently writes in his journal for 1842 that "The moral law does not want any champion. Its asserters do not go to war" (*Journal*, I, 334). Thoreau does not qualify this with an escape clause such as "when possible." Nor is his "direct personal action in all cases whatsoever" manifested in his weary response to the conflict between the North and South that had just begun in 1861. Thoreau's letter to Parker Pillsbury, an abolitionist friend of the family, is remarkable for its escape clauses: "I do not so much regret the present condition of things in this country (provided I regret it at all) as I do that I ever heard of it." Thoreau goes so far as to counsel Pillsbury that the only fatal weapon that one can direct against evil is to ignore it. Lynd's paragon of direct action is capable here of little more than some grumpy rumblings about "Fort Sumpter, and Old Abe, and all that" before quickly turning to *Six Years in the Deserts of North America*, reading it as hard as he can, in order to quench his thirst for spirit and to "counterbalance" the New York *Tribune*.27

Lynd's attempts to make Thoreau relevant to the new radicalism of the sixties are not entirely convincing; his version of Thoreau as a revolutionary activist "stripped for action" (p. 26) is a Thoreau also stripped of complexity and, some might want to add, confusion. Lynd is reductive in his treatment of Thoreau, and it is understandable why he is, because his purpose is to offer an American writer with whom all activists can identify in a common cause aimed directly against injustices everywhere, whether it is "refusing to torture Algerians, hurling bricks at Soviet tanks, clambering aboard Polaris submarines, [or] choosing jail without bail in Mississippi" (p. 25). When one's constituency is so broad, it is not wise to make too many distinctions, and Lynd does not. It is entirely possible to support the morality and sense of personal commitment that informs the function of Lynd's article while at the same time recognizing that his purpose in invoking Thoreau as a revolutionary activist is to get his readers first on their feet rather than on their toes. His description of Thoreau is designed to offer a precedent for urging his readers off the fence, not onto one, and, as Lynd writes elsewhere on the function of his work, his ideal reader, the "critic of the American present," wants something more satisfying than "detached analysis"; his reader "wants history to do something more than caution against complete commitment." 28

Lynd's efforts to create a sense of solidarity among radicals by using social activism as a rallying point rather than Thoreau's alleged pacifism or his support of Brown is an attempt, as he explained in a defense of the article, "to point to something in our own lives: the tension between an absolute ethic and the demands of social revolution." 29 Although Lynd is an "advocate of the nonviolent idea," 30 he, like William Stuart Nelson, does not reject violence categorically if it becomes a necessary means of stopping injustice which is violently imposed. Lynd is less concerned with ultimate strategies than with the required tactics of the moment, and that is how he perceives Thoreau:

> If one is convinced that anarcho-pacifism on the one hand, or violent revolution on the other, is The Answer, then Thoreau's faith may well seem an unsatisfactory "halfway covenant." But if one feels (as I do) that both contain essential truth, then Thoreau's lonely struggle looms large as example and inspiration. [31]

Lynd avoids diluting Thoreau's full-strength support of Brown's methods even though it runs counter to the popular view of Thoreau as a pacifist.

Two of the published responses to Lynd's article demonstrate, once again, that there is a strong tendency to preserve Thoreau's reputation as a nonviolent reformer. One writer concedes to Lynd that Thoreau's "enthusiasm" for Brown was "a rather serious departure," but she then insists that the reason he "momentarily" supported violence was because Thoreau was most impressed with "Brown's willingness to risk his [own] neck in a direct confrontation with evil." [32] She brings Brown's hanging, not his killing, into focus in an attempt to soften the image of Thoreau as a spokesman for violent reform. Another commentator who objects to Lynd's treatment of Thoreau poses his Thoreau in a pacifistic background by superimposing an extraordinarily loose definition of pacifism into the picture. He argues that Thoreau's support of Brown

> is comparable to the support some pacifists today give to Castro or Robert Williams. Pacifists are not so much critical of violence as they are of systems or philosophies which depend upon violence for their existence, and they will not hesitate to stand behind forceful revolutionaries, while at the same time offering nonviolent solutions. [33]

This approach to pacifism overlooks the fact that it is principally a *mode* of reform. In addition to this objection, one might also ask where Thoreau offers a nonviolent solution in "A Plea for Captain John Brown."

The strongest response to Lynd's article is written by Truman Nelson (not to be confused with William Stuart Nelson already discussed), who, rather than questioning Lynd's critical examination of Thoreau's pacifist credentials, objects to what he believes to be Lynd's hesitancy to proclaim "the full gospel of Thoreau's message," which to Nelson is a violent one. [34] An advocate of violent revolution whose model is John Brown rather than Gandhi, Nelson takes Lynd to task for not being consistent in his treatment of Thoreau's support of Brown. Lynd, writes Nelson, describes Thoreau as nonpacifistic, but he then wonders "why Lynd has to drag the name of Martin Luther King [and other pacifists] into the reflected glory of Thoreau's aura and does not mention Robert Williams or William Worthy" (p. 23), both of whom had pledged themselves to violent resistance in the name of freedom for the black person in America. Nelson is eager to disassociate Thoreau from "the standard [pacifist] heroes of genteel radicalism, the ones that are *always* mentioned" in connection with Thoreau and to replace them with names such as Jomo Kenyatta, W.E.B. DuBois, and Fidel Castro (p. 24). Nelson's use of Thoreau is one of the few treatments of his support of violence that positively accents Thoreau's willingness to employ dynamite and guns to usher justice into the world. Nelson's was a minority report, but he saw to it that his position on Thoreau at least had to be taken into consideration by the majority view.

When the *Massachusetts Review* articles that had originally appeared in 1962 were collected in book form as *Thoreau in Our Season* in 1966, there were two essays added to the book. One of them was by Truman Nelson, and it was entitled "Thoreau and John Brown." History, as well as Nelson, helped to put it there. Between 1962 and 1966 violence continued to rip its way to the surface of American life: in addition to President Kennedy, Malcolm X and numerous civil rights workers were assassinated; Harlem and Watts were torn by riots; and a plot to blow up the Statue of Liberty, the Washington Monument, and the Liberty Bell was uncovered. [35] None of these events can be equated except to say that violence informed them and that they represent one aspect of the mood of the period that would make Thoreau's interest in Brown seem relevant. Symbolic action was becoming for some less of a

means of calling attention to an injustice than it was a means of an-
nihilating it.

Truman Nelson discusses Thoreau from the perspective of a
white middle-aged radical who is convinced that the injustices
heaped upon blacks in the United States of the sixties are cause
enough for the fire next time to be Now. In *The Right of Revolution*
(1968), a book which serves as a summary statement of Nelson's
sense of outrage and passionate conviction that conditions in
America warrant a black revolution, he uses John Brown as a
touchstone in order to measure his reader's commitment to justice.
He begins the book with several quotations that call attention to
Brown's means as much as his cause; here are two of them: (1) "If
you are for me and my problem — when I say me, I mean *us*, our
people — then you have to be willing to do as old John Brown did"
(Malcolm X, *Malcolm X Speaks*); (2) "If you can't see yourself as
being in the context of John Brown, then bring me the guns" (H.
Rap Brown, *National Guardian*, November 4, 1967).[36] Like Lynd,
Nelson believes that "History is on our side, if we know how to use
it" (p. 121). Looking back for precedents that establish the right to
revolt, Nelson finds many, and among them is Thoreau. He em-
phasizes the political writings that came after "Civil Disobedience."
The title of his last chapter is a quotation from "Slavery in
Massachusetts" which succinctly expresses his own position on
what he perceives as the necessary means of reform: "I NEED NOT
SAY WHAT MATCH I WOULD TOUCH, WHAT SYSTEM EN-
DEAVOR TO BLOW UP" (p. 131).

In his article in *Thoreau in Our Season*, Nelson raids the nonviolent camp of the civil rights movement to liberate what he considers
to be a more mature Thoreau from the limitations of peaceful resistance: "If there are any doubts that Thoreau rejected non-resistance
and even passive resistance, his position toward John Brown has
blasted them forever."[37] "Rejected" is a carefully chosen word to
describe Thoreau's later stand on nonviolence. Nelson states his
case in strong terms; he is purposely blunt so that there is no mistake about the meaning he sees in Thoreau's support of the survey-
or from Kansas: "Brown tried to get people to do what they did not
want to do. They fought back and he killed them" (p. 136). Nelson's prose gets down to the real thing. He does not embarrass

those who might agree with him or confuse those who do not with euphemistic abstractions about "moral resourcefulness." He keeps his matches on the table.

While tracing Thoreau's interest in slavery, Nelson praises the "revolutionary incitements" of "Civil Disobedience," an essay which leaves "none of the sacred cows unscathed," but he is critical of its individualistic approach to issues because the "completely self-orbed transcendentalist-individualist" is estranged from collective action and the specific needs of the people. But with "Slavery in Massachusetts" Nelson sees a "profound revolutionary growth" in Thoreau's tactics, because the staunch transcendental individualist is now addressing himself to what Thoreau calls in the essay the "united sentiment of the people" and is urging them to eliminate slavery and all its trappings no matter what means are necessary to achieve abolition (pp. 138-140). After quoting Thoreau's statement concerning his readiness to blow up the system if need be, Nelson speculates on it ("one of the most violent statements ever written") and suggests that Thoreau could have used the mood of the 1960s as much as it could use him:

There is no telling what would have happened to Thoreau as a writer and as a man if he had been approached directly after his inflammatory speech by some of the breed of youth we see around today on picket lines, sit-ins, sleep-ins, teach-ins, or traveling perilously to Mississippi or Cuba. If some of these, in the blue jeans and sneakers of that day had come and said, "Like man we want to enforce the law when the government breaks it," he might have been, in the realm of action, much more than Captain of a Huckleberry Party. At least, for once, he would have had a direct reply to one of his rare collective proposals. (p. 143)

Nelson's point — aside from wondering how Thoreau would have reacted — is that although Thoreau did not have a radical audience in 1854, it is not too late to respond to him in 1966 "in this accursed racist country where the black man still has no rights that the white man has to respect" (p. 152).

Nelson describes Thoreau as tragically unhappy, isolated, and alienated in his later life owing to his rigid individualism, but in his

loyalty to Brown, Thoreau was capable of "an exalted form of individualism which merges into universality and becomes one with
it." The universality to which Thoreau ascends emanates from the
aspirations of men and women whose "broad shoulders" elevate
the selfless revolutionary as a symbol of the "broad base below
him" (p. 152). In spite of his rigid individualism, Thoreau is for
Nelson a man of the people almost as much as Brown, because
neither man would run away from what had to be done in the name
of justice for all the people:

Revolutions are bloody awful, no one argues that, but things
have to be twice that bloody awful to make them work. This
was the way things were with John Brown and Henry Thoreau. Both were real men in a real world. You have to take
them as that or leave them alone. (p. 153)

This conclusion to the article asserts that if one accepts Thoreau as
relevant to the sixties, then one must also accept revolutionary
violence. Nelson made the same point more firmly at the end of his
1963 article for *Liberation*, in which he insisted that if we reject
what Thoreau praised in Brown, "then Thoreau is the wrong saint
for us and to claim him as our own is a pious fraud." Unless the
tools are going to be put into the hands of those who can use them,
Thoreau is better off left alone. Curiously, Nelson is as exclusive in
his revolutionary use of Thoreau as the pacifists are in their desire
to portray him as nonviolent. [38]
  But few Americans were interested in Thoreau on Nelson's
terms. There was no more of a mandate for Nelson's version of
Thoreau on the domestic scene than there had been in 1964 for
Barry Goldwater's version of foreign policy, a policy nicely summed up in one of his campaign slogans: "extremism in the defense
of liberty is no vice." And despite the increasing violence during the
last half of the sixties, when the Black Panthers carried guns and the
New York Review of Books featured on its front page a diagram for
making Molotov cocktails (August 24, 1967), despite the violent
demonstrations, bombings, and other assorted revolutionary gestures, those who were convinced that violence was both inevitable
and the only way to reform the country's ills were not convinced
that Thoreau was a model for them. It is not difficult to understand

why this was so. Already the hero of the nonviolent protesters, Thoreau was famous for being an individualist rather than a collectivist, and he was probably perceived as being too provincial compared to Fidel Castro, Che Guevara, Ho Chi Minh, or Mao Tse-tung. These were the faces in the wall posters that were to be found in the quarters of militants. It is very likely that most Americans, especially students, who placed Thoreau in a political context did so based on a reading of "Civil Disobedience" rather than "A Plea for Captain John Brown." The latter essay was relatively obscure for college students because it was reprinted with much less frequency than the former in anthologies of American literature. Indeed, it is more accurate to say that it was rarely reprinted. It is quite possible that many students — and certainly the public at large — were not aware that Thoreau had ever come out in support of violent reform. One of the most popular collegiate anthologies devoted entirely to Thoreau's writings provides considerable evidence for the idea that Thoreau's relationship to Brown did not attract very much attention.

The Portable Thoreau, edited and introduced by Carl Bode, was first published in 1947 and had gone through seventeen printings by the end of 1972. In its original edition this widely used collection contained Bode's introduction; several of the nature essays; the complete text of *Walden*; excerpts from *A Week*, *Yankee in Canada*, and *Cape Cod*; some poems, letters, and journal entries; and "Civil Disobedience." The collection was revised once in 1964; the major change was that the letters were dropped to make room for "The Last Days of John Brown" and an epilogue written by Bode which was a reprint of an article he wrote for the *Massachusetts Review* in 1962.[39] The anthology, which according to a description of it by the publisher was intended to be "representative" of Thoreau's entire work, was reprinted for seventeen years before its readers were introduced to Thoreau's writing on John Brown. After seventeen years of a half-hidden Thoreau, even the piece on Brown reprinted was "The Last Days of John Brown," a work written more in sorrow than in anger. Thoreau does not emerge from "The Last Days of John Brown" as an advocate of violence as he does in "A Plea for Captain John Brown." Like many of his colleagues, Bode did not take Thoreau's championing of Brown's means very seriously in a social and political context. This is reflected in Bode's introduction and the epilogue to the 1964 edition.

The only significant revision — and one of the very few revisions — in the 1964 twenty-seven page introduction has to do with Bode's one-paragraph discussion of Thoreau's relationship to John Brown. In the 1947 edition Bode describes Brown as "a fanatic but clearly dedicated to a cause" (p. 25). Bode is not attempting to be humorous; nor is he aware that this description of Brown is tautological. He could not have thought very carefully about Brown and still have come up with such an excuse for fanatical behavior. What fanatic is not "dedicated" to his cause? In the 1964 edition, with the civil rights movement near its peak, the sentence is revised to read: "Brown was a fanatic but in a noble cause" (p. 25). Apparently, Bode had thought some more about Thoreau and Brown, and although he has no reservations about their "noble cause," his epilogue shows him raising some questions and his psychoanalytic eyebrows at Thoreau's support of Brown.

Writing from a Freudian perspective, Bode acknowledges that he draws heavily from an extended Freudian study of Thoreau by Raymond Gozzi. Employing Gozzi's findings, which were based on an analysis of Thoreau's imagery and certain facts of his life, Bode writes on the first page of his analysis that he seeks to demonstrate that "Thoreau was not a normal man — though his writing was the richer for it." [40] Asserting that Thoreau suffered from an unresolved Oedipal problem, Bode argues that "Thoreau never outgrew his mother-fixation" (p. 109), and because of this he was attracted to older women — including "mother-nature." While the "same mother-fixation . . . barred a normal sexual partnership with a woman [it] also prejudiced a normal friendship with a man by charging it with undue emphasis and tension." On an unconscious level Thoreau was plagued by an "incipient homosexuality" (p. 111). As a result of the sexual paralysis generated by a "marked Oedipus complex," Thoreau was compelled to "look for a mother in older women instead of a mate [Lidian Emerson, for example] and look for a father in Emerson (and later in John Brown). It allowed him to compensate, however, by developing an extraordinary aggressiveness and independence; and it allowed him to sublimate through literary creation" (p. 112).

According to Bode, Thoreau coped with the "Oedipal hatred" he felt for his father by channeling it into a hatred of the state. The aggression and independence that might have otherwise been turned on his father were directed instead toward authority in general and a government that supported slavery in particular. Bode accounts for Thoreau's support of Brown by arguing that Thoreau found a "father-substitute" in him; in addition, he could identify with Brown because he was stronger than John Thoreau and because Brown radically rejected authority. "There can be little doubt that the strongest aggressions in him found an outlet through Brown" (p. 114). Bode is able to place Thoreau's nearly lifelong quarrel with the state in this context. Briefly tracing Thoreau's course of action from "Civil Disobedience" to John Brown, Bode charts that movement on an exclusively psychological level:

Fighting audaciously against the state, he had been punished like a stubborn child, by being shut up [overnight in the Concord jail]. His imprisonment helped to embitter and harden Thoreau to such an extent that in the next decade he could approve of armed rebellion, of war itself. And that was what John Brown determined to wage against the United States of America. (p. 114)

The effect of Bode's analysis is to remove Thoreau from a historical and political context. Thoreau is presented as a writer with "psychological problems" (p. 116) whose relationship to the state and the issues of his day is informed by his own neuroses rather than any external historical factors. After having read Bode's essay, a reader would find it difficult not to consider Thoreau's insistence upon being an adversary of the government as little more than psychic spillage from a crackpot.

In the headnote to "The Last Days of John Brown," Bode writes that the piece ends the selections in *The Portable Thoreau* because it makes "a natural bridge to the Epilogue" (p. 676). And from that epilogue the many students of Thoreau who have read it are left with the impression that Thoreau's support of Brown need not be taken too seriously, because it emanated more from his unconscious Oedipal problems than it did from his convictions. Readers of the epilogue are not asked to confront the dilemma that Thoreau's approval of Brown's violence presents; instead one is encouraged to nod one's head knowingly and to marvel at Thoreau's power to sublimate his Oedipal complex into art. In a sense, this is another way of suggesting that Thoreau did not really mean what he said about lighting matches and pulling triggers for Brown's cause; Thoreau is easier to accept that way. If Thoreau was guilty of unconsciously suppressing the emotional significance of his support for Brown, Bode's epilogue unconsciously reduces one of the most disturbing aspects of Thoreau's social and political thought to a psychological idiosyncrasy.

Although Bode scrutinizes Thoreau's alleged unconscious motivations concerning his attraction to Brown, he avoids attacking Thoreau for his support of Brown. Bode focuses primarily on Brown's resistance to authority rather than the means of his resistance as the reason for Thoreau's interest in him. But C. Roland Wagner, another critic employing Raymond Gozzi's psychoanalytic perspective suggesting that much of Thoreau's writing represents his unconscious struggle for a sexual identity, uses the opportunity to repudiate Thoreau's approach to social and political problems. Wagner cites and agrees with Heinz Eulau that Thoreau's political essays are "morally and politically naive," and Wagner accounts for these failings by attempting to show that Thoreau's politics are the product of "infantile wishes" which Thoreau was unable to outgrow because he never resolved his Oedipal complex. It is not necessary to reproduce the psychoanalytic chart that Wagner writes up for Thoreau in order to understand the diagnosis: in the political essays, according to Wagner, "Thoreau's struggle for inward identity, his rage against the ideas of passive submission and apparently arbitrary authority, almost makes him lose contact with the real world and express his fantasies only."[41] Thoreau had a "child's view of political and social reality" (p. 131), and his insistence upon moral purity in every aspect of his life led to his courtship of violence; indeed, Thoreau's "need for violence came first, the good end second; violence had to find the good end to justify itself. John Brown expressed publicly what Thoreau felt privately" (p. 132). He was "a monstrous mirror of Thoreau's inner life" (p. 133) whose violent activities reflected Thoreau's deepest feelings and requirements for violence.

One gets a stronger sense from Wagner than from Bode that

Thoreau's politics, in addition to being impractical, as Eulau had noted, were pathological. Psychological approaches to Thoreau — the few that there are — seem to preclude a favorable attitude toward his social and political thought; perhaps one explanation for this is that it is easier to identify with a figure who is presented as a strident hero than with someone who is wheeled out as a patient. By witnessing the uncovering of the alleged true motivations of any political action, it is difficult to remember that simply because a belief or action gratifies an emotional need it does not automatically mean that the belief or action is a mistake. If a man has an unresolved Oedipus complex and as a result secretly hates his father and rejects authority, and if he also finds himself in conflict with a totalitarian government, does he repudiate the government simply because he is neurotic? An affirmative answer to this question would be as much an oversimplification as it would be to assume that all people who fight in a noble cause do so because their motives are pure. The point is that because the psychoanalytic approach to Thoreau's social thought focuses primarily on his personal history while neglecting public history, it places his social thought in a vacuum. Other critics of Thoreau's social thought have found him to be wrong and politically useless, not because he had an unresolved Oedipus complex, but because his politics were judged to be destructive in a social and historical context. The efficacy of a person's politics is, I think, more properly judged in a social sphere than a psychological sphere. Without a serious consideration of the historical context, the psychoanalytic approach to Thoreau's social thought seems to present itself as more of an attempt to discredit than to explain his social thought. Intentionally or not, this is the effect. [42]

Those having negative reactions to Thoreau's social and political thought in the sixties were in a distinct minority compared with those who enlisted Thoreau in a cause and found him useful. The politics of the sixties vitalized Thoreau's social thought and made it appear as if he were finally understood and appreciated in his native land. He seemed portable indeed. "Civil Disobedience," used as a showpiece, functioned for Thoreau as a passport into a decade in which many activists believed that if a person was not part of the solution, then he was part of the problem. Whatever lapses that might have been perceived in his thinking were usually overlooked or minimized out of a sense of gratitude to Thoreau for having said so well what so many social activists were trying to achieve. If Thoreau's early reputation had gotten off to a bad start with James Russell Lowell and Robert Louis Stevenson, he was subjected to an equally extreme — but opposite — assessment in the 1960s when he was seen as part of the solution to the country's ills, and therefore his social and political thought was perceived as presenting few significant problems. It is, of course, understandable that those who share Thoreau's rightfully indignant position on unjust governments and slavery (of any kind) would not call attention to an ally's shortcomings, but if one's friend does not, then someone else usually will — and in stronger terms. As early as 1957, one commentator, Vincent Buranelli, complained that Thoreau's reputation was inflated by readers who refuse to acknowledge the problems that his thought presents and, instead, insist upon viewing them as "hardly more than spots on the sun." [43] Buranelli suggests that owing to the country's mood Thoreau's "anarchic individualism" has been accepted too uncritically. In their haste to break away from drab conventions and the boredom created by excessive conformity, too many Americans have failed to consider the dangers implicit in Thoreau's position.

Seeing more than spots on Thoreau's sun, Buranelli argues that Thoreau's political thought is an eclipse of it. Not concerned with whether or not Thoreau was a prig or a cynic, Buranelli goes deeper than Lowell or Stevenson in an attempt to demonstrate from a philosophical perspective that much of Thoreau's thinking was "egregious nonsense" because Thoreau was solipsistic in his insistence upon making the world over into "his own image" (p. 261). Since Thoreau was blinded by his own self-righteousness, he was incapable of either making "discrimination[s] among partial truth" or "intertwining" ideas that seemed incompatible at first glance. Thoreau's "psychological rigidity" (p. 262), his inability to suspect that he might be wrong on an issue, led him to support Brown, the "lunatic of Harper's Ferry" (p. 263). Buranelli sees Thoreau's failures emanating from his "pledging his allegiance to inspiration [Higher Law] rather than to ratiocination and factual evidence" (p. 262). Buranelli's case against Thoreau raises many of the same points that Heinz Eulau had put forward in 1949, but Buranelli uses stronger language and is considerably more vehement in his condemnation of Thoreau's politics, particularly in relation to Brown. His lightest moment is when he quotes Bishop Butler's warning to John Wesley, another enthusiast: "Sir, the pretending to extraordinary revelations and gifts of the Holy Ghost is a horrid thing, a very horrid thing" (p. 264).

Buranelli is more than half-serious, however, for he ultimately judges Thoreau to be an "unmitigated fanatic" whose insistence upon the primacy of the individual will over majority rule is the most "insidious political theory" imaginable. Buranelli objects to Thoreau's politics in theory and does not attack him for irresponsible political activity, but rather for sloppy political thinking. His analysis is aimed at those who would use Thoreau, more than it is aimed at Thoreau himself. The caveat he issues concerning Thoreau's belief that action based on individual conscience transcends the jurisdiction of the law is at the core of many objections to Thoreau's social and political thinking. Buranelli argues that when individual consciences conflict with one another, each believing in its own righteousness, it is usually the strongest that imposes its will on the masses. Buranelli invokes Rousseau's "Legislator," Lenin's "genius Theoretician," and Hitler as destructive landmarks along this path of righteousness:

Thoreau had as profound a disdain for ordinary law as these tyrants. Of course he would have insisted that he meant only "bad" law, and that they erected the most monstrous legislation into a system as soon as they had seized power. But this is no answer, for in subordinating law to conscience as he did, by denigrating majority rule and institutional checks, he opened the door to the agile demagogue who generally does not defer to the author of *Civil Disobedience* when it comes to claiming infallibility. For the Concord Transcendentalists peculiar notions like Thoreau's may have sounded pleasantly philosophical and intellectually titillating. For the world of the twentieth century they have been politically scarifying.[44]

Although Buranelli labels Thoreau an "unmitigated fanatic," he does grant that "Thoreau had one saving grace," and that was his "self-centeredness" which kept him from the total commitment that

Brown engaged in until his death (p. 267). But Buranelli warns that "the frenetic zealots of the Thoreau cult" can "sing hosannahs" to him only because they have ignored the potential dangers of their idol's transcendental politics — only because "they have never taken a good look at its feet" (p. 268).

A little more than ten years after Buranelli's article dealing with the potential, theoretical dangers of Thoreau's politics, some of those dangers were realized, according to several commentators, in the political activities of some protestors of the late sixties. The riots that erupted in Newark, Detroit, and other Northern cities during the summer of 1967 seemed finally to put an end to the idealistic faith in nonviolent civil disobedience that had characterized the earlier part of the decade, and if the riots were not enough, Martin Luther King's assassination the following spring (followed by Robert Kennedy's in the summer) left the country with a numbed awareness that the era of Kennedy's New Frontier and Lyndon Johnson's Great Society had ended. Concurrent with a decline in popularity of the peaceful faction of the civil rights movement was an increase in violent confrontations with the government over the war in Vietnam, a war that would eventually turn out to be the most unpopular war that the United States had ever fought. The unresponsiveness of the government generated a growing disillusionment on the part of numerous Americans, particularly those associated with colleges and universities, and caused a minority of them to feel that "Amerika" had to be stopped even if, to use Thoreau's words in "Civil Disobedience," stopping the country's alleged imperialism (both at home and abroad) "cost them their existence as a people." Capitalizing on the average American's reaction to the violence and disorders that ensued, Richard M. Nixon was elected President in November 1968 on a platform of law and order designed to assure the "silent majority" that the Nixon administration would return the country to normalcy. The Democratic party had also expressed concern about violence and disorders, but the party's disastrous 1968 Chicago Convention disallowed the law-and-order issue as a fundamental plank in the platform.

However, the Johnson administration's 1968 *Report of the National Advisory Commission on Civil Disorders* describes and laments several aspects of the national mood in the late sixties, aspects which account for the tolerance for violence, among some groups, as a method of social protest:

A climate that tends toward the approval and encouragement of violence as a form of protest has been created by white terrorism directed against nonviolent protest, including instances of abuse and even murder of some civil rights workers in the South, by the open defiance of law and Federal authority by state and local officials resisting desegregation, and by some protest groups engaging in civil disobedience who turn their backs on nonviolence, go beyond constitutionally protected rights of petition and free assembly and resort to violence to attempt to compel alteration of laws and policies with which they disagree. This condition has been reenforced by a general erosion of respect for authority in American society and the reduced effectiveness of social standards and community restraints on violence and crime.[45]

In 1968 the solicitor general of the United States, Erwin N. Griswold, addressed himself to what he perceived as a growing tendency to legitimate violence as a means of social protest, and he cited Thoreau's attitude toward civil disobedience as one source of the irresponsible expressions of dissent in contemporary America.

The focus of Griswold's article is not Thoreau but the question of whether civil disobedience is efficacious in a particular situation and how — assuming it is — it ought to be carried out. As solicitor general, Griswold is naturally concerned with the preservation and obedience to law, and the society which the law presumably protects and orders. Like Buranelli he worries that the dissenter who is loyal only to his own conscience may fail to recognize that his "judgment has not merely a personal significance but also portends grave consequences for his fellows."[46] But Griswold does not specifically subpoena Thoreau as a prototypical exponent of violence. It is curious that he does not, since it would serve to reenforce one of the primary dangers associated with civil disobedience that he seeks to outline in the article — the tendency to legitimize violence. It is likely that the reason he does not cite "A Plea for Captain John Brown" or "Slavery in Massachusetts" is simply that he was not familiar with them. Instead, what he does challenge is Thoreau's "passionate attempt to dissociate himself from society." Griswold insists that such a position is impossible because no citizen can voluntarily withdraw from the "social compact"; he is part of society whether he likes it or not. Thoreau's attempt to sign off is irresponsible as well as futile: "Complex problems demand rational attention that can come only from personal focus on solutions and never from stubbornly turning one's back on harsh and unpleasant realities." Griswold sees a strong connection between Thoreau's attempt to drop out and "the essential irrationality of the 'hippie movement' " (p. 737). For Griswold this apolitical, antisocial streak in Thoreau nullifies his relevance for serious, responsible contemporary dissenters.

Only one month after Griswold's repudiation of Thoreau another political figure, Eugene V. Rostow, undersecretary for political affairs for the Department of State, also attacked Thoreau's views on civil disobedience. In an Independence Day address at the Thomas Jefferson Memorial Foundation in Charlottesville, Virginia, Rostow cautioned his audience against "Giving full and sympathetic weight to Thoreau's plea for the autonomy of the individual, [because] no society of consent could live acording to Thoreau's principle, and no other society would care enough about the rights of a non-conformist to consider it." [47] In a sense, Thoreau's "Civil Disobedience" had helped to force Lyndon Johnson's announcement in March 1968 that he would not run again for office, and the administration was not grateful. This is not to suggest, however, that the U.S. government waged a campaign against Thoreau; in fact, the post office, responding to Thoreau's popularity, issued a commemorative stamp in honor of him in 1967. Yet it is not difficult to imagine that many politicians wished that his admirers would settle down with *Walden* and leave "Civil Disobedience" on the shelf for awhile; but his admirers did not, at least not right away. As late as 1971 the *New York Times* reported that Senator Byrd of West Virginia "deplored the 'national climate' which brought about the issuance of a postage stamp to honor Henry David Thoreau — 'who had a thoroughly anti-social personality' — rather than one honoring the cops." [48]

It is hardly surprising that those who were in one way or another subjected to the tactics of protesters who claimed Thoreau as one of their strategists found him dangerous. From the perspective of some governmental officials, the jagged edges of anarchy could be seen emerging from the fringes of mass demonstrations, and for those few governmental officials who challenged Thoreau in print, "Civil Disobedience" represented the voice of the mob. Unfortunately for their own purposes those who worried about the dangers implicit in "Civil Disobedience" ignored "Slavery in Massachusetts" and "A Plea for Captain John Brown," two essays that would have provided ammunition in support of the extrapolations which they drew from "Civil Disobedience." It was unnecessary for them to speculate on the potential for violence in the early essay; Thoreau spells it out for them in the later two essays. No less than many who believed that violent reform was essential, many who deplored violence were ignorant of Thoreau's acceptance of it as a tactic.

The same kind of objections that Griswold, Rostov, and Byrd raised can be found in William F. Buckley's conservative *National Review* in an article by Frederick K. Sanders, a professor of English at the University of Georgia. In the summer of 1968 the *National Review* featured a cover story on Thoreau, and on the cover was a huge lighted time bomb with a photograph of Benjamin Spock's face in the center of it. The title of the article was "Mr. Thoreau's Timebomb." Spock's antiwar activities and Thoreau's "Civil Disobedience" were presented as a volatile mixture. Sanders argued that the philosophical implications of the essay were "profoundly heretical," because Thoreau's ideas could lead to violence and anarchy. [49] Like his contemporaries, Sanders ignored Thoreau's later essays even though they might have been useful, from Sanders' perspective, in making his point.

The *National Review* seemed to relish its attack on Thoreau, because the magazine saw itself embarrassing the liberals who claimed Thoreau as a hero. A reply to Sanders by James Lundquist was subsequently printed which argued that Thoreau's version of civil disobedience did not, at least in principle, necessarily lead to violence as it had on the contemporary scene. The article is introduced to *National Review* readers by the following editorial commentary describing its author:

James Lundquist — now get this — is a) really somebody with a different name who b) is a student of philosophy at a promi-

nent Eastern University [in the lexicon of the *National Review*
a phrase synonymous for liberal and radical thought in the
late sixties], who c) is taking issue with Professor Sanders'
hostile essay on Thoreau (*NR* June 4), but d) is afraid to sign
his own name to the reply on the grounds that it might dam-
age his prospects of academic advancement if he were caught
writing for *NR*. Which means that writing for *NR* even in
order to disagree with it and to praise Thoreau is net-danger-
ous. Got it? [50]

Thus it is suggested that the writer reveals himself as a coward and
shows a lack of integrity, while those he presumably represents are
narrow-minded and oppressive. What the reader is supposed to
"get" is that these are the qualities of the characters and the minds
of those who agree with Thoreau's politics, those labeled by
Sanders as the "discontents of the 1960's."

An article in *Human Events*, another conservative magazine,
takes a different approach from the *National Review* in refuting
Thoreau's "Civil Disobedience." Fred DeArmond, a former associate editor of *Nation's Business*, in the title of his challenge asks
"professional dissenters" who use the essay as an article of faith:
"Can Dissenters Really Claim Thoreau?" [51] After having seen an ad
that had recently appeared in two New York newspapers which invoked Thoreau as an inspiration for withholding that part of one's
income tax used to support the war in Vietnam, DeArmond wonders how many of the dissenters who signed the ad (described by
DeArmond as "448 radical writers, journalists and other off-color
characters such as Victor Perlo, Dr. Benjamin Spock and Allen
Ginsberg") "know anything about the real Henry Thoreau and his
representative writings?" DeArmond likes the "original" and "trenchant" qualities of *Walden*, but he views "Civil Disobedience" as an
"absurdity" and anarchistic. In order to take Thoreau away from
all those unsavory dissenters, DeArmond's tack is to insist (not
argue) that because Thoreau supported the Union cause in 1861,
"he wholly repudiated his civil disobedience theory of 1849." In this
way DeArmond can have his Thoreau and use him too while simultaneously rejecting civil disobedience.

Judging from the few examples that did appear in print, there
was a tendency among those who believed that civil disobedience

was a threat to the stability of government and society to warn against Thoreau's "romantic extravagances," which they feared might liquidate all law and order in the country. [52] Their concern was not widely shared by very many other commentators on Thoreau. On occasion a liberal publication might include an article speculating on a problem perceived in Thoreau's version of civil disobedience, but that was rare. [53] Throughout the decade there were relatively few detailed and extended examinations of his social and political thought. Given the volume of Thoreau scholarship during the sixties, it is remarkable that no comprehensive book was published on the subject — from any point of view. There were, however, scattered brief negative assessments of Thoreau's social and political thought. During the decade his thinking was considered anarchistic, ineffectual, escapist, chaotic, futile, and grossly overestimated; he was also called, among other epithets, a secret conformist and an impossible egotist who was totally irrelevant to the needs of the sixties. [54] This catalog is not complete, but even if it were, it would appear scant compared with the commentaries that are essentially uncritical of Thoreau's social and political ideas.

Neither the negative assessments of Thoreau's politics nor the rare attempts to use him as an advocate of violent reform had much — if any — impact on his popular reputation. Throughout the decade and throughout the country he was most famous for his nonviolent civil disobedience. And related to this reputation was another one he enjoyed among many of the college-age youth whom Theodore Roszak called the "counterculture." Thoreau was perceived by many hippies (a silly, overly general term but still useful for my purposes) as one of the links between their values and the nonmaterialistic philosophies of the East. Generally, the hippies and those who fashioned themselves after them rejected what they considered to be the predominant characteristics of American life: its materialism, its consumerism, its cold rationality, its competitiveness, and its violence. Wanting no part of the corporate adult world because it seemed diametrically opposed to a simple, meaningful, organic life style, hippies dropped out and attempted to establish communal Waldens where they could live free from the quiet desperation of a nine-to-five world. What Thoreau sought alone, they did together. As broad as this description is of the hippies, a distinction ought to be made between their fleeing from the political world — or attempting to ward it off by holding up flowers to it — and their radical contemporaries who actively protested what they opposed with direct confrontations; but this distinction is not especially useful in terms of Thoreau's reputation. One might expect that "Civil Disobedience" would be the primary text for the latter group, whereas *Walden* would be the manual for the quietism of the hippies, but there seems to be no significant evidence to confirm that such a distinction was made; Thoreau was simply used as another way of saying no to an America that had failed to meet both groups' expectations. There was plenty of overlapping. Just as the length of one's hair became less of an accurate index to a person's politics as the sixties wore on, so too did the length to which Thoreau was used become less of a means of determining a person's ideology. By the end of the decade Thoreau's relevance to the movement was amorphous; for most he was as comfortable and as functional as a pair of dungarees and a chambray shirt, and few worried about whether or not he fit. His image was marketed more than his writings were read.

In Greenwich Village Thoreau became "a fast-selling hippie objet d'art" in 1967 when the *East Village Other* featured on its front page an enlargement of the U.S. postal stamp "picturing a frail, bearded" Thoreau; the newspaper claimed Thoreau as "One of America's first hippies."[55] Thoreau looked like a hippie and frequently sounded like one in his disdain for conventional stultifying life styles. That was enough. It did not matter that he loathed cities or considered two a crowd; it did not matter that from among all of the country's writers he was probably the most virginal (even Michael Wigglesworth begat eight children). And least of all did it matter that Thoreau viewed the use of artificial stimulants of any type as unnecessary and harmful to spiritual fulfillment: the contemporary use of drugs would have been for Thoreau — a debauchee of dew — the equivalent of surrounding his hut with plastic flowers and astro-turf. Like so many others who used Thoreau for their own purposes, the hippies quickly embraced Thoreau with the cheerful alacrity of a spider rolling up a prey that had landed on a remote circumference of its web.[56]

Exploiting his popularity, the world of commodity prepackaged

Thoreau for the young and reduced him to a series of attractive antiestablishment postures into which the young could project themselves. Perhaps the best example of this can be seen in a collection of brief quotatons from Thoreau's writings edited by Rod McKuen, one of the chief purveyors of pap at the end of the sixties. [57] Garnished with sentimental photographs concerning race relations, war, and conformity, McKuen's edition managed to drain the toughness of Thoreau's prose and make it seem like a hip version of *Poor Richard's Almanack*. Sentimentalizing an issue is another way of depoliticizing it — one can ignore an issue this way and still feel good about it. McKuen put the edition together for Stanyan Books, and it was part of a series that included among its inspirational readings quotations from the Bible, which were entitled *God's Greatest Hits*, a title which suggests the nature of the series.

Like God, Thoreau found himself in the top forty. Indeed, Thoreau was so popular that he was in danger of suffering from overexposure among college-age students by the end of the decade. In *Course X: A Left Field Guide to Freshman English*, a half-serious spoof on the agonies of teaching and taking freshman English, Thoreau was mentioned frequently and rated a chapter entitled "Chances Are, You'll Read Thoreau." Like freshman English, Thoreau was getting to be somewhat of a bore. He was also well enough known to warrant a satire in the *National Lampoon*, but in spite of the kind of familiarity that often breeds contempt, the seriousness of the issues which the country faced from Harlem to Hanoi caused him to be taken seriously for the most part. [58] As issues and fads surfaced in the sixties Thoreau was right there: he emerged as both a spokesman and an antagonist of capitalism; a food faddist; an anarchist; a sexual libertarian advocating a "bodily-orgasmic response to life"; a man with "Soul"; a nudist; an ecologist; and, in general, an all-purpose savior capable of redeeming humanity from the frenzy of a troubled world.[59] All of these were in some way related to a concern for the *quality* of life, a concern that particularly characterized Thoreau and the 1960s.

Yet is was principally Martin Luther King's version of a politicized Thoreau engaging in nonviolent civil disobedience that prevailed, and by the end of the decade Thoreau was associated with the antiwar movement as much as he had been linked earlier to the civil rights movement. In 1970 Jerome Lawrence and Robert E. Lee coauthored a play which capitalized on Thoreau's popularity and the increasing popular dissatisfaction with the war in Vietnam; the play's title suggests its emphasis: *The Night Thoreau Spent in Jail*.[60] In the preface to the play ("The Now Thoreau") the authors recount the outrages and injustices of the Mexican War; these are intended to be juxtaposed silently in the reader's mind to the war in Vietnam. Thoreau's "outrage is closely akin to the anger of many young people today" (p. vii). Thoreau is first and foremost offered as a pacifistic, intensely moral individualist who is sensitive to social injustices, the desecrations of nature, and the potential desecrations of himself if he compromises. The last point is made at Emerson's expense. The "Production Notes from the Playwrights" point out that the subtext of the play is Thoreau's "evolution from withdrawal [Walden Pond] to return, the journey from hermitizing to social conscience" (p. 103). He is presented, according to Jerome Lawrence, as a "folk-hero" for the young. There is, needless to say, not even standing room for a John Brown in this production.

Walter Harding commented on the play before it was produced and found the image of Thoreau presented in the play attractive: "Although we have not seen the play as yet, we have read it and recommend it heartily as demonstrating a profound understanding of Thoreau the man, what he stood for, and the pertinence of his ideas today.[61] These comments are consistent with his preference for those writings about Thoreau which use him as a paragon of nonviolence. This was also the public's preference.

The Night Thoreau Spent in Jail had its first run in the spring of 1970 at Ohio State University. Its opening there and then made Thoreau seem particularly relevant, because within several weeks of the first performance the United States had invaded Cambodia, and during the student demonstrations that ensued the National Guard had shot to death four students at Kent State University. By the end of 1972 the play had been produced more than 2000 times by 141 separate producers in university and regional theaters all over the country. There were also plans to make the play into a film.[62] The play was enormously popular, particularly on campuses. The *New York Times* noted that Jerome Lawrence, after having seen a number of productions of the play "reported that audience reactons have been uncommonly personal. On one college campus, where there had been demonstrations and violence some months before the production, he was told by a student, 'This is our play. It proves that you can dissent without violence.' " [63]

Without question, one of the primary reasons for the overwhelming number of positive impressions of Thoreau's politics is that, to quote Leon Edel's words in a different context, "The world has wisely chosen to remember 'Civil Disobedience' rather than the three John Brown lectures — 'A Plea for Captain Brown,' [sic] 'The Last Days of John Brown,' and 'After the Death of John Brown.' " [64] Edel thinks it wise to ignore Thoreau's "defense of John Brown, with his espousal of violence in that instance, [because it] is hardly the voice of the same man" (p. 38). Edel's remarks, coming at the end of the 1960s, point to the fact that the later political essays were considered dangerous if Thoreau was to be useful to the sixties, and so rather than have a useless Thoreau the decade chose an edited Thoreau.

I am aware of no literary critic within the academy who in print either vigorously endorsed Thoreau's views on violence in the later essays or who insisted that they were relevant and useful for solving the problems faced by the civil rights or the antiwar movements of the sixties (Truman Nelson is not a literary critic, nor does he have any academic affiliation). But one critic almost did. Paul Lauter, writing in a book (1972) designed to place literature in a left-wing political perspective and to help in "reconstructing the canon of what is studied and taught," describes how he nearly wrote an essay on Thoreau's politics which might have told "us something about the condition and development of our own movement. . . ." Lauter explains how the essay would have been relevant to the shift in the sixties from a firm belief in nonviolence to a serious consideraton of violence as a tactic:

I had done one [essay] some ten years ago ("Thoreau's Prophetic Testimony") which argued that Thoreau was consistent in all his writings since, like a Hebrew prophet, he was attempting to awaken and change his readers. Thus his speeches supporting John Brown were not at odds with the pacifism of "Civil Disobedience" or with *Walden*, as had been charged, but were sharper attempts to penetrate the consciousness of a still-slumbering people. But lately it had seemed to me less important to protect Thoreau's nonviolent consistency; indeed, what intrigued me was his development from the somewhat private "Civil Disobedience," through the more directly political but frustrated "Slavery in Massachusetts," and to the explicit commitment to armed struggle in John Brown. [65]

But the essay was never written because while Lauter was investigating mid-nineteenth-century American politics and society for the background of Thoreau's development, he "got fired" (p. 12).

Accurately or not, by linking the almost-written article to his being fired from the University of Maryland at Baltimore, Lauter implies that the academy has a low tolerance of radical politics which entertain the relevancy of violence. Certainly, in terms of the small amount of published scholarship on the possible meanings of Thoreau's interest in Brown, the critics' response seems to have been one of studied indifference. It may be only a small exaggeration to say that they wished that it would all go away. Alfred Kazin's perspective seems to be more representative of that of the majority of his colleagues in the academy than Lauter's:

it is impossible to imagine the most passionately anti-Vietnam writer saying today that in the face of such evil, "I need not say what match I would touch, what system endeavor to blow up." We have all lived too long with violence to be persuaded by the violence of language. [66]

It is significant that Kazin restricts his comments to writers. Those who might have found Thoreau's statements on violence useful as an endorsement of their own tactics — the revolutionary Weathermen, for example — were not the type to be dashing off articles for *Atlantic* or the *Saturday Review* introducing interested, prospective revolutionaries to Thoreau. (Truman Nelson, who of course was not a Weatherman, is an exception here.) Nor was the Weatherman interested in shaping the past to make it useful for the present; the cultivated anti-intellectual and irrational aspects of the organization precluded such an approach. What David Horowitz (a Marxist) says about the Weatherman's rejection of history and politics is a fair assessment of what many in the academy probably felt (but did not often express) about the quality of Thoreau's politics in terms of his support of Brown's revolutionary violence. What was important to the Weatherman "was not the political consequence of the deed, but its *Karma*. What was important was the *will* to bomb. Revolution here has almost ceased to be a strategy for social change and has become instead a yoga of perfection."[67] Brown was for Thoreau, it must be remembered, "a transcendentalist above all."

Now that the freneticism of the sixties has waned and that decade is becoming more and more a subject of inquiry rather than a source of anxiety, it seems likely that there will be a number of assessments examining various aspects of the reform movements of the sixties. And, as that happens, perhaps the comprehensive book which has not yet been written on Thoreau's social and political thought will appear, if the topic is not ignored as it was in the fifties.

The supercharged political atmosphere of the sixties has subsided. Even the Thoreau Society reflects this. Since its inception in 1941, the society has often provided a forum for speakers, and the *Bulletin*, for articles, dealing with contemporary social problems ranging from ecological dangers to racial issues. Until the sixties, however, the society never attempted to endorse — as an organization — a particular political point of view, but during that decade it made tentative moves toward politicization in response to the pressures that it and many other organizations experienced, pressures that called for the society to stand up and be counted on the issues of war, racism, poverty, and ecology. The society seemed to move toward just that when at the 1969 annual meeting it voted in an unprecedented action to "donate to the National Farm Workers Association five hundred dollars in honor of Cesar Chavez for working for human rights in the tradition of Henry David Thoreau."[68] But at the society's meeting the following year, concord gave way to discord when one of its members made clear that he believed that the society was not moving quickly enough toward a political identity; he distributed handbills entitled "A Protest Against the Thoreau Society's Annual Meeting." In the handbill Charles W. White charged that the society paid too much attention to Thoreau's interest in nature and not enough to his concern with social injustices. He argued that if the society was not to "become a House-and-Garden Club" and "be co-opted into boosterism for the Concord Chamber of Commerce," it had to address itself to "the problems of modern America." He proposed formal resolutions condemning the war in Vietnam and elected officials in Washington who tolerated and encouraged racism; he also urged the society's members to demonstrate "en masse at the business office of some major polluter."[69]

Like many of Thoreau's public addresses, White's resolutions were confronted by a phlegmatic audience which sat near the doors. One member later described the "unsettled atmosphere" of the meeting as "emotion-torn," and indeed it must have been with White and his supporters attempting to flush the Thoreau Society out of the woods while "the reaction of the majority of the Society was one of fear driven determination not to hear, not to listen, not to confront, not to consider" and not to move.[70] The resolutions were ruled out of order and were sent to the executive committee for further consideration. However, White's campaign was not a complete failure, for included in the 1971 agenda for the meeting was a forum on the relevance of Thoreau's ideas, and, more importantly, White's supporters managed to have his resolutions from the previous year sent to the members as a mail ballot. Apparently, a significant number of the membership agreed with one member who wrote that "To be a Thoreauvian is to be a warrior for the truth in a world of milksops, hypocrites, and conformists."[71] One-third of the membership voted and passed the resolutions.[72]

This was a short-lived victory, though, for in 1973 there was an amendment added to the Thoreau Society bylaws, a portion of which read: "No part of the activities of this corporation shall be for the carrying on of propaganda or otherwise of attempting to influence legislation."[73] The purpose of this amendment was to remove the Thoreau Society explicitly from any political issues so that it could meet the requirements of section 501 of the Internal Revenue Code for tax-exempt corporations. The reader is invited to supply his own favorite, appropriate quotation from Thoreau here.

The reformist impulses of the 1960s have been checked, and the Thoreau Society serves as a microcosm of that process. Although the country still faces many of the same problems, rightly or not there are many fewer Americans who feel compelled to disobey laws in order to preserve the integrity of their own consciences or to effect a particular social change. With a slackening of the intensity of the issues, there will, perhaps, be more time to read Thoreau before using him. The publication of the Princeton edition of Thoreau's complete works should also foster a reappraisal of Thoreau's social and political thought. It may be that one reason why a book on Thoreau's politics was not written in the sixties is that the events of the decade made his ideas — especially those in "Civil Disobedience" — seem too critical to be examined critically. For all the causes that Thoreau has been signed onto (or expelled from), the commentaries on Thoreau's politics have yet to explain the significance of both the strengths and the deficiencies of his politics for Americans. If that comprehensive book is to be a good one, its author will tell us something about our own politics as well as Thoreau's. Shorn of the need to trim Thoreau's thinking so that it conforms to the outlines of a particular ideology, such a book may end up offering Americans the most useful Thoreau to date, but that will be for the next decade to decide. Thoreau's mistakes may turn out to be as valuable as his insights. His sense of morality will probably always be edifying for his readers, but there is also much that is important and chastening to be learned from Thoreau's apolitical temperament, a temperament which resulted in his unwillingness to take politics seriously and his subsequent impulse to champion violence as a means of surgically removing evil from the world.

For now, however, Thoreau can have the last words; I offer them as a rationale for my own study of the responses to his social and political thought and as a possible rationale for the title page of that future comprehensive study of Thoreau's politics: "We have heard of a Society for the Diffusion of Useful Knowledge. It is said that Knowledge is power; and the like. Methinks there is equal need of a Society for the Diffusion of Useful Ignorance . . ." (*Writings*, V, 239).

NOTES

1. Quoted in *TSB*, 109 (Fall 1969), 7.

2. "The Cult of Thoreau: Its Background, Development, and Status," unpublished master's thesis (Brown University, 1955), p. 3.

3. "Thoreau and the Younger Generation," *TSB*, 56 (Summer 1956), 1.

4. *Stride Toward Freedom: The Montgomery Story* (New York: Harper & Row, 1958), p. 51. King was the most prominent black to connect Thoreau to the civil rights struggle, but he was not the first. For an earlier example see: C.E. Nichols, "Thoreau on the Citizen and His Government," *Phylon*, 13 (First Quarter 1952), 19-24.

5. Robert B. Downs, "Individual Versus State," in *Books That Changed the World* (New York: Mentor, 1956), p. 75. On the centennial of the publication of *Walden* Richard Merrifield speculated in *Yankee Magazine* ("100 Years After," [July 1954], 68-69) that owing to his influence on Gandhi, Thoreau "may at this moment . . . be one of the most powerful anti-totalitarian forces in Asia" (p. 69). Again, the usefulness of Thoreau's essay on civil disobedience is located outside the United States. Even as late as 1959 it was not unusual to read in reference to "Civil Disobedience" that Thoreau's "most important contribution was made not to his native land but to India." See Robert S. Laforte, "The Political Thought of Henry David Thoreau: A Study in Paradox," *Educational Leader*, 23 (July 1959), 50.

6. Felix Morley, *Nation's Business*, 46 (April 1953), 17-18.

7. Ernest Earnest, "Thoreau and Little Rock," *Best Articles & Stories*, 3 (November 1959), 42-43. For another negative treatment of Thoreau because he could not live in a "give-and-take society," see Richard C. Crowely, "Thoreau's Correspondence," *Commonweal*, 70 (May 1959), 186. And for an earlier and more theoretical denunciaton of Thoreau see Vincent Buranelli, "The Case Against Thoreau," *Ethics*, 67 (July 1957), 257-268. Buranelli's essay is discussed later in this chapter.

8. John P. Sisk, "Beatniks and Tradition," *Commonweal*, 70 (April 1959), p. 75. See also Anders Ehnmark, "Rebels in American Literature," *Western Review*, 23 (August 1958), 43-56; and Carl Bode, "Thoreau: The Double Negative," in *The Young Rebel in American Literature*, ed. Carl Bode (New York: Frederick A. Praeger, 1960), pp. 3-22. Bode collects seven essays by various critics on writers such as Lewis, Dreiser, Mencken, and Steinbeck; he prefaces the essays with "A Word of Explanation," the first paragraph of which captures the impulse that informed many attempts to rediscover the past in the 1960s: "The assertions that this is an age of conformity are so frequent and the evidences cited so numerous that they

ought to be taken seriously. However, it is worth reminding ourselves that there is a vigorous American tradition of nonconformity, of dissent and criticism, as well. Certainly the literary heritage has not been a tame one. Both in the lives of American authors and in their works the evidences of rebellion are ample" (p. v). See also Henry S. Kariel, "Rebellion and Compulsion: The Dramatic Pattern of American Thought," *American Quarterly*, 14 (Winter 1962), 608-611.

There is no shortage of evidence documenting the tendency to present Thoreau as rebellious; the notes to this chapter will clearly establish that, but two book titles that appeared within one year of each other in the early sixties are especially appropriate here: August Derleth, *Concord Rebel: A Life of Henry D. Thoreau* (Philadelphia: Chilton, 1962), and Thomas Morris Longstreth, *Henry Thoreau: American Rebel* (New York: Dodd, Mead, 1963).

9. "New Light on Thoreau," *New Leader*, June 15, 1959, p. 16.

10. For a reading of "Thoreau's Social Criticism as Poetry" see Lawrence Bowling, *Yale Review*, 55 (Winter 1966), 255-264. As this chapter will demonstrate, there were no shortages of almost any type of approach to Thoreau in the sixties. The following books, articles, and dissertations suggest the range — but not the bulk — of work on Thoreau which deals with the form and function of his prose and, occasionally, his poetry: Richard C. Cook, "Thoreau and His Imagery: The Anatomy of an Imagination," *TSB*, 70 (Winter 1960), 1-3; Lauriat Lane, "On the Organic Structure of *Walden*," *College English*, 21 (January 1960), 195-202; John C. Broderick, "The Movement of Thoreau's Prose," *American Literature*, 33 (May 1961), 133-142; Walter L. Shear, "Henry David Thoreau's Imagery and Symbolism," dissertation (University of Wisconsin, 1961); Larzer Ziff, *Walden: A Writer's Edition* (New York: Holt, Rinehart and Winston, 1961); W. H. Bonner, "Mariners and Terreners: Some Aspects of Nautical Imagery in Thoreau," *American Literature*, 34 (January 1963), 507-519; Arthur L. Ford, "A Critical Study of the Poetry of Henry Thoreau," dissertation (Bowling Green State University, 1964); Joseph J. Moldenhauer, "The Rhetoric of *Walden*," dissertation (Columbia University, 1964); J.J. Boies, "Circular Imagery in Thoreau's *Week*," *College English*, 26 (February 1965), 350-355; Reginald L. Cook, "Ancient Rites at *Walden*," *Emerson Society Quarterly*, 39 (Second Quarter 1965), 52-56; Sidney B. Poger, "Thoreau: Two Modes of Discourse," dissertation (Columbia University, 1965); Francis D. Ross, "Rhetorical Procedure in Thoreau's 'Battle of the Ants,'" *College Composition and Communication*, 16 (February 1965), 14-18; Herman L. Eisenlohr, "The Development of Thoreau's Prose," dissertation (University of Pennsylvania, 1966); David Mason Greene, *The Frail Duration: A Key to Symbolic Structure in Walden*, San Diego State

College Humanities Monographs, 1, no. 2 (1966); Alan Holder, "The Writer as Loon: Witty Structure in *Walden*," *Emerson Society Quarterly*, 43 (Second Quarter 1966), 73-77; Ronald Earl Clapper, "The Development of *Walden*: A Genetic Text," dissertation (UCLA, 1967); Howard R. Houston, "Metaphors in *Walden*," dissertation (Claremont Graduate School, 1967); Melvin E. Lyon, "Walden Pond as Symbol," *PMLA*, 82 (May 1967), 289-300; Donald Ross, "The Style of Thoreau's *Walden*," dissertation (University of Michigan, 1967); Charles R. Anderson, *The Magic Circle of Walden* (New York: Holt, Rinehart and Winston, 1968); Joyce M. Holland, "Pattern and Meaning of Thoreau's *A Week*," *Emerson Society Quarterly*, 50 (First Quarter 1968), 48-55; and Lauriat Lane, "The Structure of Protest: Thoreau's Polemic Essays," *Humanities Association Bulletin*, 20 (Fall 1969), 34-40.

The number of dissertations examining the artistry of Thoreau's style suggests the strong influence that earlier critics such as F.O. Matthiessen and Sherman Paul have exerted on academic approaches to Thoreau in the sixties. The emphasis on form in the dissertations just cited is in stark contrast to Wendell Glick's 1950 dissertation for Northwestern University entitled "Thoreau and Radical Abolitionism," in which Glick states that no reader of *Walden* would argue that the book is worth studying for its "architectonics" (p. 227). But Glick's assumption is no more extreme than some of the more enthusiastic readings of Thoreau's style that have tended to squeeze analyses from Thoreau's prose. Consider the following passage by J. Golden Taylor in an article entitled "Thoreau's Sour Grapes" (*Proceedings of the Utah Academy of Sciences, Arts, and Letters*, 42 [1965], 38-49): "It is my purpose in this paper to describe how Thoreau evolved one of his outstanding technical achievements, the use of the sour grapes symbol in 'Economy,' the first chapter of *Walden*, which I believe has not been treated elsewhere" (p. 38). For an article which articulates some sense of the frustrations felt by more than one critic about readings of *Walden*, see Raymond P. Tripp, Jr., "A Recipe for *Walden* Criticism," *New England Review*, 1 (July 1969), 11-14.

11. John C. Broderick, "Teaching Thoreau," *Emerson Society Quarterly*, 18 (First Quarter 1960), 3.

12. Walter Harding, "On Teaching *Walden*," 11-12. Harding's essay and the following articles which deal with approaches to the teaching of Thoreau appear in the same issue of *ESQ* (see note 11): Raymond Adams, "Thoreau — Surveyor in the Survey Course," 2-3; Robert P. Cobb, "Thoreau and 'The Wild,' " 5-7; Reginald L. Cook, "Teaching Thoreau at Middlebury," 7-9; Frank Davidson, "A Reading of *Walden*," 9-11; Alexander Kern, "Introducing Thoreau as Artist and Man," 12-14; Kenneth Kurtz, "Thoreau and Individualism Today," 14-15; Andrew Schiller, "Thoreau in

the Undergraduate Survey Course," 17-19; and Ethel Seybold, "Thoreau for Everyone," 19-21.

13. "Critic at Large," *New York Times*, December 2, 1960, p. 26.

14. Both incidents are cited in the *TSB*. The rowboat episode is in 73 (Fall 1960), 6; Uphaus is mentioned in 71 (Spring 1960), 4; and 75 (Spring 1961), 1. For a detailed account of Uphaus' reasons for going to jail see his "Conscience and Disobedience," *Massachusetts Review*, 4 (Autumn 1962), 104-108. Again, the *TSB* serves as the most useful source of information in order to suggest the pervasive interest in Thoreau. Its brief notations on the popular uses of Thoreau occasionally read like Melville's "Extracts" in *Moby Dick*: Thoreau seems to be ubiquitous. There are numerous examples to cite concerning Thoreau's popularity among the various voices of dissent in the sixties, but there are two conveniently found in the same issue of *TSB* (91 [Spring 1965], 4). Walter Harding notes that included with the bulletin, for its subscribers, is a sample of "Thoreau Money," upon which was printed a pacifist manifesto issued by the Committee for Non-Violent Action. On the same page that this is mentioned there is reproduced a valentine distributed by Hallmark Contemporary Cards featuring a cartoon of a young woman with hair flowing below her waist wearing a short skirt and a sweatshirt bearing a drawing of a bust of Thoreau. Below the cartoon is the caption: "I DREAMED I WAS YOUR VALENTINE IN MY HENRY THOREAU SWEATSHIRT." It is only a valentine card, but the assumption behind it is that if one goes to the demonstration (or at least sympathizes with it) and one appreciates and invokes Thoreau, then one is accepted and loved. By 1965 Thoreau was a familiar part of the youth culture; he was one of the hallmarks of it. And, interestingly enough, by 1972 it was no longer necessary to dream of wearing a Thoreau sweatshirt, because Donald Stoddard of the English department of Skidmore College had silk screened a daguerreotype of Thoreau onto not only sweatshirts but also T-shirts and was selling them for $5.00 and $3.50 respectively (see *TSB*, 119 [Spring 1972], 8). Stoddard and some of the girls at Skidmore sweated for the values they shared with Thoreau, not the money.

15. "Letter to the Editor," *New York Herald Tribune*, June 8, 1945.

16. Don Kleine, "Civil Disobedience: The Way to Walden," *Modern Language Notes*, 75 (April 1960), 297-304. An example of this shift in focus can be found later in the decade in a paperback edition of Thoreau's *Walden* and "Civil Disobedience" entitled *Essay on the Duty of Civil Disobedience and Walden* (New York: Lancer Books, 1968). As Walter Harding points out (*TSB*, 112 [Summer 1970], 5), the title clearly attempts to suggest to the prospective reader that the book is primarily about civil disobedience rather than life in the woods.

Even *Reader's Digest* mentioned "Civil Disobedience" in a discussion of Thoreau; see Bruce Bliven, "Mr. Thoreau of Walden Pond," 79 (December

1961), 225-234. Earlier treatments of Thoreau by the *Reader's Digest* managed to avoid "Civil Disobedience," and although Thoreau was reduced to a self-help formula in 1961 as he had been before, "Civil Disobedience" did, at least, appear as a variable in the equation.

17. John H. Hicks, "Introduction," *Thoreau in Our Season* (Amherst: University of Massachusetts Press, 1966), p. 1. This collects the pieces on Thoreau that appeared in the *Massachusetts Review*, 4 (Autumn 1962). I have cited the book because it is more readily available than the journal and Hicks's introduction is useful. All page references are to the book.

Another indication of the growing tendency to place Thoreau in a political context can be seen almost immediately after the appearance of the articles in the *Massachusetts Review*. An excellent anthology of Thoreau's essays, journal entries, and letters relating to politics was edited (in both cloth and paper) by Milton Meltzer and entitled *Thoreau: People, Principles and Politics* (New York: Hill & Wang, 1963). This was the first of its kind.

18. Thoreau enthusiasts often universalize him. In one of the essays in *Thoreau in Our Season*, "Five Ways of Looking at *Walden*" (pp. 44-57), Walter Harding writes that *Walden* "Can and does mean all things to all men. Therein lies its very strength" (p. 57) and, one might add, Thoreau's indiscriminate reputation.

19. Martin Luther King, Jr., "A Legacy of Creative Protest," in Hicks, p. 13.

20. The telegram is quoted in Walter Harding, "The Centennial of Thoreau's Death," *TSB*, 79 (Spring 1962), 1. For a similar salute to Thoreau which also connects Thoreau to Gandhi's principle of nonviolent resistance, see remarks made by Hubert H. Humphrey in 1957 for the *Congressional Record* (vol. 103, pt. 2 [pp. 14471-14475]) in which Humphrey praises Thoreau and asks that a reprint of a 1957 address to the Thoreau Society by G.L. Mehta, then ambassador of India to the United States, be included in the *Record*.

21. "An Eccentric Kinship: H.D.T.'s 'A Plea for Captain John Brown,' " *Southern Speech Journal*, 27 (Winter 1961), 151. In a more well-known essay, Richard Drinnon in "Thoreau's Politics of the Upright Man" dismisses the essay by insisting that although "It is true that Thoreau himself was unclear about violence," it is more important that "like Antigone he left us the powerful, burning, irresistible appeal of his example" of civil disobedience (in Hicks, p. 168).

22. "Thoreau," *Eight American Authors*, ed. James Woodress, rev. ed. (New York: Norton, 1971), p. 163. The following is a representative list of critical and popular views of Thoreau which , in various degrees, either insist on Thoreau as an advocate of peaceful reform or simply ignore his support of Brown. The list does not begin to suggest the number of times

Thoreau was cited as an American prophet of nonviolent resistance, but it
does point to the widely accepted view of him in that role; as one pacifist
described "Civil Disobedience," the essay "is today in all likelihood the
most influential text for the pacifist conscience after the Sermon on the
Mount" (Peter Mayer, ed., *The Pacifist Conscience* [New York: Holt,
Rinehart and Winston, 1966], p. 21). See Arthur Volkman, ed., *Thoreau
on Man and Nature* (Mount Vernon: Peter Pauper Press, 1960); Karl
Shapiro, "On the Revival of Anarchism," in *The Anarchists*, ed. Irving
Horowitz (New York: Dell Publishing Co., 1964), pp. 572-581 (this is re-
printed from the February 1961 issue of *Liberation*); Eleanor Woods, "Cost
What It May," *Humanist*, 21 (March 1961), 77-86; Leo A. Bressler,
"*Walden*, Neglected American Classic," *English Journal*, 51 (January
1962), 14-20; Betty Schechter, *The Peaceable Revolution* (Boston:
Houghton Mifflin, 1963), passim; Bradford Smith, "Thoreau: Civil
Disobedience," in *Men of Peace* (Philadelphia: Lippincott, 1964), pp.
144-156; R.C. Whittemore, "Henry David Thoreau" in *Makers of the
American Mind* (New York: William Morrow & Co., 1964), pp. 185-196;
Charles Poore, "Thoreau's Ideas Still Shake the World," *New York Times*,
November 16, 1965, p. 45; James Finn, ed., *Protest: Pacifism and Politics*
(New York: Random House, 1967), passim; Carl Markle, Jr., "The Shores
of Walden — and Beyond: A Study of Henry David Thoreau's 'Civil
Disobedience' and Its Influence," unpublished master's thesis (Oakland
University, 1967); William Packard, "Infinite Expectation and Thoreau,"
Wall Street Journal, 12 July 1967, p. 14; Berel Lang, "Thoreau and the
Body Politic," *Colorado Quarterly*, 18 (Summer 1969), 51-57; Robert B.
Downs, "Resistance to Civil Government," in *Books That Changed
America* (New York: Macmillan, 1970), pp. 78-88; and Sidney Poger,
"Thoreau's Resistance to Civil Government," *The Leaflet*, 69 (February
1970), 11-16.

The widely held critical and popular view in the sixties of Thoreau as
nonviolent was consistent with earlier assumptions in the forties and fifties
concerning his approach toward reform. Before the forties Thoreau's
attitudes toward modes of reform — in terms of violence — were not given
much thought by anyone, because he was primarily considered as either a
nature writer or a master of the art of living. See Chapter 3 for a discussion
of the image of a nonviolent Thoreau in the forties, and see the following
articles from the fifties, which serve as a prelude to the sixties' view of Thoreau: Joseph L. Blau, "Henry David Thoreau: Anarchist," in *Men and
Movements in American Philosophy* (Englewood Cliffs, N.J.: Prentice-
Hall, 1952), pp. 131-141; Michael F. Moloney, "Walden: A Centenary,"
America, 90 (1954), 683-685; Francis B. Dedmond, "Thoreau and the Ethical Concept of Government," *Personalist*, 36 (Winter 1955), 36-46;
Michael F. Moloney, "Christian *Malgré Lui*" in *American Classics Recon-*

sidered: A Christian Appraisal, ed. Harold C. Gardiner (New York: Charles Scribner's Sons, 1958), pp. 193-209; "The Duty of Civil Disobedience," *Catholic Worker,* 26 (August 1959), 1, 6; and Robert Stowell, "Modern Civil Disobedience and Thoreau," *TSB,* 69 (Fall 1959), 1.

23. William Stuart Nelson, "Thoreau and American Non-Violent Resistance," in Hicks, p. 18.

24. "Thoreau and the Current Non-Violent Struggle for Integration," *TSB,* 88 (Summer 1964), 1-3. This is a reprint of the text of the address as it appeared in the *Concord Journal* for July 11, 1964.

25. *Liberation,* 7 (February 1963), 21-26. The magazine is briefly described in a useful anthology of the New Left edited by Massimo Teodori entitled *The New Left: A Documentary History* (New York: Bobbs-Merrill, 1969), p. 493.

26. For another approach which also finds Thoreau's thinking unified see Paul Lauter, "Thoreau's Prophetic Testimony," *Massachusetts Review,* 4 (Autumn 1962), 111-123; this is also reprinted in Hicks, pp. 80-90.

27. Walter Harding and Carl Bode, eds., *The Correspondence of Henry David Thoreau* (New York: New York University Press, 1957), p. 611.

28. Staughton Lynd, *Intellectual Origins of American Radicalism* (New York: Random House, 1968), p. 162.

29. "Response by Staughton Lynd," *Liberation,* 8 (April 1963), 29. This is in reply to several brief commentaries on Lynd's original article in the February issue of *Liberation.*

30. Lynd is described as an advocate of nonviolence by the general editors in the preface of a book edited by Lynd entitled *Nonviolence in America: A Documentary History* (New York: Bobbs-Merrill, 1966), p. viii. Lynd's sympathies and aspirations are clearly allied with nonviolence, but he makes clear in his introduction that he is aware that the movements in the 1960s may be heading toward violence just as they did one hundred years earlier (see p. xiii).

31. "Response by Staughton Lynd," p. 29.

32. Holley Cantine, "The Direct Actionists and the Bird Watchers," *Liberation,* 8 (April 1963), 22.

33. Victor Richman, "More Than Our Minds Can Map," *Liberation,* 8 (April 1963), 28. Despite Richman's claims, pacifists are generally critical of violence whether it is used by the "system" or by those who want to reform it. See, for example, Martin Luther King, Jr., *Where Do We Go from Here: Chaos or Community* (New York: Harper & Row, 1967), pp. 55-66.

34. "A Society Not Yet Formed," *Liberation,* 8 (April 1963), 23-25.

35. A very readable account of the sixties will be found in William L. O'Neill's *Coming Apart: An Informal History of America in the 1960's* (Chicago: Quadrangle Books, 1971). O'Neill cites the plot to blow up the monuments (p. 172-173). O'Neill's book is one of the few good general

overviews of the sixties to appear so far, but there are numerous specific
articles and books dealing with features of the decade relevant to this chapter; they are, however, too numerous to cite. Yet two are especially worth
mentioning owing to their usefulness in understanding the New Left and
the student movement; the first item is filled with primary sources, and the
second is a series of bibliographical essays. For the primary materials see
Mitchell Goodman, ed., *The Movement Toward a New America: The Beginnings of a Long Revolution* (New York and Philadelphia: Knopf and
Pilgrim Press, 1970); and for the bibliographical essays see the following
articles, all of which appeared in *Radical America* under the general title of
"A History of the New Left, 1960-1968" by James P. O'Brien: "The New
Left's Early Years," 2 (May-June 1968), 1-25; "The New Left, 1965-67," 2
(September-October 1968), 1-22; and "The New Left, 1967-1968," 2 (Nov-
ember-December 1968), 28-43. These are supplemented by Allen Hunter
and James O'Brien in "Reading About the New Left," *Radical America*, 6
(July-August 1972), 73-94.

36. *The Right of Revolution* (Boston: Beacon Press, 1968), p. 3. Nelson
is also the author of several historical novels, one of which is a highly sym-
pathetic treatment of John Brown: *The Surveyor* (Garden City, N.Y.:
Doubleday, 1960). Nelson later complained that his writing on Brown
could not gain a wide readership because publishers and critics are afraid
of truly revolutionary works; see "On Creating Revolutionary Art and
Going Out of Print," *TriQuarterly*, 23/24 (Winter/Spring 1972), 92-110.
For an account of Nelson's sympathies for Thoreau see Rita Doucette,
Parallel Lives: A Comparison of Henry David Thoreau to Truman Nelson
(Salem, Mass.: R. Doucette, 1964).

37. "Thoreau and John Brown," in Hicks, p. 135. A less detailed version
of this article appeared in *Ramparts*, one of the many voices of the New
Left, as "Thoreau and the Paralysis of Individualism," 4 (March 1966),
16-26.

38. For a less polemical but similar view of Thoreau see Joseph DeFalco,
"Thoreau's Ethic and the 'Bloody Revolution,' " *Topic: A Journal of the
Liberal Arts*, 6 (Fall 1966), 43-49. Following Lynd and writing at the same
time as Truman Nelson, DeFalco sets out to free Thoreau from the popular
notion that "mistakenly" associates him "with a kind of weak, pacifistic,
and pious idealism that has no bearing on direct social action" (p. 44). He
argues that Thoreau's support of Brown reveals that "realistic insights [into
the necessity for violence] temper his idealism. Not a blind and pious
moralizer, he views his commitments in the light of practical situations" (p.
48). DeFalco calls this a "sliding scale of ethical relativism," which allowed
Thoreau to remain constant in his reformist goals but flexible in his means
"no matter to what violent extreme this may lead" (p. 49).

And for two academic studies which describe rather than invoke Thoreau's willingness to support violence, see the following unpublished master's theses: Francis Marion Williams, "Thoreau's Views on Violence" (San Diego State College, 1963); and Hermes R. Berlin, "Aspects of Henry David Thoreau's Social Thought" (University of Iowa, 1965).

39. Carl Bode, ed., *The Portable Thoreau* (New York: Viking Press, 1947); see also the revised edition of 1964. The epilogue which appears in the 1964 edition (pp. 683-696) was originally printed as "The Half-Hidden Thoreau," *Massachusetts Review*, 4 (Autumn 1962), 68-80.

40. "The Half-Hidden Thoreau" is also reprinted in Hicks, pp. 104-116. Page numbers in the text refer to the pagination in Hicks. Gozzi's Freudian approach to Thoreau was an unpublished doctoral dissertation for New York University (1957) entitled "Tropes and Figures: A Psychological Study of David Henry Thoreau." Two chapters of it were revised and later published in Walter Harding, ed., *Henry David Thoreau: A Profile* (New York: Hill & Wang, 1971), pp. 150-187. Bode's article is, in effect, a summary of the dissertation. Although Gozzi seems to discover genitalia lurking in almost every bush surrounding Walden Pond, the dissertation makes an interesting case for a Freudian reading of Thoreau. For anyone interested in a psychological approach to Thoreau's life and writings, Gozzi's dissertation is the place to begin.

41. "Lucky Fox at Walden," in Hicks, p. 130. Wagner's essay, along with Truman Nelson's, was added to *Thoreau in Our Season* in 1966. Neither essay appeared in the 1962 *Massachusetts Review*. The addition of these two essays — though each is ideologically opposed — indicates a modest increase in interest concerning Thoreau's relationship to Brown.

42. For a useful discussion (to which I am indebted) dealing with the problem of psychoanalytic approaches to historical interpretation, see Martin B. Duberman, "The Abolitionist and Psychology," *The Journal of Negro History*, 47 (July 1962), 183-191.

43. "The Case Against Thoreau," *Ethics*, 67 (July 1957), 257.

44. Buranelli, pp. 266-267. These "peculiar notions" were also "scarifying" for those in the nineteenth century who were fair game for the terrible swift sword of transcendental politics. Mary Boykin Chesnut's description of Northern reformers in *A Dairy from Dixie* captures one Southern point of view in 1861 by a woman who shared many of the racist assumptions of slavery but who deplored the institution itself. Referring to Stowe, Greeley, Thoreau, Emerson, and Sumner, Chesnut complains that all of them "live in nice New England homes, clean, sweet-smelling, shut up in libraries, writing books which ease their hearts of their bitterness against us. What self-denial they do practice is to tell John Brown to come down here and cut our throats in Christ's name" (quoted in Edmund Wilson, *Patriotic Gore: Studies in the Literature of the American Civil War* [New York: Oxford University Press, 1962], p. 292). Chesnut's reaction to

Brown's Christian philanthropy recalls, ironically, a passage from *Walden* (p. 74); "If I knew for a certainty that a man was coming to my house with the conscious design of doing me good, I should run for my life. . . ."

45. Quoted in Erwin N. Griswold, "Dissent — 1968," *Tulane Law Review*, 42 (June 1968), 727). It is noteworthy that four years after Staughton Lynd's documentary history of *Nonviolence in America* there appeared a book edited by Richard Hofstadter and Michael Wallace entitled *American Violence: A Documentary History* (New York: Alfred A. Knopf, 1970), and it was not the first of its kind.

46. Griswold, "Dissent — 1968," pp. 737-738.

47. Quoted in *TSB*, 104 (Summer 1968), 7.

48. Robert Sherrill, "The Embodiment of Poor White Power," *New York Times*, February 28, 1971, sec. 6, p. 49.

49. *National Review*, June 4, 1968, pp. 541-547. Sanders' article adds nothing new to the objections raised about Thoreau's individualism; his treatment seems to combine a contemporary concern about mass demonstrations with a reworking of materials from two earlier articles, one being Vincent Buranelli's and the other M.A. Goldberg's "Egotisms: Ancient and Modern," *Colorado Quarterly*, 10 (Winter 1962), 285-295. Goldberg traces the preoccupation with the self in Western thought in order to discredit Thoreau's individualism and urge upon his readers an awareness of human limitations and a sense of humility. For another earlier objection similar to Sanders' article see George B. Bringmann, "Thoreau's Civil Disobedience: A Principle, Not a Technique," *Fragments*, 3 (July 1965), 4.

50. *National Review*, August 13, 1968, p. 775. The Lundquist article, "An Apology for Henry," is on pp. 806 and 819.

51. *Human Events*, May 25, 1968, p. 330. The magazine describes its conservative principles under its masthead on p. 2. On the same page included among "Capital Briefs" will be found a slur on Robert Kennedy similar in technique to the one used by the *National Review* on supporters of Thoreau in reference to "Lundquist": "Latest celebrity to jump aboard the Kennedy for President bandwagon: underground film maker *Andy Warhol* who specializes in far-out 'flicks' about sexual deviation."

52. The quoted phrase is from George Anastaplo's essay, "On Civil Disobedience: Thoreau and Socrates," *Southwest Review*, 54 (Spring 1969), 203-214. Anastaplo cites the ancients to support the virtue of "law-abidingness."

53. In the liberal publication of the Center for the Study of Democratic Institutions, Harry Kalven, Jr., a professor of law at the University of Chicago, finds that "Civil Disobedience" is an effective polemic, but he argues that it raises more legal and ethical questions than it answers. He is particularly concerned about what civil disobedience leads to if nonviolent means do not work ("Thoreau," *Center Magazine*, 3 [May 1970], 62-65).

Kalven's essay was originally written in 1966 as part of an "Occasional Paper." Concern was also expressed by some who were sympathetic with Thoreau's version of civil disobedience that contemporary practitioners of it be as responsible as Thoreau and be willing to accept the legal consequences of their actions; see, for example, Joseph Wood Krutch, "If You Don't Mind My Saying So," *American Scholar*, 37 (Winter 1967), 15-18; and John A. Christie, "Thoreau on Civil Resistance," *Emerson Society Quarterly*, 54 (First Quarter 1969), 5-12.

It is interesting that several of the few close criticisms of Thoreau's social thought and politics have come from political scientists and lawyers, professions committed to systems and to precedent, unlike the humanities, which tend, like Thoreau, to encourage a "broad margin." This strikes me as a rather facile over-simplification (which is why I bury the idea in a note); nevertheless, it may be that the temperament of most academicians in the humanities has something to do with the reason why few literary critics have examined at length Thoreau's politics and found them wanting from a social perspective. Two unpublished doctoral dissertations dealing with Thoreau as a social thinker and writer offer some tentative — if scanty — support for this idea. The first was written for an English department, and the second was written for a political science department; the latter is much more critical of Thoreau's politics. See Douglas A. Noverr, "Thoreau's Development as an Observer and Critic of American Society" (Miami University, 1972); and Charles M. Evans, "The Political Theory of Henry David Thoreau: An Exposition and Criticism" (University of Oklahoma, 1973).

54. The following articles are in the order of the charges cited in the text: Richard M. Weaver, "Two Types of American Individualism," *Modern Age*, 7 (Spring 1963), 119-134; Perry Miller, "The Responsibility of Mind," *American Scholar*, 31 (Winter 1961-1962), 51-69; Lucie Scott Brown, "The Peter Pan of American Literature," *CEA Critic*, 32 (January 1970), 13; Hubert H. Hoeltje, "Misconceptions in Current Thoreau Criticism," *Philological Quarterly*, 47 (October 1968), 563-570; Robert D. Callahan, "*Walden*: Portrait of the Critic's Saint as a Young Daydreamer," *Paunch*, 24 (October 1965), 27-39; Wade C. Thompson, " 'The Uniqueness' of Henry David Thoreau," *Paunch*, 24 (October 1965), 18-26; L.W. Michaelson, "The Man Who Burned the Woods," *English Record*, (February 1970), 72-75; Theodore Baird, "Corn Grows in the Night," in Hicks, pp. 68-79; and Quentin Anderson, "Thoreau on July 4," *New York Times*, July 4, 1971, sec. 7, pp. 1, 16-18.

55. "Postal 'Hippie' Art Is Going Over Big with Hippies Here," *New York Times*, July 16, 1967, p. 51. The reproduction of the stamp was on the cover of the July 15-20, 1967 *East Village Other*.

56. For discussions of Thoreau's relevancy to the hippie movement see

John T. McCutcheson, "Was Thoreau a Hippy?" *Chicago Tribune*, July 27, 1967, sec. 1, p. 14; Paul Woodring, "Was Thoreau a Hippie?" *Saturday Review*, December 16, 1967, p. 68; Herbert S. Bailey, Jr., "Thoreau Changed the World and the World Changed Him," *University: A Princeton Quarterly*, 38 (Fall 1968), 15-19; Debert L. Earisman, *Hippies in Our Midst* (Philadelphia: Fortress, 1968), 127-131; F.T. McGill, "Rutgers Professor Contends Thoreau Was Not a Hippie," *New York Times*, January 5, 1968, p. 24; Guy Wright, "Thoreau the Square," *San Francisco Examiner*, 16 May 1968, p. 33; and Paul H. Wild, "Flower Power: A Student's Guide to Pre-Hippie Transcendentalism," *English Journal*, 58 (January 1969), 62-68.

57. *The Wind That Blows Is All That Anybody Knows: The Thoughts of Henry David Thoreau* (Los Angeles: Stanyan Books, 1970).

58. See Leonard A. Greenbaum and Rudolf B. Schmerl, *Course X: A Left Field Guide to Freshman English* (New York: Lippincott, 1970); and "Walden, Schmalden,"*National Lampoon*, 1 (June 1970), 24.

59. For views of Thoreau as anticapitalistic see Edwin S. Smith, "A Thoreau for Today," *Mainstream* (April 1960), 1-24, (May 1960), 42-55; and Staughton Lynd, *Intellectual Origins of American Radicalism* (New York: Random House, 1968), 92-95. Robin Linstromberg and James Ballowe argue that Thoreau confirmed the basic premises of capitalism in "Thoreau and Etzler: Alternative Views of Economic Reform," *Midcontinent American Studies Journal*, 11 (Spring 1970), 20-29. Thoreau lends support to a food faddist's manual in Edwin Flatto, *The New Walden* (Laredo, Tex.: South Publications, 1963). Dachine Rainer insists that Thoreau is an anarchist in "Who Are the Anarchists?" *Liberation*, 8 (April 1963), 26-27; D.T. Wieck, in the same issue argues that Thoreau is not: "The Community of Principle" (p. 29). Kingsley Widmer places Thoreau in a tradition of "orgasmic prophecy" in "The Prophet's Passional Ethos: Henry David Thoreau," *Paunch*, 24 (October 1965), 40-50. For a Thoreau who has "soul" see "An Arbitrary Guide to Soul," *Time*, June 28, 1968, p. 66; and for a Thoreau without any clothes on see Mark Reid, "Fish in the Sky" in Charles Cropsey and Jill Browner, eds., *The Shameless Nude* (Los Angeles: Elysium, 1963), pp. 112-119; Robert T. Mayrand, "Thoreau on Clothing," *Sol*, 64 (1964), 46-53; Mischa Murphy, "Thoreau: The Thinking Man's Nudist," *Mr. Sun*, 1 (December 1966), 18-20; Joseph Salak, "The Nudist Philosopher," *American Sun Bather*, 18 (March 1966), 32-34; and Thomas D. Austin, "Thoreau, the First Hippie," *ANKH*, 1 (Spring 1968), 12-21. (I am indebted to Walter Harding for pointing out these nudist articles in a correspondence with me.) The most succinct and direct evidence for Thoreau's reputation among those concerned with ecology comes from *TSB*, 110 (Winter 1970), 4: "Former Secretary of the Interior Stewart Udall in a

NBC 'Frontiers of Faith' program on environmental pollution, ended his broadcast with this advice to his listeners; 'Read Thoreau!' " See also, for example, Victor A. Croley, "The Freedom Way," *Mother Earth News*, 1 (January 1970), 46-55; and Wade Van Dore, "Walden as the American Bible: A Gospel of Ecology," *Churchman*, 185 (November 1971), 8-10. For representative views of Thoreau as a general cure for the ills of modern life see Donald J. Adams, "Speaking of Books," *New York Times*, May 6, 1962, sec. 7, p. 2; Frank Chodorov, *Out of Step* (New York: Devon-Adair, 1962), 197-205; Reginald Cook, "Think of This Yankees!" *Massachusetts Review*, 4 (Autumn 1962), 42-52 (reprinted in Hicks, pp. 29-37); Winfield Townley Scott, "Walden Pond in the Nuclear Age," *New York Times*, May 6, 1962, sec. 6, pp. 34-35, 84, 86, 88, 90; Joseph Wood Krutch, "Wilderness as a Tonic," *Saturday Review*, June 8, 1963, pp. 15-17; Richard J. Fein, *"Walden* and the Village of the Mind," *Ball State University Forum*, 8 (Winter 1967), 55-61; Joseph Wood Krutch, "Who Was Henry Thoreau?" *Saturday Review*, August 19, 1967, pp. 18-19, 46; Samuel R. Ogden, "The Road to Walden," *Vermont Life* (Summer 1971), 24-25; and Charles B. Seib, *The Woods: One Man's Escape to Nature* (Garden City, N.Y.: Doubleday, 1971). A somewhat belated repudiation of most of these uses of Thoreau is in E. Merrill Root, "Henry Thoreau: Upon Finding a Fish in the Milk," *American Opinion*, 16 (February 1973), 19-30. The magazine is the house organ of the John Birch Society. Root signs Thoreau on to the Birch Society by signing him off everything else that the "Bearded Establishment" has associated with him. Root claims that Thoreau is the "greatest reactionary" in all America, and he means it as a compliment.

60. *The Night Thoreau Spent in Jail* (New York: Hill & Wang, 1971).

61. *TSB*, 111 (Spring 1970), 8. It is noteworthy that Harding dedicated his biography of Thoreau (*The Days of Henry Thoreau* [New York: Knopf, 1965]) to two men, Edwin May Teale and Martin Luther King.

62. For an account of the opening night at Ohio State see Edmund Schofield, "The First Run of 'The Night Thoreau Spent in Jail,' " *TSB*, 119 (Spring 1972), 5. The success and popularity of the play are noted in *TSB*, 118 (Winter 1972), 8.

63. Howard Taubman, "On Stage: Thoreau Speaks Today," *New York Times*, December 23, 1970, p. 16. For two more articles in the *Times* on the popularity of the play see Lewis Funk, "Thoreauly Modern," October 18, 1970, sec. 2, pp. 1, 36; and Clive Barnes, "Stage: Thoreau in Jail," November 2, 1970, p. 66. Barnes, tongue in cheek, writes that given the fashionable popularity of the play he "can even foresee a musical version called 'Walden' starring Peter Fonda." For a detailed critique of the play for which I am grateful but not indebted see Charles Clerc, "The Now Thoreau: Caveat Emptor," *Midwest Quarterly*, 16 (Summer 1975), 371-388.

64. Leon Edel, *Henry D. Thoreau*, University of Minnesota Pamphlets on American Writers, No. 90 (Minneapolis: University of Minnesota Press, 1970), p. 39.

65. Louis Kampf and Paul Lauter, eds., "Introduction," *The Politics of Literature: Dissenting Essays on the Teaching of English* (New York: Random House, 1972), pp. 10-11.

66. "Thoreau and American Power," *Atlantic Monthly*, 223 (May 1969),

67. Kazin also gently suggests that "Civil Disobedience" is not a practical guide to contemporary politics, because Thoreau did not anticipate the overwhelming power of the modern state and because he did not realize the necessity for a collective response to social problems.

67. Quoted in Frederick Crews, "Offing Culture: Literary Study and the Movement," *TriQuarterly*, 23/24 (Winter/Spring 1972), 38. In the same issue of *TriQuarterly* see John Seelye's "Some Green Thoughts on a Green Theme" (576-638) for a study that goes a long way in explaining the backgrounds of Thoreau's apolitical temperament. Concerning Thoreau's relationship to Brown, Seelye writes that his "plea for Brown is a classic example of primitivist politics . . . its insistence that the righteousness of the cause transcends the means used to implement that cause, brings us close to a militant form of mystical fascism, the seeds of which may be found in his own sense of divinity . . . his intense, evangelical conviction of personal rectitude, and his Romantic (elitist) individualism" (p. 634).

68. *TSB*, 108 (Summer 1969), 1.

69. The handbill is reprinted in *TSB*, 113 (Fall 1970), 4.

70. See the letter to the editor by H. Nicoll Hoppner for an account of the meeting in *TSB*, 114 (Winter 1971), 3. Another letter in the same issue — the only other one — by Elaine Shaw, tends to confirm Hoppner's version of the meeting (pp. 5-6).

71. See Harlan L. Umansky's letter to the editor in *TSB*, 115 (Spring 1971), 3.

72. For the exact wording of the resolutions and a tally of the votes see *TSB*, 116 (Summer 1971), 7-8.

73. *TSB*, 124 (Summer 1973), 5.

Index

Seelye, John, 206n.67
Seib, Charles B., 205n.59
Seldes, Gilbert, 79n.32
Seybold, Ethel, 196n.12
Sex, Thoreau on, 185, 186. *See also* Psychoanalytic criticism
Shanley, J. Lyndon, 144n.14
Shapiro, Karl, 198n.22
Shear, Walter L., 194n.10
Shepard, Odell, 20-22, 33, 34, 41, 75n.14, 148n.35
Shores of America, The. See Paul, Sherman
Sillen, Samuel, 133-35
Sinclair, Upton, 30
Sisk, John P., 155
Skwire, David, 144n.14
Slavery, 86, 88, 90, 129-30, 140-41. *See also* "Slavery in Massachusetts"
"Slavery in Massachusetts," 20, 36, 56, 87-88, 119, 138, 160, 169, 170, 180, 182, 189
Smith, Bernard, 61, 76n.21
Smith, Bradford, 198n.22
Smith, Edwin, 204n.59
Smith, Henry Nash, 5-6, 95
Socialism, 97-98
Society, Thoreau as critic of: Macy on, 18-19; Shepard on, 20-21; Phelps on, 22-23; *The Freeman* on, 24-25; Finger on, 31; Vivas on, 32-35; Atkinson on, 36-38; Parrington on, 38-44; Brooks on, 53; McKaye on, 55-56; Blankenship on, 57-58; Williams on, 58; Schuster on, 58; Lerner on, 58-59, 77n.24; academic critics of 1930s on, 59, 75n.15; Boyd on, 60-61; Calverton on, 62-65; Krutch on, 66-67, 126-33; Canby on, 67-70, 73-74, 86-88; Lewis on, 71-73; Dreiser

on, 72-73; Collins on, 83-85; Cosman on, 86; Schlesinger on, 89; H. Miller on, 89-91; Harding on, 93-95; Matthiessen on, 95-102; Hyman on, 110-14; Paul on, 119-21; Hollis on, 122-23; Eulau on, 123-26; Houston on, 125-26; Sillen on, 133-35; Adams on, 135-37; Thoreauvians on, 137-38; Stoller on, 140-42; students of 1950s on, 153; King on, 153-54, 160; Hicks on, 159-61; W.S. Nelson on, 162-64; Lynd on, 164-68; T. Nelson on, 168-71; Bode on, 172-75; Wagner on, 175-76; Buranelli on, 177-79; *National Review* on, 182-83; Lawrence and Lee on, 187-88; Lauter on, 188-89. *See also* Politics; Thoreau, Henry David; Violence, Thoreau's support of
Socrates, 28, 29
Southern agrarians, 63-64
Southworth, J.G., 75n.15
Spock, Dr. Benjamin, 182, 183
Stein, William Bysshe, 12n.2, 144n.14
Steinbeck, John, 155
Stevenson, Robert Louis, 177
Stewart, Randall, 12n.2, 80n.34
Stimson, Henry L., 90
Stoddard, Donald, 196n.14
Stoic, Thoreau as, 9
Stoller, Leo, 140-42
Stowell, Robert, 199n.22
Stromberg, R.N., 146n.25
Student response to Thoreau: in 1920s, 32-33; in 1930s, 53; in 1950s, 152-153; in 1960s, 152, 172, 184-88
Studies in Philology, 59
"Succession of Forest Trees, The," 19

About the Author

Michael Meyer, assistant professor of English at the University of North Carolina at Charlotte, specializes in nineteenth-century American literature. He is presently working on a book-length study of Thoreau's social and political thought in the context of nineteenth-century politics.

Several More Lives to Live is the winner of the second Ralph Henry Gabriel Prize in American Studies. The prize is awarded by Greenwood Press in conjunction with the American Studies Association to the author of the book-length original manuscript judged best each year by a special prize committee of the American Studies Association.

DATE			